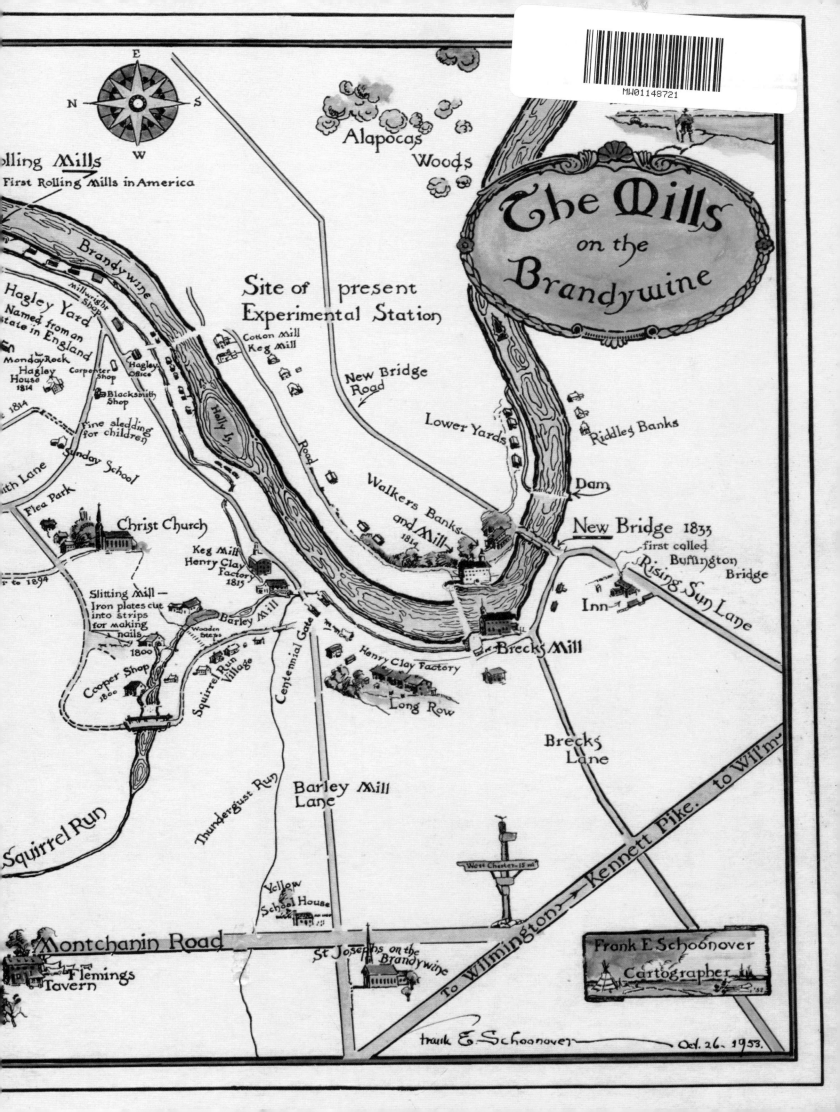

The Mills on the Brandywine

Alapocas Woods

olling Mills
First Rolling Mills in America

Brandywine

Millwright Shop

Hagley Yard
Named from an
state in England

Monday Rock
Hagley House 1814

Carpenter Shop

Hagley Office

Blacksmith Shop

Fine sledding for children

uth Lane

Sunday School

Flea Park

r to 1894

Christ Church

Keg Mill Henry Clay Factory 1815

Slitting Mill —
Iron plates cut
into strips
for making
nails
1800

Cooper Shop 1800

Wooden Steps

Barley Mill

Squirrel Run Village

Centennial Gate

Site of present Experimental Station

Cotton Mill Keg Mill

Holly Is.

Road

New Bridge Road

Lower Yards

Riddles Banks

Walkers Banks and Mill 1814

Dam

New Bridge 1833
first called
Buffington Bridge

Rising Sun Lane

Inn

Brecks Mill

Henry Clay Factory

Long Row

Brecks Lane

Squirrel Run

Thundergust Run

Barley Mill Lane

West Chester - 15 mi.

Yellow School House

Montchanin Road

Flemings Tavern

St Josephs on the Brandywine

To Wilmington

Kennett Pike

to Wil'm

Frank E Schoonover
Cartographer

frank E. Schoonover

Oct. 26, 1953.

CHATEAU COUNTRY

DU PONT ESTATES IN THE BRANDYWINE VALLEY

To Susan,
My longtime friend—
enjoy the book—
a tribute for your
fine work over the
years.
Joe Melloy

DANIEL DEKALB MILLER

Schiffer Publishing Ltd

4880 Lower Valley Road • Atglen, PA 19310

Chateau Country photography by

Terrence Roberts Photography

except where otherwise noted.

Line drawings by Joseph Malloy, Sr.

Cover Photographs:
 Front. Top: *Oberod*; center left: *Granogue*; center right: *Crooked Billet*; bottom left: *Winterthur*; bottom right: *Nemours*
 Back. Top: *Longwood*; bottom: *Mount Cuba*
 Inside Cover: *The Mills of the Brandywine* by Frank Schoonover, Credit: Hagley Museum and Library

Cover and book designed by: Bruce Waters
Type set in Minion Pro

ISBN: 978-0-7643-4415-2
Printed in China

Published by Schiffer Publishing, Ltd.
4880 Lower Valley Road
Atglen, PA 19310
Phone: (610) 593-1777; Fax: (610) 593-2002
E-mail: *Info@schifferbooks.com*

For our complete selection of fine books on this and related subjects, please visit our website at www.schifferbooks.com. You may also write for a free catalog.

This book may be purchased from the publisher. Please try your bookstore first.

We are always looking for people to write books on new and related subjects. If you have an idea for a book, please contact us at proposals@schifferbooks.com

Schiffer Publishing's titles are available at special discounts for bulk purchases for sales promotions or premiums. Special editions, including personalized covers, corporate imprints, and excerpts can be created in large quantities for special needs. For more information, contact the publisher.

In Europe, Schiffer books are distributed by
Bushwood Books
6 Marksbury Ave.
Kew Gardens
Surrey TW9 4JF England
Phone: 44 (0) 20 8392 8585; Fax: 44 (0) 20 8392 9876
E-mail: *info@bushwoodbooks.co.uk*
Website: www.bushwoodbooks.co.uk

TO ANNE
You spread the sunshine

CONTENTS

Introduction 5

Applecross 9

Ashland Red Clay Creek.................17

Bellevue Hall.................................25

Boxwood 31

Brantwyn (Bois des Fossés) 39

Crooked Billet 47

Dauneport 53

Dilwyne Farms 59

    and The Ball Farm 65

Eleutherian Mills.................................73

Gibraltar 81

Goodstay.................................87

Granogue 93

Greenville House 101

Hod House 107

Hotel du Pont 115

The Inn at Montchanin Village 121

Lower Louviers 125

Mount Cuba.................................133

Nemours 141

Oberod.................................153

Owl's Nest 161

Peirce-du Pont House and Longwood Gardens..........169

Rokeby 181

Saint Amour 191

Squirrel Run 197

Staglyn (Fiskekill) 205

Strand Millis.................................211

Upper Louviers (Louviers Upper House) 217

Windmar.................................223

Winterthur.................................229

Winterthur Cottage.................................237

Xanadu.................................245

Appendix 1: The Siege of Guyencourt.................252

Appendix 2: Glossary 254

Appendix 3: Directory of du Pont Houses.................260

Acknowledgments.................................263

Resources.................................264

Index.................................266

INTRODUCTION

I think Chateau Country is one of the few great country landscapes in America and that's largely due to the du Ponts.
David Ames
Director, Center for Historic Architecture & Design
University of Delaware

The Brandywine Valley encompasses an expanse of magnificent scenery rivaling any in America. Extending from just south of the city of Wilmington, Delaware, corporate home of E. I. du Pont de Nemours & Co., as well as more than half of the nation's largest corporations, the region stretches north to Delaware and Chester counties in Pennsylvania.

It could just as well be called the du Pont[1] Valley, as this is the seat of one of the world's wealthiest families, whose residences mushroom over the gently rolling hills, frequently sequestered behind stone walls[2] at the end of long allees or winding driveways. Unlike Newport, Palm Beach, and Long Island's North Shore, where fabled families included the likes of Vanderbilts, Astors, Morgans, and Whitneys, the estates of the Brandywine Valley are dominated by just one family—the du Ponts.

In 1925, approximately sixty du Pont families lived in and around Wilmington. Thirty years later it was estimated that the number of descendants of the families of Irénée and Victor was approximately 1200 and increasing at the rate of thirty per year. Based on this formula the extended family today would number some 3000 persons living throughout the United States and abroad, but Wilmington remains the family stronghold.

Not without reason is the area often called "Chateau Country," a reference to France's Loire Valley with its imposing chateaux and the roots of many of the du Ponts. Though all houses are not of equal importance, the sobriquet is legitimate. And like their Newport and North Shore counterparts, most of the du Ponts have based their domicile designs on Colonial Revival, English, and French architectural styles and interpretations and many of them are very grand indeed.

When Pierre Samuel du Pont[3] left France in October, 1799,[4] he could scarcely have imagined what lay ahead for him and his family in the New World. Boarding the barely seaworthy commercial schooner, *American Eagle*, accompanied by twelve family members, including sons Victor and Eleuthere Irénée and their families, the voyage took ninety-one days, twice as long as expected and nearly a month longer than it had taken Christopher Columbus to sail from Spain to the Bahamas three centuries earlier.

The family made their way to North Bergen (now Bayonne), New Jersey, from their slightly off-course landing in Newport, Rhode Island (January 1, 1800). Du Pont's wife, along with son-in-law, Bureaux de Pusy, had preceded him, and there the weary party was welcomed to *Goodstay,* the sprawling house they had purchased. Pierre, and elder son Victor and his family, soon moved to New York, nine miles away, to pursue business under the name Du Pont de Nemours Pere, Fils et Cie. A year later the brothers returned to France to seek additional financing.

Irénée, with a background in black powder-making in Essonne, France, was most successful, obtaining backing for a powder mill from Swiss banker Jacques Bidermann and the French government, which was anxious to thwart its production by the British. Returning to *Goodstay*, he began exploring the Hudson River Valley, Virginia, and Maryland for a place that would be suitable for a production facility. Family friend Peter Bauduy urged him to look in the Brandywine Valley where Jacob Broom had built the first cotton mill in the United States in 1795. Here Irénée found the undulating hills and coursing water of the Brandywine Creek a perfect site for the manufacture of the black explosive powder that became the foundation of the chemical company and, subsequently, the family fortune. He struck a deal to purchase Broom's defunct facility, which was made even more appealing by Bauduy's offer for financial aid if he would locate his facility in Wilmington.

With plans formed, Irénée returned to New Jersey, gathered his wife, Sophie, and their young children—Victorine, Evelina and Alfred—and said goodbye to *Goodstay*. After a four-day journey by wagon, Sophie and Irénée in front, worldly goods in the middle, and children dangling their feet over the back of the wagon, they made their way to Delaware. In establishing E.I. du Pont de Nemours and Company, Irénée not only laid the cornerstone for one of the country's most important manufacturers, but started a dynasty whose relatives and heirs reside in countries throughout the western hemisphere.

The first du Pont dwelling in Delaware (1802), the former Broom farm, was a rough, two-story dwelling with bare plank floors and low ceilings, located near the Brandywine River within the shadow of the proposed DuPont Powder Mills. This served as temporary shelter while the new house, *Eleutherian Mills*, was being constructed. By the summer of 1803, it was ready for occupancy.

Originally the company owned and controlled all employee housing, but as the DuPont business prospered this gradually changed. Through the years, as family fortunes increased, so too did their dwellings, gardens, and indulgences. Distinguished landscape architects were hired to create estate gardens. Plots producing vegetables and flowers for the table were enthusiastically supplanted by elaborately designed and carefully manicured landscapes rivaling those in Europe, with fountains, parterres, and follies. Architectural and landscape components were integrated with careful consideration given to both interior and exterior views.

Tennis courts, swimming pools, greenhouses, multiple-car garages, stables, workers' cottages, gatehouses, a private golf course, and a polo field became parts of various du Pont country house landscapes. These required a retinue of servants—maids, cooks, butlers, housekeepers, chauffeurs, footmen, gardeners—to maintain the properties and attend to the owners' needs and desires. *Winterthur's* household staff numbered thirty-six at one time. Several du Pont estates had their own airstrips and, in a period when most homeowners were content with a single-car garage, *Saint Amour* had five, plus stables. *Bellevue Hall* was rebuilt from a Gothic Revival house into a Colonial Revival style mansion in a replication of *Montpelier*, former Virginia home of President James Madison. And, reflecting its owner's interest in the sport of kings, a 1.25 mile racetrack, complete with bleachers was added.

Many mansions of the du Ponts and family members are not visible on a casual drive, though it isn't unusual to see well-tended fields of corn or grazing sheep and horses belonging to their estates paralleling the Brandywine's back-country roads. On a stretch of Center Meeting Road, between Kennett Pike and Montchanin Road, at *Meown Farm*, a herd of Belted Galloways—the prized hornless Scottish cattle with a broad stripe encircling their mid-sections—grazes contentedly on a hillside, oblivious to the interest they arouse for passers-by. These idyllic properties are often euphemistically referred to as farms in Delaware, though in Maryland and Virginia they are called plantations.

Most of the family houses were not designed to impress; however, *Nemours* (1909) is an exception and it established an elevated benchmark to which other du Pont country residences were compared. Surrounded by 320 acres, its French formal gardens are the largest in North America, extending a third of a mile from the main house. Imperial gates, fourteen feet high and ten feet wide, formerly installed at an estate owned by Catherine the Great of Russia, flank the entrance driveway.

As the gunpowder mill continued its enormous success, family residential areas moved northward from the original Brandywine location, often to the Greenville and Centreville areas, and at times crossing into neighboring Pennsylvania and Maryland. In the 1940s, almost two dozen du Pont houses lined Kennett Pike in this eight-mile stretch and more than seventy family houses in the area were surrounded by twenty or more acres.

In most instances these mansions were built in the era of the American Country Place, from 1895 to the end of World War II, and designed for a specific du Pont family, though at times existing residences were purchased and added onto. For house names ancestral ties (*Pelleport, Bellevue*) or places in France of significance to the family (*Chevannes, Saint Amour*) were usually chosen. *Goodstay,* originally called *Green Hill* (c. 1783),

was enlarged and re-named for the homestead in Bergen Point, after being purchased by the du Pont family. A few residences were designated only by the names of the inhabitants or by street addresses.

Since Irénée du Pont built *Eleutherian Mills,* almost one hundred houses in the Brandywine Valley have been built or rebuilt and occupied by the du Ponts. Regrettably a number of these have been razed, victims of the economy and the changing tastes of our times. A few are now house museums or are within conservancies open to the public, while others have been transformed into private clubs or incorporated into other commercial complexes. Fortunately many have been well preserved and still serve as private dwellings—for the most part occupied by du Ponts and their extended families.

Chateau Country describes residences past and present of the du Pont family. Whether readers visit the existent houses personally or simply take vicarious pleasure in looking through the pages of this book, they will come away with an appreciation of the manners and mores of an era gone by, before television and the internet demanded so much of our time, and, above all, before the graduated income tax made most of these houses unaffordable to all save the very, very wealthy, which of course, still includes many of the du Ponts.

Daniel D. Miller

Notes

1. Through the years the name du Pont has been spelled in different ways. The Wilmington telephone directory lists five spellings, i.e. DuPont, Du Pont, Dupont, duPont and du Pont among thirty-three family listings. Most have indicated that they prefer the du Pont spelling. The corporate name is E.I. du Pont de Nemours and Company, but when referred to in abbreviated form is DuPont.

2. Stone for these walls was quarried along the Brandywine River below Alapocas at the Brandywine Granite Co.; du Pont family members were major shareholders in the company.

3. To the family name of du Pont, Pierre added de Nemours to distinguish his family from two other members serving in the French Chamber of Deputies with the name Dupont.

4. Pierre Samuel du Pont de Nemours arrived in Newport, R.I., January 1, 1800, with his two sons, Victor and Eleuthere Irénée, and their families, but returned to France in 1802 to be with his wife who had returned. Here in the United States the family first stayed in Bergen Point, New Jersey, nine miles from New York City in a house purchased by Bureaux de Pusy.

The original 1807 stone farmhouse has been expanded from approximately 1,000 square feet to ten thousand.

APPLECROSS

An 1807 farmhouse transformed into a 21st century showplace

In 1928, when Wilhelmina Haedrick du Pont and Donald Peabody Ross were married, the DuPont powder mill had been idle for just seven years and across Kennett Pike, in the recently opened Westover Hills development, houses were still under construction. For a wedding present, the newlyweds were given seventy-seven acres of land[1] on which the only structures were a simple 1807 stone farmhouse, with approximately 1,000 square feet, and a bank barn. As neighbors they had the *Ball Farm*, across the railroad tracks with sixty-five acres of open space and simple farm buildings, and, across Montchanin Road, their Carpenter cousins' six-year-old *Dilwyne Farms* surrounded by 300 largely undeveloped acres.

Today the estate contains a complex of buildings that includes the original house, now expanded to 10,000 square feet, a three-car garage near the house, gardener's cottage with attached garage, chauffeur's apartment and three-car garage, summer house, and the completely rebuilt and remodeled bank barn. Additionally there is a swimming pool and extensive gardens. For the current owners, Christopher and Penny Saridakis, it has been a five-year project. For Wilhelmina and Donald Ross it was a lifetime effort.

Mina was the daughter of William Kemble and Ethel Fleet Hallock du Pont, the youngest of four children. She was just one year old when her father died and the young family, then living at what was formerly the Second Office, moved to *St. Amour* at the urging of her grandmother, Mary Belin du Pont, widow of Lammot, and her uncle, Pierre Samuel. Buck Road was considered dangerous and too far out in the county for a young widow and her small children to live.[2] Twenty-one years later Mina became mistress of the seventy-seven-acre estate that became known as *Applecross*, just a half mile from the Second Office. An astute and independent young woman, she enjoyed her role as overseer and administrator.

To convert the farmhouse into their home, the Rosses chose architect James Thompson, a Greenville, Delaware, native, who was then practicing in New York with the firm, Holden, McLaughlin & Associates. Thompson increased the size of the house to 6200 square feet by putting a wing on each side of the original building. On the first floor the east wing enlarged the kitchen and added servants' quarters, a butler's pantry, and a den. The west wing included an entrance hall and increased the square footage of the living and dining rooms. Additional bedrooms, bathrooms, and storage space were created on the second level.

Soon after completing the *Applecross* project, Jim Thompson resigned from his job in New York to join the armed forces in the Second World War. He was recruited to serve in the Office of Strategic Services, later the Central Intelligence Agency, serving in Thailand, and, after discharge, remained there. Drawing upon his knowledge of fabric production from his father, a successful textile manufacturer, Thompson founded the Thai Silk Company with a partner. It was highly successful, but on a 1967 weekend trip with friends to Malaysia's Cameroon Highlands, "the silk king," as he had come to be known, disappeared. No clues were found to his disappearance and despite extensive and conscientious investigation the mystery has never been solved.

Donald Ross was an enthusiast of horses—raising, riding, and designing courses. Working in partnership with William duPont, Jr., they designed Delaware Park Racetrack, a 700-acre layout just seven miles from Wilmington that opened on June 26, 1937. And with Bayard Sharp, a first cousin by marriage, he owned Troilus, a Kentucky Derby contender. Included in the *Applecross* renovation was a plan for the barn that divided the lower level so that it had stalls to accommodate three horses.

While her husband was occupied with equine interests, Mina Ross devoted her time outside the household to creating award-winning gardens. She came by her horticultural interest and skill naturally. Her mother, Ethel du Pont, having moved to Still Pond, was famous for the tree peonies she brought to Delaware from Japan, among other garden accomplishments. A woody plant with majestic blooms up to eight inches across, the peonies originated in China, but were then brought to the Japanese emperor's garden. The plants were so popular that she returned and purchased more. Some of these she shared with her daughter and they are still thriving at *Applecross* today. She was also an enthusiast of daylillies and a deep fuchsia hybrid plant, Mrs. William Kemble du Pont, was named for her.

To help in the design of the *Applecross* gardens Mina hired New York City landscape architect Noel Chamberlin in 1929. Chamberlin had worked for Mina's sister, Paulina du Pont Dean, at *Old Nemours (Nemours House)* where he created a formal garden on the site of an old croquet court and she undoubtedly recommended him. Among his other commissions was the William Lybrand 1880 farmhouse in Darien, Connecticut, listed in the Smithsonian Institution's *Archives of American Gardens*, that is similar to the *Applecross* setting.

The gardens that Chamberlin created were extensive and, over time, included a water garden, rose garden, vegetable and cutting garden, and a native plant garden. They also included sculpture, fountains, and the Lord & Burnham greenhouses brought to *Applecross* from Still Pond after Ethel du Pont's death in 1951. Two giant clamshells from the South Seas were used as bird baths.

Nationally known landscape designer Marian Cruger Coffin created the tree peony garden below the summer house in 1952.[3] Nearly one hundred specimens were planted in a garden that featured a rectangular reflection pool with rounded ends. Marian Coffin worked with a number of du Pont families at their estates, including *Mt. Cuba, Winterthur, Gibraltar,* and *St. Amour* as well as at the du Pont family cemetery and the University of Delaware.

In preparation for a visit by members of the Garden Club of America in 1953, Mina Ross wrote: "The green garden, with the barn wall as a background, contains mostly hybrid rhododendrons. The formal part of the garden is planted for spring and fall effects. The tree peony garden contains nearly one hundred plants, most of which came from the collection of the late Mrs. W. K. du Pont (Mina's mother). They are largely Japanese."

Donald Ross died in 1973 and Mina in 2000. The *Applecross* estate was then inherited by their two daughters and a grandson. Though the idea of placing *Applecross* in a land conservancy had been discussed on several occasions, Mrs. Ross decided to leave the decision as to its disposition up to her heirs. Their final decision in 2004, to sell the land to a developer, is still a cause for regret among many Greenville residents. The property was divided into twenty-two one acre lots, all of which have now been built upon, with approximately forty acres of open space.

In 2006, Christopher and Penny Saridakis purchased three-and-a-half acres with the original farmhouse and bank barn. Four years later, they added another three-and-a-half acres that included the gardener's cottage and chauffeur's quarters and they have now completed all rebuilding and renovation. When the Rosses owned *Applecross,* all major utilities were located in the garage, including the steam pump for heating, water well, electric utilities, and sewer system with lines connecting the services to the main house. These have now been relocated to individual buildings.

The former entrance drive to the front door has recently been reconfigured. Rather than approaching the house by driving past the barn, the driveway now goes by the gardener's cottage and garage to a circle and the *Applecross* entrance. The bank barn is now in back of and to the right of the house.

Chris and Penny Saridakis's first priority was to expand the main house. As architect they selected Jeffrey Beitel, who designed a master plan for the twenty-two *Applecross* houses following the guidelines of the developer. In increasing the size of the house, Beitel took the original 1919 *Longwood Gardens* conservatory built by Mina Ross's Uncle Pierre as an inspiration.

In order to construct an entrance hall, an enclosed porch was added at the front of the house with a main door and columned overhang complementing the three arched-roof dormers. Flagstone floors were then installed. Inside and to the right, the original front entrance became a doorway leading into the stair hall and main part of the house. The handsome curved stairway is now enhanced by a mural executed by Vicki Vinton.

On the second floor there were five bedrooms and five full bathrooms. The Saridakises raised the roof of the master bedroom by three feet and converted the sitting room into the master bathroom. Another bedroom is now a walk-in closet. The attic was divided into a playroom, and a bedroom and a full bath were added.

To the left of the stair hall on the first floor, a small hallway leads to the original pine-paneled study with built-in bookshelves and a corner fireplace. A second door from the study opens to the enlarged butler's pantry with doors to the kitchen on the left and the dining room on the right. At one end of the kitchen, an outside door connects to a covered walkway and a three-car garage whose three dormer windows match those on the house. The original servants' quarters next to the kitchen have been remodeled as a mud room and laundry area.

From the kitchen there is a double-width doorway to the breakfast room and a new terraced addition with an innovative skylit corridor designed by architect Beitel. A garden room addition, reflective of the contemporary architecture of that period, was constructed in 1949. This was removed and a step-down great room has been built in its place. The breakfast room, great room, and a new conservatory are all accessible from the open corridor with the former stone exterior wall at the back of the house used as the corridor's supporting wall. Original windows and house shutters, rejuvenated and repainted, are a stunning accent with a skylight above each of the four windows. On one wall of the conservatory, Penny has had a hutch cabinet installed with the open middle shelf plumbed to accommodate a Delft tureen, now used as a bar sink.

The original dining room and living room, each of which has a fireplace, have not been changed with the exception of adding French doors to the terrace at one end of the living room. A safe built into a dining room closet is large enough to accommodate large silver trays, hollowware, and serving pieces in addition to flatware.

French doors at the end of the corridor open onto a flagstone terrace with a reflecting pool in the center. The bronze sculpture, *Spring Ballet*, was created by André Harvey. It is forty-nine inches high and features a pair of jumping frogs, each weighing 225 pounds and replaces a Charles C. Parks sculpture.

The terrace leads to the original bank barn that has been completely rebuilt. When Chris and Penny bought *Applecross* the sides of the barn were bowing out, the roof leaked badly and the floor was unstable, but they considered it an important part of their master plan for redevelopment of the estate. The Montchanin Design Group was consulted and was instrumental in creating a plan that converted the barn into a center of activity for the Saridakis children, while at the same time functioning as a gathering place for adults.

The undertaking required considerable engineering skill. To accomplish this the barn roof was raised while steel supporting girders were put in place on the outside of the building; these were later faced with stone matching the barn. The roof was then repositioned and eleven inches of compressed insulation added. Finally, the old roof slate was removed and 7,000 square feet of new slate installed. This was brought from Christ Church, two miles away, which was replacing the slate on its main structure and the parish house.

The barn has three levels. A loft has been installed that is currently used for guests. On the main level Chris Saridakis has a corner office with floor-to-ceiling glass walls looking over the swimming pool and gardens. The kitchen, seating area, and bar next to the office are made of reclaimed wood. Open space is equipped with a ping pong table, pool table, foosball, air hockey, table basketball, and a retractable screen for movies or television. On the lower level there is a three-car garage, two bathrooms and two showers, all convenient to the swimming pool. The horse stalls are now in use as a storage area, but there's room for a pony.

Applecross

Owners:	Donald P. and Wilhelmina du Pont Ross, original
	Mr. and Mrs. Christopher Saridakis, current
Constructed:	c. 1807, 1928, 2006
Architects:	1928: James Thompson
	2006: Jeffrey Beitel
	2008: Montchanin Design Group
Location:	Greenville, Delaware

Notes

1. The seventy-seven acres of land given to Wilhelmina and Donald Ross as a wedding present were part of the original land grant given to William Penn's Quaker colony in 1685. It was then granted by Penn to William Gregg. Through the years ownership passed to the DuPont Company and Henry A. du Pont and subsequently to Henry F. du Pont, who sold it in order for it to be given to the Rosses as a wedding present.

2. In a letter dated September 22, 1998, addressed to the grandson of Hugh Rodney Sharp (*Gibraltar*) Wilhelmina Ross wrote, "Granny and Uncle Pierre were living down in *Saint Amour* and they felt it was dangerous for my mother and three small children to live so far in the county! ... So we moved into *Saint Amour*."

3. *Money, Manure & Maintenance, ingredients for successful gardens of Marian Coffin*, Fleming, Nancy. Country Place Books,

The great room of the barn overlooks the swimming pool. Next to the pool an outdoor pavilion overlooks gardens designed by landscape architects Marian Coffin (1923) and Noel Chamberlin (1929).

The original exterior wall at the back of the house became an interior wall with shutters left intact. The newly created hallway connects the kitchen, breakfast room, living room and conservatory.

The re-designed kitchen was expanded, with the former servants' quarters converted into a laundry and mud room. A covered walkway leads from the kitchen to garage.

The bank barn was completely rebuilt as a combination activity center for children and gathering place for adults with changing rooms and showers for the nearby swimming pool.

A reflection pool between the house and barn is the setting for André Harvey's bronze sculpture, *Spring Ballet,* featuring a pair of jumping frogs.

Stone used for construction of *Ashland Red Clay Creek* is called a "Brandywine Mix." Much
of it is Brandywine blue rock which, when first quarried, is bright blue to blue-gray in color.

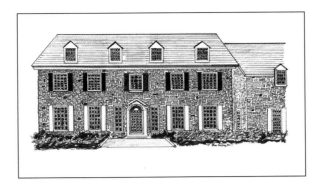

ASHLAND RED CLAY CREEK

Overlooking the rural valley of Delaware's Piedmont region

When Henry Belin du Pont, Jr., chose a site for his estate, it was the only family-owned property in the Delaware region of the Piedmont plateau.[1] Situated on the fall line between the ancient Appalachian Mountains to the west and the generally wet Atlantic coastal plain on the east, the area is characterized by undulating hills and upland valleys primarily used for agriculture. The Ashland and Red Clay Creek farms were absorbed into du Pont's holdings, providing a spectacular setting for his country seat.

As architect for his residence du Pont selected R. Brognard Okie. A native of New Jersey, Okie made Philadelphia his base of operation and most of his commissions were in a tri-state area that included Delaware, where he designed three du Pont houses and modified several others.[2] Okie specialized in Colonial Revival style with particular reference to original Pennsylvania farmhouses and incorporated many of their details in his work. To learn more about them he often spent time driving through southeastern parts of the state to study their common characteristics in place. *Ashland Red Clay Creek* typifies his interpretation of the style.

In the Henry B. du Pont, Jr., house, now owned by his grandson, Henry du Pont IV, Okie's design is evidenced by the random appearance of the stone construction, an uneven roofline, massive chimneys, and internal dormer windows that begin below the roofline and project into the roof.

Crossing Red Clay Creek,[3] the half-mile driveway to the residence passes through an allee of eighty-foot London plane trees surrounded by woodlands interspersed with low shrubs, ferns, and wildflowers, gradually climbing and bending to the right before ending in a formal circle at the front entrance.

Ashland Red Clay Creek has five stories including the basement and attic. It has eight bedrooms in the main part of the house and seven in the staff quarters; there are eleven fireplaces. A vestibule at the front opens to the entrance hall that extends the full width of the house. On the left side of the hall is a formal stairway to the

second floor and to the right of the stairway an outside door opens to a back terrace with a sweeping view of the Red Clay Valley.[4]

An arched doorway to the left of the front entrance leads to the library and living room hallway. Mural wallpaper in shades of black and white depicts classic architecture and formal gardens. The powder room, on the left side, is large enough to have a settee in the anteroom. Resting on it is a pillow with the aphorism, "Despite the cost of living, it's still popular." At the end of the corridor on the same side, there is an elevator, installed at a later date, that operates from the basement to the second floor. Before its installation the area was occupied by a telephone room.

The thirty by forty-five-foot living room has eleven-foot ceilings surrounded by dentil molding, and the fireplace, facing the entry, is surrounded by painted wood paneling with pilasters on each side. When you enter the room on the left wall there is a full-length portrait of Henry's great grandmother, Eleuthera du Pont Bradford. Oak floors, laid in random widths that vary from six to fourteen inches, are complemented by Persian carpets and traditional period furniture. An outside door leads to a front terrace and a second door opens to a screened-in porch.

The dark, richly stained pine paneled library reflects two major interests of both Henry Jr. and Henry IV—sailing and antique firearms. In addition to shelves filled with books, many of them sea-oriented, a number of naval prints from Henry Jr.'s collection are prominently displayed. A tempera on panel of Henry B. du Pont, Jr., known as Hank, hangs above the fireplace. The painting was done by George A. Weymouth (Frolic), a cousin, in 1970. To the left of the fireplace is a glass-fronted bookcase and to the right is an exterior door. A pair of early dueling pistols is mounted on the facing below the mantelshelf.

On either side of the front door there is a pair of brass salutatory cannons. Dated 1860, they were used aboard ship and were part of Henry Jr.'s extensive collection of sixty. Robert A. Howard, an archivist and former curator at Hagley Museum, who dealt with archaic technologies and black powder, was hired to document the collection. A privately printed book, handsomely bound in red morocco, describes each cannon, giving the provenance where available. The oldest one mentioned is a 1720 beer mug or stein breech cannon. The name derives from a cannon in which the breech end is left open and the projectile is loaded from the breech with a handle resembling a beer mug or stein.

In an article Howard later wrote for *The Artilleryman* journal, he recounted an incident that took place on Hank's forty-six-foot sloop, *Cyane* (meaning azure-blue and named for the flagship of Admiral Francis du Pont). There was a custom aboard the yacht that, after every drink, those aboard would load one of a pair of bronze guns with one ounce more powder than the last charge and fire the gun. On one occasion, following a day Howard describes as especially "social," a tremendous load was put in the gun and fired. The canon recoiled right through the bulkhead of the deckhouse.[5] The tradition ended that afternoon.

Most of Henry IV's sailing is done on his 1927 William Hand motorsailer, *Nor'easter*. Hand was considered the premier yacht designer of the 1920s and 30s. His boats were the strongest and most beautifully built and were credited with being the ultimate in form and function. Henry had *Nor'easter* restored in 1991 and it has served as the Committee boat for the Connecticut-based OSC (Off Soundings Club) for more than fifty years.

Across from the front stairs at *Ashland Red Clay Creek*, the arched doorway matches the one leading to the living room hallway and opens to the formal dining room. Its focal point is the fireplace at the end and above it the portrait of Eleuthere Irénée du Pont, founder of E.I. du Pont de Nemours and Company, a copy of the one painted by Rembrandt Peale in 1831, on display at another family member's house.

The spacious room is painted off-white with a glaze of old ivory. There are three floor-to-ceiling windows and three additional portraits. To the right of the fireplace is a flower room with a door to the outside. On the wall opposite the fireplace there is a painting of Pierre Samuel du Pont, the physiocrat[6] who brought his family to this country on New Year's Day in 1800. Across from the windows are portraits of Pierre Samuel's parents, Samuel du Pont de Nemours and his wife, Anne Alexandrine de Montchanin. Furniture in the dining room is Chippendale and the table, Henry comments, can seat eighteen comfortably, though he has squeezed in twenty-two.

Next to the dining room entrance and passageway to the service wing is a paneled office once used by Henry's step-grandmother, Emily. The office was originally painted blue, then pink and is now hunt red. Hunting prints and eclectic memorabilia in bookcases on each side of the fireplace reflect another of Henry's interests, horses. Despite an allergy to them, that has not prevented his participation in *Winterthur*'s annual Point-to-Point Steeplechase, held on the estate formerly owned by a cousin, Henry Francis du Pont.

Emily du Pont Tybout du Pont was Henry Jr.'s second wife and they shared an interest in flying and hunting that was a natural extension of family interests. His grandfather, Henry Belin du Pont, had the first private plane licensed by the U.S. Department of Commerce and he opened DuPont Airfield in 1927, which he called "the airway to everywhere." On October 22nd of that year, he welcomed Charles Lindbergh, who landed at the airport on his U.S. tour.

Skeet shooting has been an avid interest of the family, and Henry and Emily often spent Sunday afternoons at Vicmead Hunt Club joining friends who shared their interest in the sport. Two couples they often met were Brig. Gen. Milton Ashkins, wing commander of the 4710th Air Defense Wing at New Castle Air Force Base, and his wife, Jane, and Col. Roy B. Caviness, who was stationed there, and his wife, Jeannette. She still fondly remembers sixty years ago, when, after an afternoon of shooting at Vicmead's clay targets, the group would often return to Hank and Emily's where Hank would fix the group scrambled eggs in the kitchen. The main part of the house, Jeannette recalls, was sometimes closed up with rugs rolled and staff off duty, as the hosts would be leaving the next day for a cruise on *Cyane*.

It is in the kitchen area that Henry IV, an enthusiastic amateur chef, has made a number of changes. Cabinets in the butler's pantry have been modified and new cabinets built matching the original ones. In the kitchen he has had a window replaced with a door, allowing him to have direct access for barbecuing.

From his mother's and father's house in Southport, Connecticut, Henry rescued the original door used for their walk-in freezer. The massive door, built by Jamison Cold Storage Co., in Hagerstown, Maryland, is in better condition than when new. It has been refinished to a rich maple color and its heavy-duty hinges and handle have been chrome-plated. Henry enjoys entertaining here and a table has been hand-crafted for him from a black walnut tree felled on his property. Ten chairs are in the process of being made of wood from the same tree. The kitchen floors are terra cotta (saltillo) tile from Coahuila, Mexico.

In the basement level there is a fully equipped gym with a treadmill and free weights. The former children's recreation room, with pine floors, has been converted for use as a game room for adults, and the former coal cellar is now used as a storage area. The barometer hanging there, Henry points out, has accurately recorded atmospheric pressure since he was a boy.

A commanding view of the Red Clay Valley is seen from the back terrace where, at one end, there is a sculpture of a boy and two dogs called *American Youth*, sculpted in 1967 by well-known Wilmington sculptor, Charles Parks. Following retirement from the DuPont Company, Henry's grandfather accepted a position as chairman of the Greater Wilmington Development Council. In this role he was instrumental in having a park, called Fountain Plaza, built in a triangle formed by Pennsylvania Avenue, Delaware Avenue, and Harrison Street in downtown Wilmington. Parks was commissioned to do the sculpture, *American Youth*, and the original is located there.

A second park was developed by du Pont in a quadrangle bounded by Washington, West, and Tenth Streets, and Delaware Avenue, across from the Sheraton Hotel. In recognition of his civic accomplishments, the park was named the H. B. du Pont Park and it is a popular venue in June for *In The Park* lunchtime jazz concerts. Du Pont was also responsible for the trees planted on Delaware Avenue, turning the street into a tree-lined boulevard.

Ashland Red Clay Creek

Owners: Henry B. du Pont, Jr., original
Edward B. du Pont
Henry B. du Pont IV, current
Constructed: 1934-1935

Architect: Richardson Brognard Okie
Location: Red Clay Creek, Delaware

Notes

1. In 1935, Lammot and Pamela Copeland purchased 135 acres of land adjoining Henry du Pont, Jr.'s property. Soon after they announced their plans to build *Mt. Cuba*, Mrs. Copeland commented that, had it not been for the fact that cousin Henry and his wife had moved there first, she doubted that they would have located that far from the Brandywine.

2. Okie was also an expert in the reconstruction of historic buildings and was responsible for the restoration of the Betsy Ross House in Philadelphia and Pennsbury Manor, the American home of William Penn, founder of the Colony of Pennsylvania.

3. Red Clay Creek is a thirteen-and-a-half-mile tributary of White Clay Creek in northern Delaware. Southwest of Wilmington the two streams empty into the Christina River. Red Clay Creek has flowed through this area for thousands of years, creating a valley that makes up part of the *Ashland Red Clay Creek* estate.

4. The Red Clay Valley encompasses fifty-five square miles of rolling hills, woodlands, and farms in Chester County, Pennsylvania, and New Castle County, Delaware, according to the Red Clay Valley Association, West Chester, Pennsylvania.

When Henry du Pont IV acquired *Ashland Red Clay Creek* it had 256 acres; since then he has added adjoining farmland bringing the total to 500 acres. There are twenty-seven buildings on the property including the original houses of both the Ashland and Red Clay Creek farms.

5. *The Artilleryman*, Summer 2000, Vol. 22, No. 4

6. Physiocracy was a school of economists in eighteenth century France that believed all wealth derived from land and that government policy should not interfere with natural economics.

These French cannons, from Henry du Pont, Jr.'s collection, date from the mid-18th century. They are cast bronze with elaborate detailing and a bore diameter of one inch, and are approximately twenty-four inches in length.

Ashland Red Clay Creek was designed by Philadelphia architect R. Brognard Okie, who specialized in Colonial Revival style architecture based on original Pennsylvania farmhouses.

The thirty by forty-five-foot living room extends across the width of the house with a centered fireplace and door to a side porch. There are eleven fireplaces in the house.

Entered from the stair hall, the library is paneled with built-in bookshelves. Over the fireplace there is a tempera painting of original house owner Henry Belin du Pont, Jr.

The dining room seats eighteen comfortably. Chairs are Chippendale. Over the fireplace is a copy of the 1831 Rembrandt
Peale portrait of DuPont Company founder Eleuthere I. du Pont.

Henry du Pont is an enthusiastic cook and has remodeled the kitchen to professional standards
highlighted by an open grill, walk-in freezer, and commercial stove.

The stately exterior of *Bellevue Hall* was inspired by the boyhood home of William du Pont, Jr., Montpelier, the Classic Revival former home of fourth U.S. President James Madison in Virginia. It was originally built as a three-story Gothic structure.

BELLEVUE HALL

A Gothic mansion rebuilt to replicate the home of President James Madison

*B*ellevue Hall is a stately two-and-a half-story Classic Revival mansion that sits on 328 acres, the centerpiece of Delaware's Bellevue State Park. The former home of William duPont, Jr.,[1] *Bellevue Hall* is one of only a handful of du Pont residences not built by members of the du Pont family.

Hanson Robinson, whose family had owned property in Wilmington for 125 years, moved to Philadelphia in 1843 and started a wool refinery business. Seven years later he returned as a highly successful merchant and purchased land on which to build a country estate. By 1855, he had built a one hundred thousand dollar, three-story Gothic Revival castle and, acknowledging the industry that had brought him his success, named his mansion Woolton Hall.

Robinson lived here until his death in 1871 after which it was bought by Clark Robinson Griggs, a successful shipping magnate with a hobby of collecting carriages. Upon Griggs' death, it was acquired by William duPont, Sr., through a Baltimore realty company. He also purchased the carriage collection and added to the property over the years, purchasing adjacent farms as they became available.

In 1892, duPont, youngest son of "Boss" Henry, married his second wife, the former Annie Rogers Zinn, in St. George's Church, London. They remained in Europe for ten years, living in self-imposed exile to escape the wrath of Wilmington society and the du Pont family that resulted from their two divorces. After spending a few months in Paris they returned to England and from 1897 to 1901 lived in a series of rented mansions in Reading, Sussex, Surrey, and finally Binfield Park, Bracknell, near Windsor Castle. Daughter Marion was born in Wilmington in 1894, during a visit home, and their son, William, Jr., Willie, was born at Loseley Park, near Guilford, Surrey County, England two years later.

While keeping Woolton Manor, re-named *Bellevue Hall*, as his Wilmington base, William looked for another home in the United States where he could raise his family and easily return to Wilmington to watch over his financial affairs. He found it in Orange County, Virginia: Montpelier, former home of James and Dolley Madison. DuPont's secretary, William King Lennig, acted as his agent and William took title to the property in January 1901. A year later the duPonts and their children, aged six and eight, boarded a steamship in Liverpool and sailed to America to begin their new life in Virginia.

William and Annie also maintained homes near Brunswick, Georgia, and outside Philadelphia, frequently returning to London. But, Marion and Willie loved their new home and it influenced both of them for the rest of their lives. Marion recalled the time and thought William gave to Montpelier and the extensive changes that he oversaw. "My father added on several rooms and made the wings two stories high," she recalled, "He was here pretty solidly the first two years after we got the place." When duPont acquired Montpelier it had twenty-two rooms. After his renovation it had fifty-five rooms and twelve bathrooms.

In 1919 William, Jr., married Jean Liseter Austin in a New Year's Day ceremony and as a wedding gift her father, an executive of Baldwin Locomotive Works, gave the couple 600 acres of land in Rosemont, fifteen miles west of Philadelphia near Newtown Square. Six years later William, Sr., matched the gift by building the couple a house that was, at Willie's request, an exact replica of his boyhood Virginia home. As its focal point the three-story Classic Revival residence was finished with a portico supported by four-columns, matching the one at Montpelier.

The couple named their new home Liseter Hall and set about breeding race horses, show horses, jumpers, and Welsh ponies as well as Guernsey cattle and pure-bred beagles under the name Foxcatcher Farms. One of their horses, Rosemont, sporting Foxcatcher's distinctive blue and yellow silks, beat the legendary Seabiscuit by a nose in the 1937 Santa Anita Handicap.

Unfortunately, the marriage didn't last. The couple separated in 1940 and in 1941 duPont packed up tack and togs, loaded his horses, main barn, and a disassembled indoor riding rink onto vans, and moved across the border to Delaware and the 328-acre *Bellevue Hall,* having inherited it from his father in 1928, along with 240 million dollars, the equivalent of three billion dollars today. And though he made changes to the grounds, adding barns (including a Butler barn and two from Sears Roebuck) and stables, and a five-furlong horse track, it was the dramatic transformation of the house that caused the most comment among his Greenville cousins, most of whom lived across New Castle County near the Brandywine River.

Unable to move Liseter Hall, or Montpelier, that Marion had inherited, but still nostalgic for his Virginia home, Willie reconstructed the Gothic Woolton Manor into yet another replica of Montpelier. Octagonal crenellated towers disappeared, rounded corners were squared, three stories became two-and-a-half in the style of Madison's house, stone walls were stuccoed and painted yellow, and, in a defining addition, a portico over a new front entrance with four signature columns was erected to complete the replication of Montpelier's facade. A matching one was also built over the mansion's former front entrance.

As bookends to his achievement, Georgian-style gate houses were built flanking the entrance of the three-quarter mile driveway that leads from the public road past woods and rippling streams to the main residence. Each gate house, also painted yellow, had a living room, dining room, den, kitchen, pantry, three bedrooms, and a bathroom.

The transformation of *Bellevue Hall* from Gothic castle to Virginia neo-classic took three years, but duPont was delighted with the results. Still, there was more to come. The front entrance of Woolton Hall had faced northeast and the Delaware River; however, duPont changed the front entrance of *Bellevue Hall* to face west. Across from it a formal walled garden was designed in the shape of a horseshoe with boxwood planted to simulate stirrups, a hunting horn, spur, horse bit, and riding crop.

Bellevue Hall has forty rooms, then maintained by a staff of fifteen, and, though Willie changed the exterior to conform to the appearance of Montpelier, he left most of the interior spaces as they were, but used them for different purposes. His major interior alteration was to move the grand staircase from its position opposite Woolton Hall's front door to its present location opposite the *Bellevue Hall* front entrance. The former drawing room was converted to a dining room seating fifty while the walnut-paneled library remained as it was, except for squaring off its octagonal corners.

The Woolton Hall dining room was changed into a bar and smoking room. Across from the library the house was extended to create a drawing room that led to a 428-square foot trophy room, twice the size of the drawing room, with built-in display cabinets to exhibit some of the numerous trophies and ribbons awarded to Willie's horses. By the time of his death, duPont had trained horses that won first place in more than 1000 races.

There are seven bedrooms on the second floor; staff rooms were on the third floor. Willie's is by far the largest bedroom with a dramatic seven-foot wide sash window looking over a panoramic view of the Delaware River. In order to have a clear view of the river, duPont paid his neighbors to keep their trees trimmed to a height that he could see over.

The guest cottage at *Bellevue Hall,* formerly the Old Mt. Pleasant School, includes a living room, dining room, kitchen, pantry, front and back porches, three bedrooms, and two bathrooms. Near the tennis courts a thirty-five by ninety-foot swimming pool is anchored by a playhouse with a living room, kitchen, and two dressing rooms. There were three greenhouses and a potting shed, with meticulous records kept for all flowers grown at *Bellevue Hall.* Camelias were Willie's favorite flower and there were seventeen varieties, including a pink and white weeping harlequin specimen named for him.

DuPont was considered one of the wealthiest men in America and, possibly because of this, was almost paranoid about his safety and the protection of his material possessions. He reportedly had five large safes in his house, though only four have been accounted for. A silver and wine vault is located in a closet in the dining room, a walk-in safe in the trophy room held business papers, jewelry was stored in a closet safe off of the upstairs hallway, and a door from the billiard room opens to a large vault. He also had several means of escape built into the house in case of a burglary. One of these, entered from a small, second floor closet could only have been managed by a small person—Willie was five feet, nine inches tall and weighed less than 150 pounds.

Willie's love of sports was nurtured by his exposure to raising horses and hunting dogs at his father's estates. He developed a foxhound pack at Montpelier that he later moved to his 5,000-acre farm in Maryland, which became known as Fair Hill. Another of his seven estates, Walnut Hall, was located outside Boyce, Virginia, in the Shenandoah Valley. It was an area popular with wealthy individuals from the northern and western parts of the country because of its fox hunting, climate and inexpensive land.

In addition to being involved in equestrian pursuits, duPont was also absorbed in raising purebred beef cattle and he owned a premier herd of the reddish-hued and powerful Santa Gertrudis cattle. This resulted from a breeding program developed with the help of Robert J. Kleberg, Jr., who owned the famous King Ranch in Kingsville, Texas, which purchased the entire herd after duPont's death.

A talented and much-in-demand designer of flat racing tracks and steeplechase courses, duPont designed more than twenty-five such projects. Included among these was a steeplechase course in Cecil County, Maryland, and Delaware Park in Stanton, Delaware, which was developed by him in partnership with Donald P. Ross, a du Pont cousin-in-law. It opened June 26, 1937, with a thirty-day meet. The track had a one-mile dirt oval, stables for 1226 horses and a 7,500-seat grandstand. Today there are 116 days of racing. The seating capacity at one time exceeded 30,000.

Barbaro made his first career race at Delaware Park and went on to win the 2006 Kentucky Derby. Barbaro won by six-and-a-half lengths and was heavily favored to win the Preakness Stakes, but stumbled in the Pimlico race, fracturing three bones in his right rear leg, an injury that led to his death the following year.

As duPont's sports interests expanded he built a 15,000-square foot indoor facility that included courts for tennis, badminton, basketball, and squash, plus a bowling alley, a twenty by fifty-foot indoor swimming pool, and a spectator gallery. In case of inclement weather, the sports complex could be reached through a seventy-five-foot subterranean tunnel accessed from the first floor by stairways from the library and dining room that also led to a billiard room. Though the billiard room was below grade, there was an illusion of it being on ground level by the installation of windows with outdoor scenes painted opposite them on the supporting walls.

Willie's second favorite sports interest was tennis and he was involved with the Southern California Tennis Association in the late 1930s and 1940s. It was at this time that he met Margaret Osborne, who was one of the top Grand Slam champions, winning thirty-seven titles, including six singles titles, and who became his second wife. They married in 1947 and were divorced seventeen years later, having had one child, William duPont III, born July 22, 1952. While married the couple entertained a number of tennis notables including Alice Marble and William Talbert, as well as Louise Brough Clapp and Doris Hart, both of whom won thirty-five Grand Slam titles. For their use at *Bellevue Hall* there was one cement court, three grass courts, and three clay courts—two outdoor and one indoor.

An astute businessman, Willie continued two of the projects started by his father. Delaware Trust Company was purchased by Alfred I. duPont and William, Sr., in 1916. William, Sr., was president from 1920 to 1922 and was serving as board chairman at the time of his death in 1928. William, Jr., replaced him in this position.

William, Sr., also founded the Delaware Land Development Co. that developed Westover Hills, Wilmington's first suburban community designed for wealthy residents. It was planned in six stages beginning in 1926. According to W. Barksdale Maynard writing in his book, *Buildings of Delaware*, there were sixty-eight millionaires in the state in 1929, many of whom lived in this neighborhood, including Pierre S. du Pont III, Alfred Victor du Pont and William Edison, son of Thomas Edison. William, Jr., inherited this company and continued with advancement of the venture and it remains a choice residential area.

After William, Jr., died (December 31, 1965) a survey was made of the *Bellevue Hall* property. There were an astonishing seventy-four named buildings on the property including, among others, the main house, the sports building, Old Mt. Pleasant School, a playhouse, three greenhouses, main garage with six bays, a work room and a wash room, a main racing barn, yearling barn and a jockey house, a wagon storage building, trailer truck building, truck garage, dairy, creamery, help's cottage, shop, potting shed, and a ham house—a carry-over from his Virginia years. A loading siding was maintained by the Baltimore & Ohio Railroad. On acreage duPont owned across Philadelphia Pike, there were an additional forty-two buildings. Each building had its own function with the added advantage that in case of fire other structures could be saved.

William duPont III was just thirteen years old when his father died and living in Texas with his mother. No disposition could be made of *Bellevue Hall* until he reached the age of twenty-one and it lay idle during this time. By the time William III reached his majority he was not interested in relocating to Delaware and the property was sold to the State of Delaware in 1976 for $6.25 million dollars. One year later, it opened to the public as a state park.

Tours of *Bellevue Hall* are conducted on a quarterly schedule; however, third floor bedrooms are not included on the tour as this floor is considered by many to be haunted. Some staff members have reported seeing a woman in a white dress in various buildings on the estate and catering crews have been puzzled by lights going on and off, curtains moving, rearranged chairs, and strange noises. The underground tunnel between the main house and sports complex does seem eerie as it is damp, sometimes has a wet floor, is low ceilinged and narrow, and poorly lit. In 1976 a barn fire killed twenty horses; since then some employees while making their rounds have reported hearing the sounds of horses hooves as if trying to escape.

Though the third floor is normally closed, visitors curious to check out spirits for themselves do have an opportunity. Once a year at Halloween there's a Ghost Tour of *Bellevue Hall*.

Bellevue Hall

Owners:	Hanson Robinson, original
	Clark R. Griggs
	William duPont, Sr.
	William duPont, Jr.
	Bellevue State Park, State of Delaware, current
Constructed:	1855
Reconstructed:	1928-1931
Location:	Bellevue State Park
	1016 Philadelphia Pike
	800 Carr Road
	Wilmington, Delaware

Notes

1. There are five ways of spelling du Pont. William preferred spelling it without a space between du and Pont, as did his cousin, Alfred I. duPont.

Bellevue Hall is the former home of William duPont, Jr. Surrounded by 328 acres of parks and recreational facilities, it is now owned and operated by the State of Delaware.

The gazebo anchors the far end of the horseshoe garden that at one time featured garden shrubbery inspired by and shaped in the forms of a stirrup, saddle, hunting horn, crop, snaffle, bit, and a spur.

Boxwood was built in 1928, covered an entire block, about twenty acres, and prevailed over Westover Hills. It was a country estate in the middle of a suburban development.

BOXWOOD

Westover Hills' largest property covered more than twenty acres

The gates are still there. At the corner of DuPont and Westover Roads, eight-foot high wrought iron gates are surrounded by holly trees, replacing a stand of towering oaks that once flanked the driveway leading to the neighborhood's largest house on its largest property. *Boxwood* covered an entire block, approximately twenty of the 600 acres of former farmland transferred by William duPont, Sr., to the Delaware Land Development Company in 1926 for the purpose of creating Westover Hills, Wilmington's first suburban community designed for wealthy residents. At his father's death William, Jr., continued the venture.

Boxwood was designed by Philadelphia architects Brenton Wallace and Fred Warner, who, after graduating from the University of Pennsylvania, formed a partnership in 1914. Their work was represented in affluent mainline communities such as Haverford, Bryn Mawr, Rosemont, and Chestnut Hill, and extended into northern Delaware. The firm's architecture, referred to as types in their master presentation book, included English, Colonial, Georgian, French, and Italian. Other leading architects designing Westover Hills houses about the same time were R. Brognard Okie, Albert Ely Ives, and Massena and duPont.

Soon after the plot lines were drawn, Wallace & Warner was hired by F. B. Davis, Jr., a DuPont executive, to design an almost 12,000 square-foot house for him and his family. However, before moving in, Davis was offered the presidency of U.S. Rubber Company (Uniroyal) in which the DuPont Company had controlling interest. He accepted and the Davises departed for New York, leaving behind not only the house, but custom-designed furniture as well.

Within six months the house and its contents had been purchased by George Phippen Edmonds and his wife Natalie Wilson du Pont, daughter of Lammot du Pont, president of the DuPont Company. At the time of purchase, Edmonds was the president of Bond Crown & Cork Co., a subsidiary of Continental Can Company. Later, he served as president of both Bond Crown & Cork and Wilmington Trust, a

bank founded in July 1903 by T. Coleman du Pont, to manage the banking and trust needs of the du Pont family.

By 1950 Edmonds was devoting full time to his Wilmington Trust presidential duties. When making the transition, he quipped to a colleague that as a bank president he would have to shun working in his shirtsleeves as he had at Bond and learn to wear a jacket while at his desk.

The Edmonds' named their estate *Boxwood* after the terraced boxwood garden they built on two tiers in back of the house on the foundations of an old barn. It was the focal point of the back yard with diamond-shaped beds and crisscrossing paths. A pond just beyond is anchored by a spring house of the same vintage. Formal gardens were planted with flowers; vegetables, herbs, and cutting flowers were supplied from the garden and a still existent greenhouse at the northeast side of the house.

For the twenty-fifth Anniversary Meeting of the Garden Club of America, held in Philadelphia in 1938, a tour was offered to visit members' gardens in Wilmington. Among those included were the Edmonds's garden. The program noted that "Old barn walls were incorporated in the flower garden." The description also mentioned the many fine specimens of box bushes. Boxwood at the front of the house was used to edge a square courtyard, and three varieties of apple trees thrived in an orchard to the right of the front entrance.

The two-story, red brick house is built in Wallace & Warner's Colonial Revival style that combined elements of their Colonial and Georgian types. The roof is grey tile simulated to look like wood and there are dormer windows at the front and back. Shutters on the first floor windows were painted white and are solid with three panels. Those on the second floor are louvered and were originally painted dark green.

The front entrance is flanked by fluted columns and above them is a wrought iron balcony surmounted by a crown-shaped keystone. Inside are two steps up to a spacious hallway leading to French doors at the back overlooking the gardens. Over these doors is a clear glass window with leaded tracery. Outside, fluted columns with Corinthian capitals support a lintel with a carved frieze and a spread eagle as the center of interest. Above it a broken scroll pediment frames a large acorn sculpture.

The house has twenty-one rooms with twelve bedrooms, including three that were originally a sewing room and the staff living room. There are seven bathrooms. In the 1960s the Edmonds finished off the attic, formerly used for badminton, where feathered projectiles once flew beneath the rafters. This added two additional bedrooms and a playroom to accommodate the Edmonds's five grandchildren. A two-person elevator that carried laundry from the basement, food from the kitchen, and passengers to the second floor has since been removed.

In 1994, George Edmonds died and, in the same year, *Boxwood* was purchased by Charles and Diane Ciarrocchi, Jr., who have made a number of changes. The house now has approximately 17,000 square feet. Chuck Ciarrocchi explains that the house was built of structural steel with steel beams in the basement. "It made changing the upstairs rooms easy," he comments, "much easier than having to tear out supporting walls to rearrange the space."

The original four-car garage is heated and is accessible from the house through a courtyard off of the servant's wing. The apartment over the garage, then occupied by the cook, was tied in with the second floor bedroom area during the 1994 renovations. The chauffeur, who lived in the house, looked after the General Motors automobiles, which most of the du Ponts owned while the company was controlled by the DuPont Company. George Edmonds drove an Oldsmobile and Natalie a Cadillac. A new three-car garage has been added across from it with an apartment above.

To the right of the front entrance is a formal twenty by thirty-two-foot paneled living room with windows on three sides. Focal point of the room is the Adams design fireplace with a white marble surround flanked by double pilasters. When the Edmonds lived at *Boxwood* the walls were painted pale yellow with white trim and the Ciarrocchis have kept this color scheme. From the living room French doors open to a guest suite that was formerly a partially enclosed porch with arched windows. At that time, it was furnished with a sisal carpet and rattan furniture. Evergreens and ferns in jardinieres accentuated the arches that have now been adapted as windows.

Across from the living room is the entrance to the dining room. The fireplace, similar to the one in the living room, is flanked by floor to ceiling pilasters. While the Edmonds lived at *Boxwood* a hand-painted mural depicting life along the Hudson River covered the walls above the wainscot. This has been removed and is in storage and the room has been painted a raspberry color. On both sides of the fireplace are arched eight-paneled doors. One of these opens to the former morning room and the other to what was the butler's pantry. Both spaces have been incorporated into a spacious contemporary kitchen with the butler's pantry in place, but completely updated.

A wing added by the Ciarrocchis at the time they purchased *Boxwood* connects the open kitchen to a breakfast room and a large family room through three arches that were formerly outside doorways. There is a fireplace in the middle of the room, which has a coffered ceiling and cove lighting. French doors along one side lead to a terrace and pergola. Over the fireplace there is a large flat-screen television and above that a wheel window divided into six panes with a medallion in the middle.

Also accessible through the kitchen wing is the new pool room overlooking the thirty by sixty-foot swimming pool built in 2003. The pool room has three sets of French doors opening to the pool terrace. A wheel window above with radiating muntins matches the one in the family room. At one end there is a fireplace and at the other end stairs lead to a minstrel balcony. Soaring cathedral ceilings are twenty-five feet high.

Further along the entrance hallway is a paneled study with bookshelves on three walls and windows overlooking the drive; it too, has a fireplace. The original pine paneling has been painted dark green. Andrew Edmonds, Jr., who lived with his grandfather at *Boxwood* for a year, recalls that after work he would come home and he and his grandfather would dine together, always in the formal dining room. "As children," he said, "we took our meals in the breakfast room, but when we grew up we always ate in the dining room. It was a wonderful experience, getting to know my grandfather on a one-on-one basis," he comments.

With all of the fine architectural details throughout the house, the part of *Boxwood* that Andrew remembers most clearly is the basement area. "It isn't your normal cellar," he says, "It's divided in half with all of the mechanicals for the house to the left of the stairs as you go down. But, the other half is built like a miniature cobblestone street. On one side are shuttered windows with mirrored glass and window boxes; between them is an antique church bench. Opposite it, and the main feature of the street, is the tap room, as my grandparents called it, or pub, with a partial shingled overhanging roof and a door from the street that opens to an L-shaped tavern."

A large stone fireplace is in the center of the far wall and on the mantel is a collection of pewter tankards, chargers, and candlesticks. The tap room is now furnished with over-stuffed leather furniture, a wall-mounted television, and a pool table covered in red baize. Original furniture was of the traditional pub type with Windsor chairs and a tavern table. Floors in this area are tile and brick. In the bar area, they are flagstone and there are bar stools and a foosball table. Also known as table football, the international game dates back to the 1890s and, while a recent addition, is an appropriate game for the age of the house. Both rooms are paneled in pine and have exposed rough-hewn beamed ceilings.

Andrew Edmonds, Sr., who grew up at *Boxwood*, remembers spending more time in the larger room that was then called the TV room because this was where the only television in the house was located. He goes on to say that the tap room was seldom used for parties or gatherings, though he does remember a New Year's dinner being served there. While New Year's Calling was in progress upstairs, preparations were underway for dinner for the immediate family and friends in the tap room.

His parents' primary entertaining, he mentions, was at an annual Apple Blossom Party held in April or May when the orchard trees were in bloom. "Over one hundred people attended and there were caterers and bartenders all over the house. One of the things I remember most was rowing guests back and forth across the pond. My brother and I each had a rowboat. Mine was named Nipper, but I don't remember why."

In the eighty-four years since *Boxwood* was built, just two families have lived there and, though the house has been added to and modernized, it remains substantially as it was in 1928. Outdoor activities at the estate no longer center around swimming or rowing in the pond, but focus on the state-of-the-art swimming pool and a Sport Court, an innovation that didn't exist when *Boxwood's* house plans were drawn. The versatile game court can accommodate basketball, tennis, volleyball, and badminton as well as ice skating in winter and aerobics in summer.

Even after George Edmonds moved on to Wilmington Trust, he fondly remembered his days spent with Gold Bond's bottle caps. At one time, cork-lined caps were used to seal bottles on hundreds of brands of soft drinks, ranging from Apple Dandy and Big Chief Root Beer to Coca Cola and Moxie.[1] As a reminder of his association with that industry, Andrew remembers his grandfather proudly planting a cork oak tree—the species from which most cork is harvested—and carefully nurturing it through Delaware's change of seasons. While they can reach a height of some sixty feet in their native environ, Andrew says his grandfather's never grew to more than about two feet. And, sadly, no cork was ever harvested from it.

Boxwood

Owners:	Mr. and Mrs. F.B. Davis, Jr., original
	Mr. and Mrs. George P. Edmonds, Sr.
	Mr. and Mrs. Charles J. Ciarrocchi, Jr., current
Architects:	Wallace & Warner (1928)
	Arthur Bernardson & Associates (1994)
Location:	Westover Hills
	Wilmington, Delaware

Notes

1. As a result of extensive advertising "moxie" entered American usage as an expression of courage, e.g. "the guy's got moxie."

Side entrance of the Colonial Revival brick mansion that incorporates elements of Georgian and Colonial styles of architecture. It was designed by the Philadelphia architectural firm Wallace & Warner.

The dramatic stairway leads to the twelve upstairs bedrooms. A former covered porch off of the living room has been converted to a first floor guest suite.

The great room, added by the Ciarrocchis, is situated off of the kitchen through archways that were once exterior doorways.

Stairs to the lower level of the house lead to a cobblestone street with a house facade and across from it the entrance to a pub, called the tap room in 1928, with flagstone floors and a billiards table covered in red baize.

Ceilings soar twenty-five feet in an added room overlooking the swimming pool. The wheel window matches one in the great room.

The back of the house overlooks a pond and terraced boxwood gardens. French doors from the new great room open to a terrace and pergola.

The stately Colonial Revival mansion was built by Pierre du Pont III and his wife between 1936 and 1940. It was originally named *Bois des Fossés* (Wood of the Trenches) after the original du Pont homestead in France.

BRANTWYN (BOIS DES FOSSÉS)

Named after the family homestead in France

Pierre du Pont III was secretary of the DuPont Company and, though considered by *Fortune* magazine to be one of the wealthiest men in the United States, worked "not because I have to work, but because I think I can help the company." Du Pont was also a racing yachtsman, community activist, and philanthropist—and proud of his ancestry. When choosing a name for the mansion he planned to build on Rockland Road in Wilmington, across the river from the original powder works, he considered only one: *Bois des Fossés,* the name of the house in France that belonged to his great-great-great grandfather, patriarch Pierre Samuel du Pont de Nemours.

Located just outside the tranquil village of Chevannes, sixty miles south of Paris, the original *Bois des Fossés* included some 445 acres, a small chateau and numerous outbuildings. Translated as "Wood of the Trenches," the name refers to the 2,000-year-old Roman trenches that were still clearly visible in the woods on the hillside east of the house when du Pont de Nemours lived there, and as recently as fifty years ago when photographer Williams Haynes visited the site, recording his findings in a series of photographs supplemented by notes.

The house in France was torn down in 1930, but not before many family members made pilgrimages there and had their pictures taken by the front door or in the courtyard to send back to Brandywine relatives.

The New World *Bois des Fossés* property is adjacent to the DuPont Country Club which purchased the house together with sixty of the original 160 acres for two million dollars in September 1990, two years after Pierre III's death. The club, owned by the DuPont Company, renamed the house *Brantwyn* after an early settler in the area, Andreas Brainwende, (Anglicized as Brantwyn), who established one of the first grain mills on the lower part of the river.

Bois des Fossés is a quarter mile north of the intersection of Rockland and Blackgates Roads, marked by a maroon and gold

Brantwyn sign, and accessed through curved brick walls flanking the entrance. The driveway follows a rolling meadow to the imposing red brick, slate-roofed mansion whose exterior looks just as it did when it was the home of Pierre du Pont III and his wife Jane, a descendant of Charlemagne, founding father of the French monarchy, and their three children, Michele, Jane (Dedo) and Pierre IV (Pete), former two-term governor of Delaware.

The house was built in the Colonial Revival style between 1936 and 1940 and was designed by Delaware architects Gabriel Massena and Alfred Victor duPont (son of Alfred I. and Bessie G.). Massena and duPont's first commission had been to plan the sunken gardens, adapted from those at Versailles, for *Nemours*, Alfred I. duPont's French showplace further south on Rockland Road. The landscape architect for *Bois des Fossés* was Frederick Holcomb, Jane du Pont's father.

The front entrance of the 28,000 square-foot house is framed by columns topped with Corinthian detailing that support a broken scroll pediment framing a sculptured eagle. Above the doorway is a three-part Palladian window—a lintel flat on each side and arched over the center. The gabled roof has four dormer windows at the front and two at the back. Twelve shuttered windows flank the Palladian window, six on each side, symmetrically positioned above first floor windows.

The outside door opens to a vestibule with curved walls and the entrance hallway dominated by a winding staircase leading to the second floor. A large, three-tier Georgian style brass chandelier hangs above it, positioned so that it is visible from the outside through the Palladian window. From the entrance hall four doors lead to the first floor public space—the conservatory, living room, dining room, and kitchen wing.

Following its purchase of the estate, the DuPont Country Club embarked on a three-million dollar, year-long renovation that included new heating, ventilating, and air conditioning systems, plus removal of asbestos. The club now operates *Brantwyn* as a banquet facility and conference center. Since its conversion, five rooms on the first floor and seven on the second floor have been given new identities and purposes, but, fortunately, remain structurally as they were when *Bois des Fossés* was a private home.

Conference room names were chosen to reflect the heritage of the DuPont Company and the surrounding area. The largest room in the house is the 966-square foot (twenty-three feet by forty-two feet) living room now called the Essonne Room, after the powder mill in France where Pierre du Pont's great-great-grandfather, Eleuthere Irénée du Pont, first learned his trade from French scientist Antoine Lavoisier, commonly referred to as the Father of Modern Chemistry. It is entered from the entrance hall through French doors that flank the living room fireplace. Broken pediments above the doors replicate the overdoor of the front entrance with the pediments surrounding handsome carved eagles.

The dining room has a fireplace, painted beam ceiling and French doors opening to the west terrace facing formal gardens and connects with the family dining room or morning room where breakfast was served; it also has French doors leading to the terrace. Together the two rooms are now known as the Boxwood Suite, alluding to the original boxwood planting on the estate. In the kitchen wing, a walk-in silver vault is now used for storage.

The pine-paneled den is lined with bookshelves with doors that recess into the wall, a large fireplace, and, of special interest, a spiral staircase leading to the second floor master suite. This enabled Mr. du Pont to go from the den to his bedroom without having to walk back through the house to the front hall stairs. The den is now known as the Willow Wood Room, a reference to the willow wood found in abundance in the Brandywine Valley and burned for charcoal, a necessary ingredient in making the black gunpowder that was the basis of the DuPont fortune. French doors from the den lead to a side terrace accented by a reflecting pool and sun dial.

An ardent sailor, especially fond of ocean racing, Pierre du Pont captained his own sixty-four foot racing schooner, *Barlovento*, and seventy-two foot auxiliary centerboard ketch, *Barlovento II*, often competing in the Newport to Bermuda race. In 1960, *Barlovento II* participated in a twenty-day race from Bermuda to Sweden. Pete du Pont, Pierre's son[1], was a member of the twelve-man crew and remembers the voyage from Bermuda around the north of England and Scotland during which he says there were several bad storms.[2] His father also headed a syndicate, in conjunction with the New York Yacht Club, that backed construction of the *American Eagle* for the 1964 America's Cup races, a name chosen to honor the first *American Eagle* that brought the family to America in 1800.

In the library, next to the den and entered from the conservatory, Pierre kept his collection of rare and limited editions. Ship models that du Pont collected, including those given to him by friends with whom he raced, were displayed on shelves in the den and library. Many of the books reflected his interest in the sea. This room is now called the Peirce Library, for brothers Joshua and Samuel, who were the former owners of the arboretum in nearby Pennsylvania that evolved into *Longwood Gardens* under the tutelage of Pierre Samuel du Pont, uncle of Pierre du Pont III.

The Copeland Conservatory is named for Mrs. Charles Copeland, who owned the property on which the original 1921 DuPont Country Club was built. The twenty-two foot by thirty-six foot room is the second largest in *Bois des Fossés*; it has black and white marble floors with three sets of French doors at the

front and the back of the house with fan windows above. At the back these open to a flagstone terrace and the formal gardens—a perfect venue for the special event that took place here more than a half century ago.

On June 22, 1957, 1,000 guests—ladies in floor length dresses, men in white dinner jackets—paraded through the conservatory to enter a fairyland setting created for the debutante party of the du Pont's daughter, eighteen year-old Jane deDoliette (Dedo). In his book, *The Du Ponts, From Gunpowder to Nylon,* Max Dorian described the setting as "an acre of crystal decor, including chandeliers."

A floodlit tent extended across the lower garden decorated with a revolving crystal ball that reflected against mirrored walls. Statues representing the four seasons were positioned down the middle of the tent between the supporting poles and soft lights illuminated the gardens. Guests were greeted at *Bois des Fossés* by Dedo who welcomed them standing in front of a portrait of her mother. The music of society orchestra leader Meyer Davis, who played for the wedding reception of John F. Kennedy and Jacqueline Bouvier, echoed across the river and through the Brandywine Valley. Supper was served at one a.m. and dancing continued until dawn.

The glittering event was described two months later in *Life Magazine*, August 19, 1957, an issue that was largely devoted to the family, in an article entitled, "A Great American Family—The du Ponts of Delaware."

From the second floor landing, hallways lead to the family quarters on the right and the servants' wing on the left. These have been converted to conference rooms and given names to reflect the du Pont heritage. Largest of these, the former master bedroom, is designated Dauphin's Run for the small stream that crosses Rockland Road and follows a course around the estate.

The adjacent sitting room's designation as Holcomb Way was chosen for Mrs. du Pont's maiden name, and Angelique Salon, formerly her dressing room, was named for Julia Sophia Angelique du Pont, the first du Pont born in America. Governor's Station was the bedroom of Pierre "Pete" du Pont IV, Pierre's son, who became the sixty-eighth Governor of Delaware, serving two terms from 1977 to 1985. Another bedroom is now called Lebanon Run after the small stream separating the *Brantwyn* property from the Governor's present home, Patterns.

Two stairways connect the first floor with the basement level. At the bottom of the formal stairway, behind a built-in, glass-fronted cabinet, there is a scale model of *Bois des Fossés* on a turntable that can be rotated with a crank, permitting views from all angles.

Pierre du Pont was a great model train enthusiast and built an elaborate layout in the basement of *Bois des Fossés*. Included in the Model-O gauge layout he constructed were sidings, reverse loops, and crossovers. His son, Pete, says that his father enjoyed building much of the rolling stock himself, but that the engines were manufactured by the Lionel Train Company. As the only son of Pierre III, Pete was expected to inherit his father's interest in the hobby, though his layout and activities were relegated to an attic location.[3] A set of passenger coaches and a diner from Pierre's collection are now a permanent part of the room-size model train display featured each year at the Brandywine River Museum during the Christmas season.

In addition to the new heating and cooling systems installed by the club, there are numerous storage closets and a wine cellar with a capacity of 1100 bottles. A built-in, paneled bar is still in place, though not in use, and in another room there is an area separated by a railing where movies were shown and professional and amateur entertainments performed.

Formal gardens at the back of the house extend to the woods leading to the east banks of the Brandywine. Enclosed by brick walls, they are planted in beds that change in color with the seasons. Handsome specimen trees planted throughout the property after the house was completed have now reached maturity.

Before DuPont Country Club acquired *Bois des Fossés* there had been talk of razing the house and dividing the acreage into four- to six-acre lots for sale, first to family members and later to others. Fortunately this plan never materialized, and the tradition of hospitality established at *Bois des Fossés* continues to be enjoyed at *Brantwyn.*

Brantwyn (Bois des Fossés)

Owner: Mr. and Mrs. Pierre S. du Pont III, original
DuPont Country Club, current
Architects: Massena and du Pont
Landscape: Frederick W. Holcomb
Location: Rockland, Delaware

Notes

1. Pierre S. III was called "Big Pete" to differentiate him from son "Pete," Pierre S. du Pont IV.

2. Correspondence between Gov. Pete du Pont and the author, July 1, 2012.

3. Ibid

Broken pediments over the living room French doors frame carvings of the United States national bird. The emblem is a reference to the schooner *American Eagle* that brought the du Pont family to America January 1, 1800.

The living room has paired French doors opening from the stair hall. It is the largest room in the 28,000 square-foot house, measuring twenty-three feet by forty feet.

The conservatory is located at the south end of *Brantwyn* and is between the living room, library, and den. There are three sets of French doors at the front and three at the back.

The dining room opens to the breakfast room that was often used as the family dining room. French doors open from both rooms to the west terrace overlooking formal gardens.

Open shelves in the library were used not just for books, but also to display Pierre du Pont's collection of ship models, many given to him by friends with whom he raced.

French doors from the den lead to the walled side garden which has a fountain as a center of focus. The garden was designed by Mrs. du Pont's father, Frederick Holcomb.

Crooked Billet was constructed as an inn and tavern with living quarters for the owner. The original entrance, and oldest part of the house, is on the left, facing Kennett Pike.

Crooked Billet has been in the du Pont family since 1864. The estate covers twenty-two acres and was part of a land grant to William Penn.

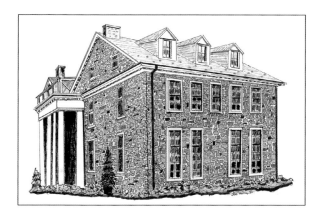

CROOKED BILLET

An 18th century farm and former inn secluded from the 21st century

Crooked Billet has been in the du Pont family for nearly 150 years, since 1864. According to National Historic Trust records[1] title to the property was given to Adam Stedham[2] in 1684 by William Penn, who received all of Delaware and Pennsylvania in a grant from James, Duke of York, the future King James II of England. It is the last farm remaining in what has become a widening suburban community.

Stedham received one hundred acres from Penn and styled it "Adam's Garden." In the same year he received title, he is believed to have constructed a two-room field stone building. At that time the Old Kennett-Wilmington Road was some 2,000 feet further west than it is today and intersected there with Center Road (Montchanin Road), which would have placed the building directly on the pike.

In 1702, the Stedham family built a larger front section to the house, a traditional four-room over four-room stone addition with an attic, that more than doubled the square footage. During this period the building began operating as an inn called *Crooked Billet*[3] and continued to do so after passing through other hands. In 1750, an eighty-acre tract was acquired by blacksmith Thomas Ogle. Though Ogle died in 1777, the estate was not settled until fourteen years later, when his children reached their majority. His widow then married James Brindley, a wealthy immigrant from England, who settled in Wilmington in 1774.

Crooked Billet continued in business, though at one time it was known as the Blue Bottle Inn. The Old Kennett-Wilmington Road was reconfigured in 1811 and moved closer to the Brandywine. At the same time it became a toll road and because of these changes it was no longer feasible to operate *Crooked Billet* as a public house. In the years following, Brindley acquired additional property for a total of some 180 acres.

Henry, Lammot, and Eleuthere du Pont II jointly purchased the Brindley farm in 1864. Eighteen years later "Boss" Henry, by then head of the DuPont Company, became the sole owner and with the acquisition of adjoining farms increased his holdings to over 300 acres. Through managing the farms, his younger son, William, developed a lifelong interest in horse and cattle breeding, and upon his father's death (1889) he inherited it.

Over the years William, following in his father's footsteps, continued to purchase more property. In 1926 he organized the Delaware Land Development Company and was able to transfer 600 acres, which he used to develop Westover Hills, Wilmington's first suburban community for affluent buyers. When he died in 1928, William left the estate to his son, William, Jr. (Willie), who was then living in Newtown Square, Pennsylvania, fifteen miles west of Philadelphia, with his first wife, the former Jean Liseter Austin.

Crooked Billet backed up to Westover Hills and duPont set aside thirty acres from the development for his own use. In addition to the main house, at that time the estate included a two-story stone carriage house built by James Brindley. It has a date stone of 1801 and two brick-arched bays. A frame bank barn has three wings and a stone foundation with stalls on the lower level. There is also a stable, water tower, riding ring, and open pasture land.

In 1943 duPont's daughter, Jean Ellen Davis, was widowed after a brief marriage, when her husband was killed in an automobile accident in California. She then returned to Delaware, accepting her father's offer of *Crooked Billet* as a place to live. It was an act of generosity that benefited both parties. In *Crooked Billet,* Jean Ellen had a project to occupy her time, and for Willie duPont it meant that he once again had his daughter nearby.

Jean Ellen married J. H. Tyler McConnell, an attorney and banker, in 1944[4] and over the next twenty years *Crooked Billet* underwent extensive remodeling in its conversion from inn to private residence. The front of the public house had faced east so that arriving guests could enter the inn parlor directly from their carriages, while the tavern door was around the corner on the north side. With their decision to make this the front of the house, the McConnells had the driveway changed so that there is now a circular drive leading to the new front entrance. It is a striking and hospitable entry hall, with the tavern's original oak-beamed ceilings, brick floor laid in herringbone design, paneling, and forty-six-inch by eighty-inch open fireplace.

To the left and one step up is the reconfigured living room. Originally there were two rooms at the front, each with its own fireplace, and a small hallway. The McConnells had the dividing walls removed and the two rooms and hallway combined into one large living room. At the same time the fireplaces were rebuilt with a single hearth.

The current owners are Marion McConnell Lassen and her husband Kai. Mrs. Lassen remembers well living there as a child and describes *Crooked Billet* as a house that has evolved over time. A case in point is the library next to the living room. When Marion was a young girl the room served as the dining room. A side porch off of this room was enclosed some years ago to provide a playroom for the Lassen children. Now grown, they suggested converting the former playroom into a media room, which has been done.

Complementing the hall entrance to the living room is an arched doorway that leads to the stairway hall and from it is a door to the library. The kitchen, pantries, and breakfast room are just beyond and were completely renovated in the 1990s. A new tiled bar area with copper accents is situated between the kitchen and a door to the media room. *Crooked Billet's* original two-inch thick exterior doors are still in place with large hand-forged iron strap hinges. The ceilings in this part of the house are just under nine feet and the 200-year-old heart of pine flooring is twelve inches wide.

In 1967, the McConnells added a new wing that was designed to replicate the original structure and once again essentially doubled the size of the house. Mrs. McConnell was exacting in her building requirements that the stonework exactly match the 18th century addition and had parts of the new masonry rebuilt as many as three times to achieve her goal. In a denouement to the reconstruction, six Doric columns, two stories high and thirty inches in diameter, were installed at the new front entrance supporting a portico and a gallery in Chippendale design that joins the two structures.

A spacious new dining room, twenty-one by thirty-six feet, was part of the renovation. It connects to the original part of the house through a passage way from the entrance hall. The focal point of the step-down dining room is a fireplace at one end flanked by open china cabinets with a shell design at the top. Above it is an oil painting of Jean Ellen's father, William duPont, Jr., astride his famous horse, Foxcatcher. In the background is Liseter Hall, Willie's Newtown Square home, a replica of Montpelier, the former home of fourth U.S. President James Madison and his wife Dolley Todd.

William and his sister, Marion duPont Somerville Scott, spent much of their childhood at Montpelier and it was here that both developed their lifelong interest in horse breeding. She was Marion Lassen's great aunt, and in 1915 became the first woman to ride astride a horse in competition in Madison Square Garden.

The room, with ten-foot ceilings, is furnished with period antiques, several from Willie duPont's house, *Bellevue Hall*, that were originally purchased in the 19th century for his parents' houses in England. Among these is a seventeenth century Dutch grandfather's clock that keeps perfect time; it is inlaid with exquisite marquetry. Eight-inch brass figures on the top represent Atlas supporting the world in the center, with Mercury, god of commerce carrying a caduceus, to his left, and Kronos (Saturn), god of time,

carrying a scythe, to his right.

On the wall facing the entrance, hanging over a sideboard, there is a painting of Mrs. Lassen's grandmother, Jean Liseter Austin duPont, on her mount, Witchcraft. Like her husband, Jean duPont was well-known as a horse breeder. She showed her first pony at the Devon Horse Show in 1907 and, through the years, won thousands of ribbons and trophies, many for her Welsh ponies. It was estimated that she once had as many as 250 of the ponies at Liseter Hall.

When the 1967 wing was added to *Crooked Billet*, a master suite, sitting room and bathroom, and new stairway were also added. The house now has three stairways, ten fireplaces, and nine bedrooms, though not all of these are used as bedrooms. One has been converted to an upstairs sitting room, another is an office, and a third was designated some time ago as a train room for young railroad buffs.

Since *Crooked Billet* has been in the duPont-McConnell-Lassen family, several more buildings have been added. A greenhouse for Marion's orchids, some of which came from Liseter Hall, has been built off of the kitchen wing and a ham house, reminiscent of ones at *Bellevue Hall* and Montpelier, was built by Willie duPont. The farm manager's cottage was added when Jean Ellen moved here. Handsome millstones at the entrance to *Crooked Billet* came from William duPont's 540-acre Walnut Hall Farms near Boyce, Virginia, in the Shenandoah Valley.

In 1950, a swimming pool and pool house were constructed. The pool house is in reality a party house with large entertainment areas. There is a great room with a fireplace and full size bar, a guest room and bathroom, and an impressive trophy room with mounted specimens hunted by Kai and his son on safaris in South America and South Africa. Among the forty-four trophies are kudu, zebra, gemsbok, Cape Buffalo, impala, sable, and blue and black wildebeest.

Jean Ellen shared the same equine interests as her father, William, Jr., and she maintained stables for both race horses and fox hunters under the name *Crooked Billet Stables*. Her racing silks were green with a white mouse on them, in recognition of the nickname given to her by her father. His silks were blue inscribed with a gold fox.

The Lassens have continued the duPont interest in horses and at present have seven, divided for use in fox hunting, riding and driving their twenty carriages. But, there is room for others. The barn has twenty-two stalls.

Crooked Billet

Owners: Adam Stedham, original (1684)
           Thomas Ogle
           James Brindley
           Henry du Pont
           William duPont
           William duPont, Jr.
           Jean Ellen duPont McConnell
           Marion duPont McConnell Lassen
Constructed: c. 1700
Later Additions   1702, 1801, 1943, 1967
Location: Greenville, Delaware

Notes

1. National Register of Historic Places, September 28, 1976.

2. Adam Stedham was born in Sweden c. 1649 and died in New Castle, Delaware, in December 1726.

3. Popular as a pub name in England. Pub signs (names) are said to have originated in ancient Roman times with a bunch of grapes indicating the arrival of the harvest. In England, they were used as a reference point for travelers, e.g. Cross Roads Inn, or a guide post such as The Horse & Hounds. One often-used symbol to mark an inn was that of a crooked billet, a limb fallen from a tree, and there are a number of inns by that name in England—Henley and Wimbledon each have one.

4. Tyler McConnell was a former Chairman of the Delaware State Highway Department and the J. H. Tyler McConnell Bridge (Delaware State Bridge 587) was named for him. It carries State Highway 141 over Brandywine Creek and was built 1951-1952. It opened to traffic December 1952 and was dedicated April 1953.

The tavern entrance of *Crooked Billet* has been retained, now as the unique entrance hall of the house. Brick floors are laid in herringbone pattern.

The living room was originally two rooms, combined into one in 1944, when the inn underwent major reconstruction as a residence. Each room had a fireplace and these were rebuilt with a single hearth.

The library of *Crooked Billet* was formerly the dining room. An adjacent open side porch was enclosed as a playroom and later adapted as a media room.

The new dining room is located in the 1944 addition to the house; it is connected by a passageway from the front entrance. Several pieces of furniture are from William duPont, Sr.'s house, Binfield Park, in England.

One of the rooms in the pool house, added in 1950, is a trophy room with forty-four trophies from hunts in South Africa and South America.

Dauneport is often compared to Mt. Vernon, from which it was copied, though Amy du Pont's house is more than 1500 square feet larger. Credit: Photograph by author

DAUNEPORT

A country house inspired by President Washington's Mount Vernon

Landowner, sportswoman, and philanthropist Amy Elizabeth du Pont was one of four daughters born to Eugene du Pont and his wife and cousin, Amelia Elizabeth du Pont. Eugene headed the DuPont Company when it was first formed as a corporation, and held this position until he died suddenly at the age of sixty-two following a one-week illness. Amy spent the last twenty-eight years of her life in California, but she was a moving force in organizing Wilmington events before then and built one of the area's most distinctive houses.

After her father's premature death, Amy, who never married, continued to live with her mother at the family home, *Old Nemours*, moving with her the next year to Pelleport, a great Gothic pile of stone situated on Kennett Pike that was designed in 1881 by Philadelphia architect Theophilus Chandler for his brother-in-law, William du Pont. Following Amelia du Pont's death in 1917, the twenty-five room house had no takers among Amy's siblings and was deeded over to her. Pelleport then became known as "Miss Amy's house," but in time it no doubt became oppressive and difficult to manage for a single woman, regardless of how self-sufficient and resilient she may have been.

In 1930, Amy acquired property for building a house on Old Kennett Pike across from her brother, Eugene, Jr., whose *Owl's Nest* mansion and outbuildings sprawled over 500 acres. In a complete departure from any other du Pont houses in the area, she decided to have her house designed in the style of a Virginia plantation. And not just any Virginia plantation, but a particular one: Mount Vernon, home of President George Washington.

As architect for her country house, Amy selected California architect Mary Craig, who, with her husband (James Osborne Craig), made significant contributions to west coast architecture, though they were natives of Deadwood, South Dakota, and were without formal training. When her husband died she took over the practice.

Mary Craig's architecture incorporated Spanish Revival characteristics and often her residences were designed around courtyards and featured slanting roofs, arches, porticoes, and prominent chimneys. It isn't known why Amy chose the west coast architect to design her Wilmington mansion, since Craig's designs were antithetical to the Virginia plantation she had in mind. One explanation is that they had met on a western visit and Amy admired her perseverance to continue the business after her husband's death. A simpler explanation is that Amy wanted a house similar to Mt. Vernon, one of the most imitated structures in the country, and asked Craig if she would be willing to undertake the assignment; the answer was "yes."

Dauneport was completed in 1933 and though not a mirror image, nevertheless, bears a great resemblance to the President's house. Both are Georgian neoclassical in design and are of clapboard construction painted white, and each has a symmetrical colonnaded porch supported by square columns. Mt. Vernon has eight columns—two more than *Dauneport*. The hip roofs of both are flanked by brick chimneys at the ends and feature three dormer windows at the front with roofs capped by cupolas offering vistas of the surrounding countryside.

The exterior footprint of Mount Vernon is ninety-four feet by thirty-three feet. *Dauneport* is 135 feet by thirty-one feet with a front piazza sixty-six feet long by ten feet wide. The back piazza is seventy-four long by eleven feet wide and overlooks an in-ground swimming pool. Mount Vernon has approximately 7,000 square feet, while the square footage of Amy du Pont's mansion is 8,650. Each has eight rooms and a center hall on the first floor.

Dauneport is reached by a long, tree-shaded driveway through an allee of maple trees that circles at the front entrance and returns by a parallel drive leading to the main road. Ionic columns flank the front door of the mansion, crowned by a broken pediment framing a spread eagle, a nod to the schooner, *American Eagle*, that first brought the du Ponts to America's shores January 1, 1800. The door knocker is also in the shape of our national bird. This is a recurring image in many du Pont houses including *Owl's Nest*, Amy's brother's nearby house, which has a copper spread eagle over the front door designed by German-born artist Oscar Bach.

An impressive entrance hallway, just over twenty-eight feet in length and eleven feet wide, bisects the house. It leads to a handsome winding stairway at the far end that ends at the second floor landing. Classic blocked wallpaper in a geometric pattern above the chair rail extends the length of the staircase. The dramatic flooring, laid in a diamond pattern, is made of 640 ten-inch square by one-inch thick Alabama marble pavers in Belgium Black and Madre Cream manufactured by Hilgartner Marble Co., Baltimore, Maryland. The oldest stone manufacturer in the United States, founded in 1863, Hilgartner supplied the stone and marble for the Washington Monument, Lincoln Memorial, and U.S. Supreme Court.

Off of the entrance hall are matching eight-foot arched doorways across from one another, each with French doors that open on the left to the living room and on the right to a dining room foyer. The generously proportioned living room is twenty-one feet wide and thirty-seven feet in length, seven feet longer than Mt. Vernon's. Elaborate paneling and molding accent the marble fireplace, and French doors open to a piazza that extends across the west side of the house.

A paneled library, with built-in bookshelves, adjoins the living room. It has a wet bar with a stainless steel counter that could double as a potting area considering its proximity to the gardens. Above it is a small built-in refrigerator with an ahead-of-its-time matching stainless steel door. The library also opens to the terrazzo-tiled sunroom with exposures on the east, south, and west. French doors are on all outside walls and those facing south are flanked by single doors. Just beyond, on the south side, steps lead down to walled gardens.

Dauneport's spacious dining room is entered through the foyer off of the front hall. Mural wallpaper above the chair rail depicts a Colonial seaport scene and built-in china closets at one end flank the fireplace. An exquisite multi-tiered crystal chandelier is positioned to hang above a dining room table. Two sets of French doors match those at the west end of the living room and open onto the west piazza.

From the dining room foyer a doorway opens to a butler's pantry and the vintage 1940 kitchen with stainless steel counters and seventy-year-old cabinets. Off of the kitchen are an office, a maid's room and bath, and the laundry room, moved some time ago from its original basement location in a concession to current standards. A stairway leads from the kitchen wing to the second floor.

There are two half-baths on the ground floor. One of these, between the library and living room, was used principally by men. The other, located off of the dining room foyer, was generally used by women. Additionally there is a small room and half-bath immediately to the right of the front door that was originally used as a receiving room or on occasion as a ladies' cloakroom.

From the large landing at the top of the grand stairway, doors open to the five bedrooms. The step-down master bedroom suite, with a fireplace, measures 460 square feet, some seventy-six feet larger than the dining room. It is entered through a large sitting room, also with a fireplace, and features a walk-in closet with

built-in drawers and a storage area for suitcases. Bedrooms facing west have French doors which open to a veranda that extends the length of the second floor above the ground floor piazza. Ceilings on the first floor are twelve feet high and on the second floor ten feet. There are seven fireplaces in the house and an upstairs back hall stairway leads to the unfinished third floor with access to the cupola via a ladder.

The *Dauneport* grounds, now just a little more than five acres, are considerably down-sized from the original acreage that was at one time extensive and often alive with activity. Amy du Pont was an ardent horsewoman and a pioneer, in Delaware, in the breeding of hackney horses, known for their distinctive high-stepping trot, style, and spirit. The Fairfield Farms Horse Show was instituted by her in 1934, and, from 1937 through 1941, she acted as the official hostess, donating the use of her property for the September event. Ice cream stands, popcorn vendors, and hot dog hawkers enlivened the *Dauneport* scene, and "Miss Amy" entertained the judges for lunch. The day's activities were highlighted by her presentation of the coveted Amy du Pont Trophy.

Amy du Pont's interest in horses extended outside Delaware. In Fairfield, Maryland, at the Fairfield Farms Horse Show, she donated the $3500 DuPont Gold Cup to the winner of the steeplechase. When this show was discontinued, the trophy became an award at the Wilmington Horse Show.

Amy entered her favorite horse, Mattie Chimes, as well as two others, Alexandre and Laddie Babbie, in a number of shows. At Atlantic City's Young's Pier (April 20, 1911) she was a winner in several categories, though in one event she was eclipsed by fellow heiress, Denver-born, Washington, D.C. hostess Evalyn Walsh McLean, who purchased a hackney one hour before she competed and won the event. An Atlantic City landmark, Young's Pier was large enough to provide space for stabling, hitching, and exercising horses, in addition to having a large auditorium with a ring big enough to show the horses. Unfortunately it was destroyed by fire the year following Amy's participation.

In addition to *Dauneport*, Amy maintained a five-acre estate, *Casa del Sueno*, (*Dreamhouse*), in the fashionable Montecito section of Santa Barbara, California. Approached by a long drive flanked by stately palms, the house was surrounded by lush gardens and complemented by avocado and olive trees in abundance. The architect for the Spanish Colonial Revival style *Casa del Sueno* was Reginald Johnson who was instrumental in designing the Santa Barbara Biltmore Hotel, Los Angeles Opera House, and several buildings at Harvard University, in addition to private residences. After Amy's death it was purchased by folk singer Burl Ives who lived there until his death in 1995.

A stunning feature of the California mansion was the interiors executed by muralist Adele Herter who often used cactus motifs in her painting. Frank Lloyd Wright considered the *Casa del Sueno* murals some of the most beautiful wall coverings in the world. *House Beautiful* magazine described them in the May 1931 issue as "covered in silver leaf with conventionalized clouds in glazed gold and low mountains of architectural character in copper color. The middle ground is sand color outlined, as are all the forms, in reddish purple and in the foreground are cactus plants drawn in their lovely natural shades of tea rose, salmon and coral with blue green foliage."

By 1939 Amy had decided to make California her permanent

home and gave *Dauneport* to her nephew, Eugene du Pont III. But, she did not sever her ties to the First State, serving on the University of Delaware Board of Trustees' Advisory Committee on the Women's College from 1939-1944 and visiting frequently until she fell from a horse at the age of seventy-eight. At her death it was discovered that "Miss Amy's" Delaware roots ran deep indeed. The University of Delaware was the chief beneficiary of her will with a bequest estimated at twenty-five million dollars.

In 1940 she established UNIDEL, the primary purpose of which was to "promote higher education in the state of Delaware and to increase, enlarge and improve the scientific and educational opportunities of its people." Her will stated that, "My father, Eugene du Pont, was the first president of the original DuPont corporation. ... he spent his life in prolonged and persistent effort to extend and enlarge the field of human knowledge. ... It is my earnest desire to pay tribute to his memory ... and create a fund to be used ... solely and exclusively for religious, charitable, scientific and educational purposes."

In 1973, with funds derived from the UNIDEL Foundation, the University of Delaware constructed a building that houses the department of music and named it the Amy E. du Pont Music Building in her honor. By 1982 the total of gifts given by Amy du Pont to the UNIDEL Foundation had appreciated to forty-two million dollars, equal to the sums given to Delaware College by Pierre du Pont and Rodney Sharp.[1]

The house has had four owners, two of whom were single women. The third owner, Marie Louise McHugh, lived there for forty-four years, longer than Amy du Pont herself. In 2011 it was placed on the market for $1,195,000. A survey, dated March 2011, refers to the property as Mt. Vernon Farm and it was sold to Dr. and Mrs. Garrett B. Lyons, Jr., in 2012. Dr. and Mrs. Lyons have restored the house to its original condition when built, at the same time renovating and redecorating it. *Dauneport* has been retained as the house name.

Dauneport

Owners:	Amy E. du Pont, original
	Eugene du Pont III
	John W. Rollins
	Marie McHugh
	Dr. and Mrs. Garrett B. Lyons, Jr., current
Constructed:	1932 - 1933
Architect:	Mary Craig
Location:	Old Kennett Pike
	Wilmington, Delaware

Notes

1. *The University of Delaware: A History*, John A. Munroe. Pg. 442

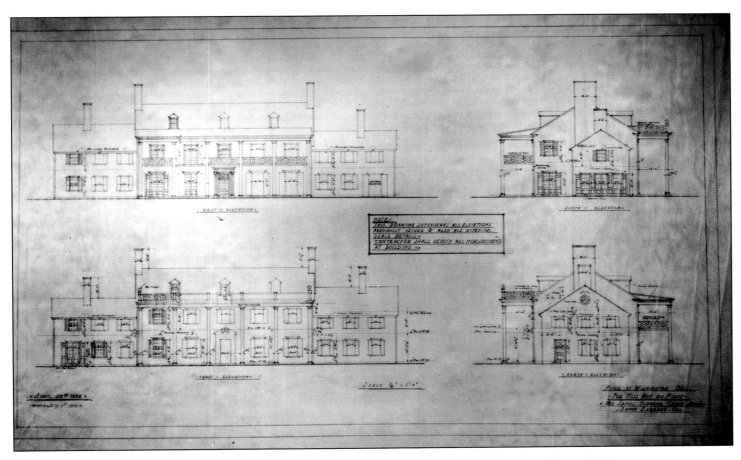

Architect for *Dauneport* was Mary Craig, Santa Barbara, California, listed on this original plan as Mrs. James Osborne Craig.
Credit: Reproduced from the Collections of the Library of Congress

An aerial view of *Dauneport* was taken September 10, 1938, by Dallin Aerial Survey Company. Credit: Hagley Museum and Library

The stair hall is dominated by a winding stairway that gracefully curves to the second floor. The hall floor is made of 640 one-inch thick marble pavers from Alabama. Credit: Photograph by author

The main house at *Dilwyne Farms* was Mediterranean in design. It was finished with dark stucco and had a red tile roof. The architects were Walter Brown and G. Morris Whiteside from Wilmington. Credit: Photograph courtesy Keith Carpenter

DILWYNE FARMS

The extraordinary estate of a DuPont executive sprawled over 300 acres

At one time the DuPont Company owned thousands of acres of land on both sides of the Brandywine Creek. Founder, French immigrant Eleuthere Irénée du Pont, was attracted to the area by the natural water power, abundance of willow trees available to produce charcoal necessary for making black powder, the great quantities of timber, granite for building mills, and the site's nearness to waterways, which could bring the other black powder ingredients, saltpeter and sulphur.

In this environment the DuPont Company produced the finest black powder available in the world's largest manufacturing facility. During the Great War, the company was never late with a shipment, neither was a pound of the explosive ever returned as being inferior in quality. Following World War I, the demand for explosives was greatly reduced and DuPont began diversifying into the production of dyestuffs, paints, and plastics.

The aging Brandywine facilities and availability of formerly essential requirements used in black powder production were no longer relevant to the company, and in 1921 the "Mills of Liberty" closed[1]. The decision was then made to sell off most of its land holdings to du Pont family members and DuPont executives in what became known as "The 1921 Distribution." Robert Ruliph Morgan Carpenter, Sr., known as "Ruly," qualified on both counts. He was married to the former Margaretta Lammot du Pont, the sister of company president, Pierre S. du Pont, and had held several positions in the company as well as serving on the board of directors.

With the thought of building a country estate, Ruly took advantage of the opportunity offered, purchasing 312 acres of former company property extending from Buck Road on the south to Kirk Road on the north. The east and west boundaries extended approximately a half mile on either side of Montchanin Road.

Significant structures on the property included the 1888 Soda House, *Strand Millis* (the oldest house west of the Brandywine), the Ball farmstead, and the Montchanin Railroad Station. Additionally, there were numerous tenant houses once occupied by DuPont workers as well as a former schoolhouse and blacksmith shop.

The site the Carpenters chose on which to build their house was across Buck Road from the Second Office with the main entrance on Buck Road. Other access roads would be from Montchanin and Rockland Roads. As architects, the Carpenters selected Brown & Whiteside, a Wilmington firm whose principals, Walter Stewart Brown and G. Morris Whiteside II, had established their firm in 1910; by 1931 it was the largest architectural firm in the state. In addition to houses, the firm's projects included plans for Tower Hill School, the Wilmington Trust Building, and the First and Central Presbyterian Church.

The Carpenters needed a large house to accommodate their growing family that included three daughters and two sons: Louisa d'Andelot, Irene (Renee), Nancy, Robert, Jr., and William. Brown & Whiteside's design for the 10,000 square-foot house was a complete departure from the stately Georgian and Colonial mansions occupied by most of the Carpenters' du Pont cousins. With a dark stucco exterior and red tile roof, coupled with an asymmetrical profile, it appeared almost Mediterranean and would have fit in well with the lavish villas lining the shores of Italy's Lake District. The formal gardens too, were designed in European style with raised gardens surrounded by cypress trees.

In a nod to their ancestral home, which was not Mediterranean but English, the Carpenters named their estate *Dilwyne Farms*. The Carpenter line began in Dilwyn, Herefordshire, six miles from Leominster, with the birth of John Carpenter in the fourteenth century, hence the name.

The main driveway to *Dilwyne Farms* was from Buck Road and ended at the front entrance with a porte cochere. From there several steps led up to a large fifteen-foot wide hallway that opened to the dining room on the left and to what was called the sitting room on the right. The hall led straight through to a garden room with steps down to the formal walled gardens. Other rooms on the first floor included a butler's pantry, breakfast room, and kitchen on the side of the dining room, and, on the right a formal living room in addition to the sitting room. The house had five bedrooms, plus an additional four for staff, and seven fireplaces. There were three large greenhouses, eight tenant houses and a garage that could accommodate ten cars plus a fire engine. When *Dilwyne* was razed in 1949 the Smithsonian Institute dismantled two of the greenhouses and moved them to Washington, D.C.

A graphic map of the estate was prepared soon after construction of the main buildings. Entitled *A Story of Dilwyne and Its People* and mounted on wallboard, it is five-and-a-half-feet high and eight-feet wide and depicts *Dilwyne's* buildings, roads and land divisions, as they were then, as well as the route of the Wilmington and Northern Railroad which bisected the property. It is of particular interest and value as it names buildings no longer existent and areas that have since been sold off and developed for other purposes. Seventy sketches border the map, depicted in a newsreel cartoon design that illustrates the various interests of the Carpenter family. Among these are tennis racquets, a cow, barn, camera, greenhouse, roller skate, violin, boot, crop and saddle, a retriever, airplane, and fire engine.

Dilwyn, Hereforshire, is a popular tourist destination in the west midlands and *Dilwyne Farms* could have equalled it in recreational facilities. Nancy ("Missy") Lickle, a granddaughter of the Carpenters, says that she "spent more time at my grandparents' than I did at home." And for good reason. In addition to the tennis court and swimming pool, there was a recreation center the family called "The Rink." The multi-purpose building contained an indoor roller rink that could be converted to three indoor badminton courts or a basketball court and on occasion a baseball game. The riding stable had twenty stalls and there were sixteen kennels to accommodate the champion Chesapeake retrievers the Carpenters bred and showed, plus a house for the dog trainer.

The Dilwyne Badminton Club was founded in the 1930s, and its first games were played in the horse barn before construction of the multi-purpose building. Though *Dilwyne Farms* has been torn down, the Dilwyne Badminton Club is still active at a school in Elsmere, Delaware, with play offered four nights a week during nine months of the year.

Dilwyne Kennels was one of the most famous names in Chesapeake breeding circles. In 1931 they began developing the best bloodlines available with emphasis on field trials, and, in 1935, built their world-class facilities. In an advertisement in the December 1936 issue of *Kennel Directory*, *Dilwyne Farms* proclaimed itself as the best equipped and largest breeder of Chesapeakes in the country. After visiting the estate, dog show judge Vinton Breese concurred. In the October 1936 issue of *Country Life*, he was enthusiastic in declaring that Dilwyne Kennels were the finest sporting dog kennels he had ever seen. Their Chesapeakes competed against the best water dogs in North America and were consistent winners, with its sire, Stacked Deck, bred from Mackenzie, one of the breed's most famous champions.

Nor were the stables neglected. The November 17, 1921, issue of the *New York Times* reported that *Dilwyne Farms* took first place in the National Horse Show with its mare Princess Sheila and second place for pony under saddle with Cutie Pie.

The October 1922 issue of *The Field Illustrated* said that at the Rochester Horse Show *Dilwyne Farms* showed saddle horses ridden by the Carpenters' daughters, Louisa and Irene, each of whom won championships for horses under 15.2 hands riding Dilwyne Dolly and Twilight Hour, and in its column, "Horse Shows and Hunts," the June 10, 1933, issue of the *New Yorker* wrote that, "*Dilwyne Farms'* hunters are thriving on the most successful season they've had in years, thanks largely to King Vulture."

Ruly Carpenter was a great sportsman, as well as sports enthusiast, and was a long time member of the Boone & Crockett Club founded in 1887 by Theodore Roosevelt. He was a big game hunter and went on numerous game expeditions and safaris, writing about them in four books and publishing them in limited editions. The titles included: *My African Safari* (1937), *Game Trails From Alaska to Africa* (1938), *Game Trails in Idaho and Alaska* (1940) and *Another Wyoming Hunt* (1943).

One of the most interesting chapters in *My African Safari* is Ruly's account of how he reached Nairobi to begin his safari: "We found ourselves climbing aboard the Imperial Airways' plane[2] at Croydon (Croydon Aerodrome, South London)," he wrote.

Paris was the farthest we got by that plane because for some reason planes are not able to cross France and Italy, so we boarded the train for Brindisi (Italy). Here we again took to the air, this time in a seaplane. Via Athens, we crossed the Mediterranean to Alexandria (Egypt), with a short stop at Crete (Greece) for fuel and tea. An Englishman must have his tea.

At Alexandria, after a short rest, we again boarded a land plane at four in the morning and started the long trip through the Sudan for Nairobi. Several stops were made, however. On landing at Wadi Halfi (Sudan) we felt as if we had stepped into a furnace. ... At the end of the desert we crossed a huge swamp, possibly four hundred miles long, abounding in game. Hippos, buffalo, antelope, giraffe and once a herd of two hundred elephants. ... In six days from London we reached Nairobi[3]. ... A night in Nairobi and we were off by noon, our safari composed of ... two white hunters, four gun bearers, a cook, six tent boys, two native skinners, a half dozen porters and a lorry driver.

While sports were the main interest of family patriarch R.R.M. Carpenter ("Pop-Pop"), Missy Lickle says that her grandmother's greatest interest was entertaining on Sundays at noon. "Sunday brunch was Gran's thing," she remembers. "It was held by the pool during the summer and in the dining room in cold weather. It didn't matter who you brought or how many showed up, Gran was always prepared. She had field ovens by the pool to keep things warm and was famous for her iced tea." Among the Sunday offerings that Missy fondly recalls were squab, crab coquettes, and chicken fricassee. "At Christmas time eggnog was substituted for iced tea," she adds.

The former Soda House, used by the DuPont mills for processing sodium nitrate, was used by Ruly Carpenter as a showcase for the big game trophies he brought back from safaris and displayed on the walls of its largest room. This space was sound-equipped and family and friends often gathered to watch first-run movies Ruly was able to get from distributors—frequently before their release in theaters.

Carpenter's greatest sports venture was his foray into major league baseball. In November 1943, he purchased the Philadelphia Phillies franchise and soon turned its operation over to his son, Bob, who was also involved with the Wilmington Blue Rocks. The family had earlier purchased a fifty per cent interest from legendary baseball manger Connie Mack, who won more games (3731) than any other manager in baseball history.

When Ruly Carpenter bought the franchise, the Phillies had lost more than one hundred games five years in a row and the purchase price reflected this: $400,000. By 1950, the team was National League champion for the second time. In the fall of 1972, Bob turned management of the team over to his son, R.R.M. Carpenter III, also known as Ruly, under whose leadership the Phillies won four division titles and became baseball's world champions in 1980. However, within a year the Carpenters sold the franchise, citing frustration with the salaries paid for players of average ability. The selling price was 32.5 million dollars.

Keith Carpenter, Ruly's grandson, has built a gracious house in southwestern style on the footprint of *Dilwyne Farms*. The 13,000 square-foot house was designed by local architect Zack Davis. It was planned and built over a two-year period from 2000 to 2002.

Dilwyne Farms

Owners:	Mr. and Mrs. R.R.M. Carpenter, Sr., original
	Keith Carpenter, current
Constructed:	1922
Razed:	1949
Architect:	Brown & Whiteside
Location:	Greenville, Delaware

Notes

1. "At the suggestion of Du pont père, the plant on the Brandywine was named *Eleutherian Mills*, which might be translated 'Mills of Liberty.'" *Du Pont One Hundred and Forty Years,* William S. Dutton, Charles Scribner's Sons, 1942

2. Imperial Airways was the early British commercial long range air transport company, operating from 1924 to 1939, serving parts of Europe, but particularly the Empire route to South Africa.

3. This would have been after a transatlantic crossing of six days.

There were three greenhouses on the property and extensive gardens, both formal and informal. The foundations of the greenhouses are still existent, but the greenhouses are gone. Credit: Photograph courtesy Keith Carpenter

Dilwyne Farms was built on part of the acreage acquired by R.R.M. Carpenter, Sr., in the DuPont Company "1921 Distribution" of property no longer needed by the company. Credit: Photograph courtesy Keith Carpenter

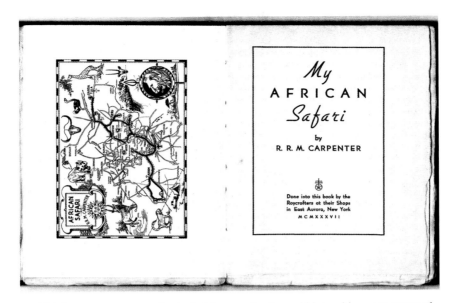

R.R.M Carpenter was an enthusiastic big game hunter and his trophies were mounted on the walls of the Soda House, then part of his property. To document his safaris he wrote four books that he had privately printed including *My African Safari* in 1937, which details the route and has an illustrated map showing animals spotted. Credit: Photograph courtesy Keith Carpenter

Dilwyne was razed in 1949 and a new house in southwestern style has been built on the same footprint. Raised gardens were a prominent feature with statuary and a fountain. Credit: Photograph courtesy Keith Carpenter

The Ball Farm was included in the 312 acres acquired by R.R.M. Carpenter, Sr., grandfather of the present owner. The original 1802 farmhouse has been greatly modified and enlarged.

THE BALL FARM

Within the 312 acres that R.R.M. Carpenter, Sr., acquired when the mills closed was a sixty-five acre parcel with outbuildings, known collectively as *The Ball Farm*. It was acquired by E.I. du Pont in 1812[1] and is now the home of Ruly III and his wife, Stephanie. Another connection Ruly III shares with his grandfather is his love of hunting and fishing and he has pursued these interests in South America and Alaska.

In addition to the main dwelling, dating back to the turn of the nineteenth century, there is a two-story calf barn, a twenty-one foot by thirty-seven foot workshop and a spring house. The handsome three-story house, finished in white stucco, is accented by tall evergreens planted close to the front entrance. It has a pitched cedar shake roof with twelve dormers and six-over-six double-hung windows. Shutters, painted black, are solid on the first floor and louvered on the second.

The Carpenters have made three additions to the house since living there. The first in the early 1960s was at the east end of the house. This included a pine-paneled den with a fireplace surround depicting game bird tiles and a master bedroom and bathroom on the second floor. Muralist Vicki Vinton painted a pastoral scene that begins in the front hallway and extends to the third floor ending with Ruly's favorite part of the mural, an osprey in flight. A late 1960s addition included a game room with fireplace, brick-floored mud room, a kitchen extension, and two bedrooms and bathrooms on the second floor.

In 1981 the Carpenters added a dining room and sitting room-sun porch that runs the length of the house with floors made of antique brick brought from Chester, Pennsylvania. The room, with a glass wall and southern exposure, opens to a flagstone terrace supported by a nine-and-a-half-foot stone retaining wall they jokingly refer to as "the Great Wall of Montchanin." The pond in the distance was created from a former marshland. A trumpeter swan and his mate were former occupants, but Ruly says that the cob became too possessive and chased grandchildren, so it was sent off to retirement in Cape May, New Jersey; the pen remained. In 1991, the former kitchen was modified to become a sitting room, making use of the original *Ball Farm* kitchen fireplace, and exposing the rough-hewn beams.

The blue rock and timber calf barn for the country estate was built in 1802 according to a date stone on its west wall that also bears the name John Simon (Simmons) scratched on it. Across from the barn is the workshop, also built of Brandywine blue rock, which has a divided fan window on the east side. A tenant house was once close by and, though razed many years ago, chards of china and the occasional fork or spoon still push through the soil after heavy rains. In 2008, a stone garage was built near this site.

Between the barn and the house there is an enclosure for the Carpenters' pet Sicilian donkey, Figgy, now thirty years old. Figgy always comes when called, Ruly explains, as long as he follows his name with the words, "cookie, cookie, cookie."

The Ball Farm

Owners: John Ball, original
DuPont Company
R.R.M. Carpenter, Sr .
Mr. and Mrs. R.R.M. Carpenter III, current
Constructed: c. 1802
Additions: 1960s, 1981
Location: Greenville, Delaware

Notes

1. Records of ownership go back to 1767.

The original kitchen has been converted to a sitting room. In one of several additions a new kitchen and mud room were added.

The west terrace has a sweeping view of the property and their pond in the distance.

The stair hall mural is by Vicki Vinton, a specialist in decorative finishes,
who has done work in a number of family houses. (opposite)

In 1981, the Carpenters added a dining room and sitting room-sun porch to the west side of the house.

When choosing a site for his house, E. I. du Pont specified that "it should be situated on the highest elevation of the property ... in such a way that the windows may overlook the entire area." *Eleutherian Mills* was constructed on a slope so that the back of the house did overlook the entire mill operation when built.

ELEUTHERIAN MILLS

First du Pont house in America and site of an annual gathering of the clan

On his French passport, Eleuthere Irénée du Pont, founder of E.I. du Pont de Nemours & Co., listed *Botaniste* as his profession in the belief that he would be heavily involved with horticulture and land development in the "Pontiana" community that his father, Pierre Samuel, envisioned as the family's American destiny. And, though he had worked for the French government's powder-making arsenal, it was E.I.'s studies at the *Jardin des Plantes* in Paris that excited him and would provide the skills necessary to supervise the agricultural activities he believed lay ahead in the family's New World "Rural Society."

Soon after the arrival of the du Ponts in America, however, their plan changed. It became apparent that a new direction needed to be followed and it was decided that, while Pierre and elder son Victor pursued a business venture in New York, Eleuthere should utilize his powder-making background as a means of earning a living.

From the family compound, *Bon Sejour (Goodstay)* in North Bergen, New Jersey, E.I. began looking for a place to establish a powder-making mill. His search ended in Delaware's Brandywine Valley where the coursing water of the Brandywine River, a nearby French-speaking settlement, convenience to water transportation, and connection with a family friend provided favorable surroundings for establishing his mill. In 1802, E.I. acquired sixty-five acres from Jacob Broom, who had operated a cotton mill there between 1795 and 1797. The price of $6,740 included a dam and millrace.

While making plans for a permanent residence, E.I., his wife, Sophie, and their family lived in a rustic house near the river on the former Broom property, said to have been damp and snake-infested. As the location for their new house, *Eleutherian Mills*, du Pont stipulated that it "should be situated on the highest elevation of the property and in one of the angles of the factory confines in such a way that the windows may overlook the entire area."

E.I. chose a site for the house between the two projects on which he was most focused: the mill for manufacturing black powder and an extensive garden with fruit trees, vegetables, and flowers to provide his family with fresh produce and bring a semblance of gracious living to the untamed surroundings.

The front of the house faced the garden planned in French style and was anchored to the west by an osage orange tree, now estimated to be 350 years old and documented as one of the two largest of its specie in the country. Wood from osage orange trees was prized by native Americans for bows and clubs, and the sharp pointed spikes of it planted as hedge rows led to the invention of barbed wire. Today the tree is seventy-two feet tall with a circumference of 26.58 feet and a spread of eighty-five feet.

Construction on *Eleutherian Mills* began soon after du Pont purchased the land, but it was not ready for occupancy until summer of the following year. The house was designed in Classic Revival or Federal style, popular in the United States between 1790 and 1830, particularly in New England, Georgia, and Virginia, where family friend and confidant Thomas Jefferson was in the second stage of building Monticello. The du Pont house was two-and-a-half stories, built of blue granite found on the property, and finished with cream-colored stucco, similar to *Bois des Fossés*, the family home of Pierre Samuel in France.

During its two hundred years of existence *Eleutherian Mills* has been modified as a result of explosions at the mill, the varying tastes and needs of the five generations of du Pont families who lived there, its conversion to a clubhouse for mill workers, and finally, the protective ownership by Louise du Pont Crowninshield and her husband, Frank. Essentially the house is the way it was when lived in by E.I. and later renovated by Henry in 1853-54.

Eleutherian Mills is set between the front garden on the west and the Brandywine River on the east. The pedimented front door has a sunburst fanlight set within an arched frame supported by Ionic columns and flanked by two double-hung, six-over-six windows on either side. On the second floor are five windows, and on the third floor four dormer windows face the garden. There are two chimneys at each end of the gable roof. When built, the five-bay house was forty-six feet wide and thirty-one feet deep. As it is positioned on a steep hillside, the east and west fronts are completely different.

The front door opens to a through hallway with double doors at the end leading to a piazza. The vista was enthusiastically described by Sophie in a letter to her brother, Charles Dalmas. "You cannot imagine the view of the countryside which we have now that some of the trees next to the site have been cut down—we overlook the entire Brandywine and the valley," she wrote. Next to the piazza doors stairways lead to the second floor and lower level.

To the right of the front door was E.I. and Sophie's bedroom and across from their bedroom was the entrance to the parlor. The dining room and office were located in a lean-to wing on the downstream side entered through a hallway parallel to E.I. and Sophie's bedroom when it was on the first floor. Additional bedrooms and a library were on the second floor.

The March 1818 explosion at the mills—known as the great explosion—was the first major one, causing extensive damage and taking the lives of thirty-two men and one woman. The glazing mill, dust mill, pounding mill, granary, and magazine all exploded. *Eleutherian Mills* sustained considerable damage to windows, sashes, ceilings, and walls, and it took three months to repair the damage and make it habitable. The health of E.I.'s wife was also affected and she was never again able to fully perform her role as wife and mother.

Sophie died in 1828 and six years later E.I. died while on a business trip to Philadelphia. Their eldest son, Alfred Victor, took over the company responsibilities after a period of transition in which he was assisted by James Bidermann. Alfred and his wife were living close by at *Nemours House* and saw no reason to move; however, in 1837 he built an office near *Eleutherian Mills*. Referred to as the First Office, it is more accurately the Second Office, since E.I. conducted the company's business affairs throughout his lifetime from an office in the house.

In 1837, Henry brought his bride, Louisa, to *Eleutherian Mills* to live and, in 1850, he took over management of the company from Alfred. Two subsequent additions were made to the new office, but by 1891 it was considered too small for the rapidly expanding company and a much larger building was constructed at 204 Buck Road. Known as the Second Office, today it is a private home.

With time and explosions having taken their toll, Henry decided it was time for some major work to be done to the house. Renovations began in 1853 and were not completed until well into 1854. The shed roof of the former office wing on the south side of the house was raised with dormer windows added to the front and rear and a matching wing built on the north side; both wings are slightly recessed from the main structure. The second floor piazza was incorporated into the house, increasing its depth fourteen feet, and the third floor renovated to create seven children's bedrooms. At this same time a front porch and wrought-iron canopy were built.

On August 22, 1857, another major explosion occurred, killing six men including Alexis I. du Pont, and in 1861 there was an explosion severe enough that doors were thrown off their hinges and all but two windows in the house broken. In October 1890, there was a third catastrophic explosion when an estimated 150 tons of powder blew up seven buildings. The blast was so great that glass was shattered in five windows at *Winterthur*, two-and-a-half miles away. *Eleutherian Mills* suffered substantial damage and

the lives of twelve men were lost. As a result Louisa G. du Pont, Henry's widow (Henry died in 1889), and her daughter, Evelina, who were then living there, decided that "enough (of explosions) was enough" and moved to the du Pont-owned Pelleport mansion on Kennett Pike.

William H. du Pont, who compiled a list of mill explosions, wrote that in the 117 years of the Brandywine Mills existence, from 1804 to 1921, there were 288 explosions with a total of 228 people killed in sixty of those explosions.

Between 1890 and 1893 the house was closed until it was converted to the Brandywine Club for DuPont employees. Under the direction of Francis G. du Pont, a grandson of E.I., dining facilities, showers, bathtubs and a library were added. A frame addition included a gymnasium with pool tables and shuffleboard courts and it was also used for employee dances and parties; however, because of decreased use, this plan was abandoned in 1910.

During World War I, *Eleutherian Mills* was used as a barracks for soldiers guarding the powder works; it was later used by the farm superintendent. After 119 years, a period of evolution that saw E.I. du Pont de Nemours and Company progress from a small family-operated mill producing gunpowder to a global science company, the powder mills were closed in 1921, and the company decided to sell several of its properties along the Brandywine River. Two years later Henry A. du Pont had the opportunity of purchasing *Eleutherian Mills* (along with fifty-two acres), and offered it to his daughter, Louise, and her husband, yachtsman-marksman Frank Crowninshield, with the understanding that they spend some time there each year.[1]

The Crowninshields lived in Boston, but also had a summer house in Marblehead, Massachusetts, and a winter house in Boca Grande, Florida; still they regularly visited Wilmington where Mrs. Crowninshield had family and many friends. Louise was very familiar with *Eleutherian Mills*, having spent her childhood at *Winterthur*, along with her brother, Henry Francis. During this time she made frequent visits to see her grandmother and fondly remembered Sunday dinners and holidays celebrated there. The idea of living at *Eleutherian Mills* greatly appealed to both of the Crowninshields and they accepted her father's offer, living there part of each year from 1923 until her death in 1958.

Louise's father had the house done over for them while they were at another of their residences. He and Henry Francis, called Harry by the family, oversaw the construction, a responsibility Harry accepted with relish and that prepared him for the major changes he was to make at *Winterthur* after his father died. Harry also chose the architectural firm for the project, Mellor, Meigs & Howe, a well-thought-of Philadelphia partnership that specialized in mid-Atlantic and New England residences.

The front porch, added during the 1853 renovations, was removed to return the front entrance to its original appearance, and the canopy was placed over the first floor piazza overlooking the Brandywine. In the entrance hallway, paneling and crown molding were added and the color changed from white to green. The handsome winding staircase installed at the end of the hallway was found in New Jersey, replacing the more simple one that was moved to the back hall. By knocking down the wall that had originally been between E.I. and Sophie's bedroom and a storeroom, and later separated twin parlors, a spacious living room was created with two fireplaces.

Off the living room, a paneled den became a retreat for Frank Crowninshield, where he could relax and enjoy a cigar. The library across the hall was converted to a writing room and, next to the 1853 dining room, a butler's pantry was built. China used by E.I. and Sophie is displayed here and includes a set of china decorated by Eder V. Haughwoot in New York, who served many wealthy clients including Mary Todd Lincoln. Another set belonged to Admiral Samuel Du Pont, some of whose furniture is on display in the second floor library.

In the dining room, created by combining two small rooms, Louise had scenic wallpaper installed. Called "Vue de l'Amerique du Nord" ("Scenes of North America), it features scenes of West Point and the Hudson River, Niagara Falls, Natural Bridge in Virginia, Boston Harbor, and New York as seen from Weehawken, New Jersey, all adapted from Currier & Ives prints. The paper was manufactured by Zuber Cie in Rixheim, France, a company that has been printing woodblocked wallpaper at the same location since 1797. Fifteen hundred woodblocks were required to print the complete series. When touring *Eleutherian Mills,* Jacqueline Kennedy was so impressed with it that she selected the same paper for installation in the Diplomatic Reception Room at the White House.

Mrs. Walter T. Hart, a cousin of Louise Crowninshield, fondly recalled breakfasts and dinners served there when she was a houseguest. "Sunday breakfast, very English on the sideboard, consisted of codfish, baked beans, a chop, great plates of toast and muffins, honeydew melon, and large cups of coffee. Dinners were beautiful," she continued. "The table was a glittering mass of fine china, the table centerpiece, priceless old things, and the crystal wine and water goblets all reflecting the candles of the lovely dining room."[2]

Bedroom space was rearranged on the second floor and three bathrooms installed; third floor bedrooms were turned over to the Crowninshield servants. Little of the original furniture remained, though through the years many pieces have been donated by family members, including portraits, chairs, and the original bedstead of E.I. du Pont and his wife. Louise, a founding trustee of the National Trust for Historic Preservation and a connoisseur of antique furniture, added Victorian, Federal, and Colonial period furniture. Her fondness for hooked rugs is evidenced by many scattered throughout the house, most of which date from the 1800s.

A room on the second floor is now called the library, though it was primarily designated as such in order to provide a showcase for the exotic Eastern furniture acquired by Admiral Samuel Francis Du Pont on trade missions to India, China, and Japan in 1857 and 1859, when he was commander of the *U.S.S. Minnesota.*

Louise was a collector with many interests and she easily filled the wall space with paintings, drawings, and eagles in a reference to the *American Eagle* schooner that brought her ancestors to America. There are forty-two eagles in the house in many forms, ranging from two-inch embossed drawer pulls on a living room secretary to a five-foot wide wood carving at the entrance to the Terrace Room on the lower level and a hitching post to the right of the front door topped by an image of our national bird. The Crowninshields' collection of hooked rugs numbered more than 100 in the house.

The Terrace Room room, a favorite of the Crowninshields, was created from storage space, with a non-working fireplace and false beams installed. It was often the venue chosen for Sunday lunches that spilled onto the terrace overlooking a swimming pool. A nearby spring house was converted to a bathhouse. In addition to the many interior alterations to *Eleutherian Mills*, the Crowninshields also made significant changes outside. In the 1800s and into the early twentieth century, horses and buggies brought *Eleutherian Mills* visitors through the massive Buck Road gates and followed a driveway that led directly to a semi-circle in front of the house. The road was flanked with silver maple trees but, according to Richard Pratt, Hagley's Supervisor of Gardens and Grounds, as these died out they were replaced with gum trees.

When Louise and her husband moved into the house, automobiles were still in their infancy; however, this soon changed and as automobile traffic to the house increased, the glare from headlamps became an annoyance as it shone directly into Louise's bedroom. The solution was apparent and the driveway took on a new course, curving to the right and ending at the front door. The allee is still existent and, though the driveway has long been covered over, its path is clearly visible.

While the house and barn were under construction, E.I. had land for a garden and orchard cleared. The garden has been restored on its original site and in a period of cultivation that would have been in the tradition of the first part of the 19th century. E.I. separated his agricultural efforts into farming and a family garden. The family garden covered an area of two acres and in this he planted ornamental and fruit-bearing trees, vegetables, berries, and flowers, many raised from seeds and cuttings sent from France and planted side by side—artichokes and asparagus next to daisies and daffodils. Roses were the family favorite with fifteen varieties represented.

The orchard included apple, peach, cherry, pear, and plum trees, and among the ornamental shrubs and trees were flowering quince, lilac, and hydrangea. One hundred-two species have been accounted for in the garden and orchard. These have been planted in accordance with excavations conducted from 1969 to 1972, which determined their location, along with the sites of paths, greenhouses, cold frames, a drainage system, and a lattice summer house.

The original barn was built at the same time as the house and was enlarged in 1844. The resulting bank barn, restored by the Crowninshields, is now used as exhibit space for carriages, wagons, and farm and powder yard conveyances similar to those first used at the mills and by earlier du Pont families who lived here. There is also a Conestoga wagon of the type that carried black powder to the Old Newcastle wharves for shipment to other American ports and overseas. Additionally, there is a collection of weathervanes, assembled by Louise Crowninshield, and agricultural tools. On the lower level of the barn are several vintage automobiles and the first duPont car manufactured, a 1928 phaeton.

Between the river and the east side of the house, the Crowninshields created a unique six-acre Italian Ruin Garden constructed over the wreckage of a mill destroyed in the 1890 explosion.

Like many of the du Ponts, Louise and Frank Crowninshield were inveterate travelers and in their wanderings through Italy visited gardens at the Villa Gamberaia outside Florence, the Villa Giulia in Rome, the Villa Aldobrandini outside Asolo, and the Villa Falconieri in Frascaati, all of which inspired them to develop a similar theme for their garden on the banks of the Brandywine.

In 1923 the area directly below *Eleutherian Mills* was cluttered with the shattered remains of the three-story saltpeter refinery but, within a year it had begun its transformation into five terraces. Reflection pools were created by flooding basements of mill houses and accented by classically inspired columns, statues, and exotic plantings. Saltpeter kettles mutated as garden urns, and, as a piece de resistance, a quarter-sized Parthenon bathhouse was constructed.

In his book, *E.I. du Pont, Botaniste: The Beginning of a Tradition*, Norman B. Wilkinson wrote that as the garden took shape, "flagstone walks bordered by low-growing box became paths between avenues of tall, tapered conifers beneath which ground flowers cluster and annuals bloom in bright and varied hues. One walk leads to a sunken pool, at the end of which is a temple ruin with a mosaic Pegasus in its tiled floor. A vista of Doric columns and towering evergreens, amid which stand statues from the pantheon of Greek and Roman heroes and mythological deities, is seen from the temple plaza. ... Pan plays his pipe ... and nearby Aphrodite poses in eternal pagan loveliness."[3]

The Italian Garden was a complete departure from the formality of those designed by the Crowninshield's cousins, many of whom no doubt shook their heads when asked for an opinion of it. Nevertheless, it made the cut when it was selected as one of the Wilmington gardens to be visited by Garden Club of America members on their 1938 pilgrimage to Philadelphia. The Crowninshields had no children, but they enjoyed one another and each had a good sense of humor. The garden was a joint effort: he designed, she planted. In a copy of Luigi Dami's *The Garden* that Louise gave to her husband, she inscribed, "To the world's greatest living classical landscape architect—from the other."

Eleutherian Mills is not only the birthplace of the DuPont Company, but is the mecca for the extended du Pont family, a place to which they return as a connection to their Franco-American roots. It's not unusual for a family member to appear on a tour of the house or to be seen strolling through the garden. Occasionally during the year, perhaps for the opening of a Hagley exhibit or dedication of a new building, a reception is held at the museum after hours, but once a year the nostalgia is brought to the surface.

On New Year's Eve, after the last museum visitor has left the property, and the gates swing closed to outsiders, the du Ponts come together en masse to commemorate the anniversary of the family's arrival in America. A cocktail party is held, usually in the Soda House or library.

Glasses are raised, and the words of Pierre S. du Pont III, spoken at the 200th anniversary celebration, though seldom confided outside the assemblage, come to mind: "The du Pont family" he said, "is entitled to a just pride in their name." Many would agree.

Eleutherian Mills

Owners: Eleuthere Irénée du Pont
Henry du Pont
Louise Gerhard du Pont
DuPont Company
Henry A. du Pont
Louise du Pont Crowninshield
Hagley Museum and Library Foundation
Constructed: 1802-03
Location: Rte. 141 near Rte. 100
Wilmington, Delaware

Notes

1. Production of black powder stopped in 1921 and, in 1923, it was decided to sell off much of the DuPont Company land holdings in what became known as "The 1921 Distribution." In August 1923, a party was held at the home of Mrs. Charles Copeland attended by family members and senior management who were sent maps in advance indicating what property would be disposed of. At the party they were asked to express their preference. In a March 11, 1958 letter to Dr. Charles David, Director, Eleutherian Mills Historical Library, Louise Crowninshield said that she and her father, Henry A. du Pont, attended. She mentioned that she had urged him to buy *Eleutherian Mills* where he had been brought up and which she so fondly remembered and he did.

2. *The Hagley Cookbook*, 1983

3. *E.I. Du Pont, Botaniste*, Norman B. Wilkinson, University Press of Virginia, 1972

The reception room is to the left of the front entrance. The Crowninshields were avid collectors and had more than one hundred hooked rugs and forty-two replicas of eagles in the house.

The living room had been two separate rooms, but the Crowninshields took down the dividing wall creating a spacious room with twin fireplaces.

The dining room is reset three times a year. All flowers in the house are raised in the greenhouse.
The decanter set in the dining room belonged to E.I. and Sophie du Pont.

The Crowninshield Italian gardens were built on the site of the
saltpeter refinery that was destroyed in the 1890 explosion when
thirty tons of powder ignited resulting in six explosions.

The millrace was constructed in 1803 to harness the power of the Brandywine River in
the production of its gunpowder. It was rebuilt in 2005.

The first office was actually located in a lean-to added by E.I. du Pont to the structure of the house. Henry "the Red" removed this and had wings added to the house. Alfred du Pont had a separate building erected and this is called the First Office.

JUMBLES

Jumbles were a favorite nineteenth century cookie. Louisa du Pont added rose water to her ingredients. Here is the classic recipe used in making the cookies served to visitors during *Eleutherian Mills'* Christmastime candlelight tours.

Recipe for Jumbles
Ingredients:
    1 cup butter
    1 Tablespoon cinnamon
    3 1/2 cups all purpose flour
    1 cup sugar
    1 Tablespoon rose water
    2 eggs

Method:
    Cream together butter and sugar. Add remaining ingredients. Make cookies using a small amount of dough (about a teaspoonful). Place on buttered cookie sheet and flatten out with the bottom of a glass dipped in granulated sugar. Bake at 350 degrees on cookie sheet until edges are slight;y brown.

Recipe from the Hagley Cookbook, *Hagley Museum and Library. Used with permission.*

Gibraltar was the home of H. Rodney and Isabella du Pont Sharp. One of the few du Pont houses previously owned, it was built in 1844 and acquired by the Sharps in 1909, who made extensive renovations to the house and gardens. Credit: Photograph by author

GIBRALTAR

Named after the rocky outcropping in the Mediterranean

Gibraltar, like its namesake, is made of limestone; but, while the peninsula is made of Jurassic rock, the Wilmington estate is built from square blocks of sedimentary limestone laced with quartz that is fine-grained with a smoky hue and was quarried just a few miles away. It is referred to locally as Brandywine blue rock or granite.

The original structure dates back some 166 years, when a prosperous Philadelphia cotton broker, John Rodney Brinckle, grand nephew of Caesar Rodney, the first governor of Delaware and a signer of the Declaration of Independence, purchased a one hundred-acre property, building a house on it with the hope of offering it as a wedding present to his new bride. Alas, it was not meant to be. The lady had other plans and refused his offer.

About 1848, Brinckle invited his brother, Rev. Samuel Crawford Brinckle, and his wife and their eight children to share the house with him. Several years later John sold the property to his brother and moved away. In a stroke of irony, Reverend Brinckle helped form Christ Church, known as the du Pont church, becoming its first rector and unwittingly beginning the connection of *Gibraltar* with the Brandywine Valley first family.

Enter Hugh Rodney Sharp. Born in Seaford, Delaware, Sharp attended Delaware College, later the University of Delaware, as a probationary student because of his age, sixteen; he graduated in June 1900 with a Bachelor of Science degree. He then pursued a teaching career in the public schools of Odessa, Delaware. Three years later, Sharp moved twenty-two miles north to Wilmington and began working for E.I. DuPont de Nemours and Company in their Accounting and Purchasing Departments.

At the time, Pierre S. du Pont was the company president and he and the new employee formed a close and lasting friendship that resulted in their becoming in-laws. Through Pierre, Rodney met his mentor's younger sister, Isabella, and on June 6, 1908, they were married at *St. Amour*, the nearby estate of the bride's mother. By then, the streets of Wilmington had already begun to cut through the Brinckle fields, but in 1909 the couple purchased *Gibraltar* and 6.24 acres of the property.

At the time, the large square house was said to have been in poor condition with no central heat or plumbing. But, in this era of the American Country Place (1890s to 1940s), the Sharps were eager to begin *Gibraltar's* transformation into a grand country estate.

In 1915, they made substantial alterations to the original house using the Philadelphia architectural firm DeArmond, Ashmead & Bickley. Servants' quarters were added, a larger kitchen installed, and the dining room was extended so that it could comfortably seat twenty-four. The addition also included a paneled library that became the family gathering place. In 1927 further changes were carried out with plans drawn by Wilmington architect Albert Ely Ives. The living room was expanded and a two-story conservatory added. *Gibraltar's* interior spaces are largely Classic and Colonial Revival in style, based on forms popular in England and the United States from the end of the nineteenth and extending into the twentieth centuries. By the time the Sharp renovations had been completed, the house had tripled in size to 17,000 square feet with fourteen bedrooms. It was listed on the National Register of Historic Places in 1998.

The grounds too, underwent major changes. A forty by sixty-foot swimming pool, ten feet deep, was added to the landscape in the summer of 1916 and at the same time the Brinckle carriage house was enlarged and converted into a pool house. Other outbuildings were also added to or relocated at this time. The pool is still existent today, but has been converted into an eighteen-inch-deep reflecting pool for safety's sake. It features twenty varieties of water lilies, both hardy and tropical, and is surrounded by Chinese wisteria and African lilies. All additions and new construction harmonized with the original Brinckle house built in 1844, and the granite came from the same quarry located on Delaware Avenue near Bancroft Parkway.

As often happens with sizable estates, *Gibraltar's* gardens became more important than the house itself. This is true partly because the estate was not designed as an entity, but was added to at different times over a period of years, and partly because the house could only be modified within a certain perimeter, whereas the gardens could be changed indefinitely—and at much less expense.

Influenced, no doubt, by his brother-in-law's extensive gardens at *Longwood,* across the border in nearby Pennsylvania, Sharp contacted Marian Cruger Coffin, one of the country's first professionally trained (M.I.T.) female landscape architects, to design a garden plan that would complement the expanding house. Coffin began working with the Sharps in 1916 and continued her association with *Gibraltar* until 1923. In effect she became the unofficial du Pont landscape gardener. During this period she also worked for Sharp's brother-in-law, Lammot du Pont, at *St. Amour* and for Lammot's first cousin, Henry du Pont, at *Winterthur*. Later on Coffin worked with Eugene du Pont at his *Owl's Nest* estate and with Lammot du Pont Copeland and his wife, Pamela, at *Mt. Cuba*.

In 1921, Sharp left the DuPont Company to devote his time and energy to overseeing *Gibraltar* renovations and to philanthropy. An extended trip to Europe at this time, with family and friends, exposed him to the continent's most exquisite houses and the elaborate gardens that showcased them, and he saw first-hand the integral relationship between houses and gardens. On his return, he discussed his observations with Marian Coffin, who incorporated some of his ideas into her garden plan.

Sharp also had a fondness for antique sculpture, filling his gardens with thirty-seven pieces he purchased locally and on trips to France, Italy, England, Hong Kong, Japan, and Singapore. After visiting the Malaysian island, Somerset Maugham wrote, "Raffles (Hotel) stands for all the fables of the exotic east." Rodney Sharp, who visited there while in Singapore, shared his thoughts, bringing home sculptures from the exotic destination to embellish his gardens. A 1996 inventory showed that, of the thirty-seven pieces he acquired, ten had disappeared either through deterioration or theft.

When Coffin began her work at *Gibraltar* she was presented with a "blank slate." Brinckle had sited the house on a rocky ledge that reminded him of the Mediterranean promontory. It looked over a rolling field and Coffin, while acknowledging that it would be a challenge, believed that it was easier to start "from scratch" than to rework another person's efforts. Her idea was to use Italian Renaissance gardens as a model in designing *Gibraltar's* gardens, a concept that greatly appealed to both Sharps.

Public access to the gardens is now from Greenhill Avenue, through hand-forged iron gates near an eight-car garage and a former tool shed, though Coffin intended guests to approach them from the house. From the east entrance guests stepped onto a boxwood-lined walk leading through a perfectly manicured lawn in English style and onto the still existent sweeping marble staircase that curves gently downward thirty feet to the pool area. Evergreens and retaining walls offered an element of surprise as visitors descended to the ground level through a series of three terraces, which also served Coffin's need to simplify grades between the house and the formal gardens and acted as a transition from the rigid architecture of the house to the more fluid components of the garden.

A few steps down from the pool terrace she designed a rectangular, sixty by one hundred-twenty-foot formal flower garden on the level of Greenhill Avenue. This is separated from the service area by a stone wall; the other end is anchored by a double-tiered fountain. Rough marble walkways outline the plat, divided into eleven bedding areas. Marble for the estate's walks—138 tons—was supplied by the Beaver Dam Marble Company in Baltimore. In her total garden plan Coffin specified over 650 species of trees, shrubs, plants, and flowers that were looked after and maintained by a staff of seventeen gardeners.

Just beyond the fountain, through a second set of iron gates affixed to stone pillars and topped by two-foot high eagles, Coffin created a 210-foot central axis flanked by 200 bald cypress trees pollarded at a height of fifteen feet for uniformity. Off of this corridor she created small areas or "garden rooms" using the sculpture acquired by Sharp as focal points. It was to one of these intimate settings that brother-in-law Pierre, following a dinner at *Gibraltar*, escorted his cousin, Alice Belin, and proposed. With greater success than Brinckle had, Pierre's offer was accepted.

At the end of the allee is an Italian garden pavilion with marble columns, three arches and a vaulted ceiling, usually referred to as a tea house, that was also enjoyed by the four Sharp children as a playhouse and by the grown-ups as a cocktail rendezvous, fitted out with oriental rugs, potted palms and wicker furniture. It is still intact, a charming and distinctive feature of the garden. Long gone, however, are the rugs, wicker and potted palms.

Besides *Gibraltar,* the Sharps owned three additional houses: a summer home in nearby Rehoboth Beach, Delaware (Colonial style, 1934); *Meown* in Centreville, Delaware, that Sharp built for his wife (Bella) as a place to entertain her friends and pursue her interest in animal husbandry; and *The Hacienda*, a residence at Boca Grande on Florida's west coast that was also popular with other du Pont families. Francis Crowninshield and his wife Louise, sister of *Winterthur's* Henry du Pont, built a cottage there in 1914, and Henry himself built one soon after. The Sharps waited until 1925.

Unlike other cottages that were generally executed in simple beach style on the west coast, Sharp built a house in the Spanish-Florida architectural style of Addison Mizner then fashionable in Palm Beach. *The Hacienda* was so ornate that other family members referred to it as the Taj Mahal. Still, it appealed to Marian Coffin who was a guest there, as well as mentor-friend Pierre, who once observed a butler carrying exotic shells on a tray and distributing them along the beach for Sharp's house guests to discover on walks later in the day.

Aside from his interest in architecture and landscaping, Sharp followed his roots back to Odessa and his days as a student at Delaware College. Lee Reese in his book, *The Horse On Rodney Square*, observed that "Sharp was an aesthete whose exquisite taste was displayed most spectacularly in his restoration of the Corbit house at Odessa." In 1938 Sharp purchased the Corbit House, renovated it, and gave it to Winterthur Museum in 1958. The museum in turn renamed it the Corbit-Sharp House in his honor. It is now registered as a National Historic Landmark by the National Park Service.

Rodney Sharp showed just as much interest in his alma mater. When he died, it was acknowledged that no one in the history of Delaware had done so much for a university and it was largely through his efforts, and his brother-in-law's, that the college gained university status. By the time of his death, a trust that he established at his wife's death (December 1946) had grown to the sum of fifty-eight million dollars. In 1953 the University of Delaware named him the outstanding alumnus of the year for his achievements as a university trustee, philanthropist, and Delaware citizen.

Sharp lived at *Gibraltar* until his death on August 9, 1968, while returning from Italy aboard the Italian liner *Cristoforo Colombo*, sister ship of the ill-fated *Andrea Doria*. Like many in the du Pont family, Rodney Sharp was an avid world traveler, and in one of his journals he noted that by 1967 he had made over fifty voyages to Europe. The *Cristoforo Columbo* would have been well-suited to his needs. At 29,191 tons, it was described by a then-current guidebook as a floating work of art, providing an atmosphere of romance embellished with fine wines and dining.

Giant evergreens originally marked the property line between *Gibraltar* and Pennsylvania Avenue, but as traffic increased these were replaced by a six-foot wall and still later by a ten-foot wall. Today the estate's gardens have been largely restored by Preservation Delaware (1997) and a devoted group of volunteers, and are open to the public the year-round from dawn until dusk. The house, on the other hand, has been neglected and vandalized since Sharp's oldest son, Hugh Rodney, Jr., died in 1990, and the house became vacant in 1994 when the caretaker moved out. Since then, a number of plans have been put forth to rehab *Gibraltar,* from conversion to an upmarket inn to modifying it for use as an office building.

Gibraltar

Owners:	John Rodney Brinckle, original
	Mr. and Mrs. H. Rodney Sharp
	Preservation Delaware, current
Constructed:	1844.
	Later additions 1915 and 1927
Architects:	DeArmond, Ashmead & Bickley, 1915. Albert Ely Ives, 1927
Landscape:	Marian Coffin, 1916 - 1923
Location:	Pennsylvania Avenue
	Wilmington, Delaware

The former swimming pool, part of the formal gardens, has been converted to a lily pond. Credit: Photograph by author

Gibraltar gardens were designed by prominent landscape architect Marian Cruger Coffin.

Garden entrance to the teahouse (in background) is flanked by symbolic
eagle sculpture atop columns. (opposite)

GOODSTAY

Named after Bon Sejour, the du Pont's first home in America

The property on which *Goodstay* was built was surveyed prior to 1685 and the house built in 1740, making it one of the oldest houses in the Brandywine Valley with du Pont connections. At one time company wives spent evenings in the parlor trimming labels for DuPont powder kegs, but today the estate, which spans three centuries, is a vibrant part of the University of Delaware's north campus.

In 1732, Andrew Lina, a communicant of Old Swedes Church, purchased 136 acres, one of two tracts of land of equal size, with the common name *Green Hill*. It's surmised that, about 1740, he built the original small stone house, still existent, for his wife and six children. Later in the century the house was nearly doubled in size, probably by Lina's grandson, who inherited it. Sixty years later *Green Hill* was purchased by John Hirons, who added a large stone barn (his initials are on an 1807 datestone) and other outbuildings, and is credited with planning the first formal English garden at the estate.

The house and eighty-eight acres, "more or less," were advertised, in 1846, for sale by George Read McLane who inherited it from his father. The property was described as "abundantly supplied with pure water and excellent springs. ... There is an apple orchard, and a great variety of other fruit trees, (such) as peaches, plums, pears, cherries, quince, etc. and the garden is stocked with currants, gooseberries and raspberries.

The description concluded:

The buildings are numerous, permanent, and convenient, consisting of a dwelling house, barn, granary, two carriage houses, hen house, smoke house, wash house, spring house, all of stone, with poultry houses, corn crib, summer house, etc. of frame. The dwelling house is large and substantial, of stone, and contains fourteen rooms ... the lawn beautifully laid out, is filled with the choicest ornamental trees. Carriage ways and foot walks have been graveled at great expense.

William Pyle, a manufacturer of patent leather, bought Green Hill in 1854 for ten thousand dollars. His son, Howard, founded the Brandywine School of Painting that included internationally renowned painters and illustrators, Maxfield Parrish, N.C. Wyeth, and Frank Schoonover.

Though Howard lived at *Green Hill* for only the first eight years of his life, he recorded his vivid memories of the house, which were published in the *Woman's Home Companion* in April 1912. In the article he recalled that there were really three houses joined together. Pyle wrote:

There was an old part built about 1740, I think. Standing against that was another part built about 1780, and then my father built an addition that stood against the 1780 part of the house, so that when you went from one of these parts, you had to go up one step and down another.

In front of the house was a grassy lawn with a terraced bank ... and there was a little grove, or park of trees, to one side, and beyond you could see the turnpike road. ...

On the other side of the house was a garden of old, old-fashioned roses and sweet shrubs that filled the air with fragrance when they were abloom. And there were beds of tulips and daffodils and there were graveled walks edged with box and a greenhouse of shining glass ... and a wooden summer-house at the end of one of the gravel walks, and altogether it was such a garden as you will hardly find outside of a story book.

Other owners lived here, tending the Tudor gardens and enlarging them, before *Green Hill* became another of the Brandywine Valley's du Pont properties in 1868. Margaretta E. Lammot du Pont (1807-1898), widow of Alfred Victor Philadelphe du Pont (1798-1856), second president of the DuPont Company and first son of the founder, lived at the original *Nemours,* built for the

Goodstay dates back to 1740 and was purchased by Margaretta E. L. du Pont in 1868. She changed the name from *Green Hill* to *Goodstay* as a connection with the first du Pont house in Bergen Point, New Jersey, named *Goodstay* by Pierre Samuel du Pont. (opposite)

couple in 1824. She remained there following his death (1856) for an additional twelve years prior to giving the house to her son and his family and moving with daughter, Emma Paulina, to the house on Kennett Pike, changing its name from *Green Hill* to *Goodstay*.

In choosing *Goodstay* for a name Mrs. du Pont looked upon the move as a new beginning, just as Pierre du Pont de Nemours had sixty-eight years before when he led the family's departure from France. Pierre's wife and son-in-law, Bureaux de Pusy, sailed ahead of other family members, selecting a place for them to live in the then village of North Bergen, New Jersey. Pleased with his wife's choice, he announced that its name should be *Bon Sejour*, translated as *Good Stay*. Margaretta du Pont, delving into the past, considered the name a good portent for her future as well.

The two du Pont women lived there until Margaretta's death, after which Emma sold *Goodstay* to her nephew, T. Coleman du Pont in 1911. During this time, an influenza virus became a pandemic and, in Wilmington, the old Wilmington Country Club, adjoining the *Goodstay* property, was mobilized as a temporary hospital for seriously ill patients. Tents were raised on the golf course adjoining *Goodstay* to make room for extra beds, and ambulances, their sirens screaming, raced up Pennsylvania Avenue at all times of day and night.

Coleman gave the property to his daughter, Ellen C. du Pont Meeds (Mrs. Hollyday Meeds), as a wedding present in 1923. Soon after Mrs. Meeds hired architect Edmond Gilchrist, to draw plans for expansion of the house, and landscape architect Robert Wheelwright, a principal in the firm Wheelwright & Stevenson, to restore the gardens to their Tudor origins.

In describing the changes made at that time, Wheelwright, who later married Ellen Meeds (October15,1937), wrote that the first remodeling was done in 1924. The kitchen and servants' quarters were placed on the north side of the house and living quarters on the south side away from the increasing traffic on Kennett Pike.

Further alterations were made to the house in 1933. A playroom was added as well as a new entrance hall and forecourt. Other changes included adding a larger living room (forty-six-and-a-half feet by twenty-five-and-a-half feet), a dining room that could seat twenty-four, a morning room, flower room, bicycle room, den and a Chinese Room (now the Gold Room) that was furnished with murals brought back by Admiral Samuel Du Pont from his Asian tour of duty.

Exterior changes made during the 1920s and 1930s included converting the old stone barn to a garage, the carriage house into an art studio for Mrs. Wheelwright, an accomplished painter, and the octagonal apple house, now a visitor reception center, into a tool house. It was during this period that *Goodstay* evolved from a farm into a country mansion and came into its own with a reputation for being one of Wilmington's major horticultural attractions.

While the house was reconstructed, the gardens were changed from exclusively vegetable gardens to flower gardens. A new vegetable garden was created and bordered by flower beds that provided cutting flowers, arranged in the old smokehouse adapted for this purpose. Wheelwright based his design on the classic Tudor plan of a square garden with three paths down and three paths crossing the square, forming enclosed spaces that he partitioned with boxwood hedges bordered by gravel paths. These individual gardens or "rooms" were designated as Rose, Iris, Peony, Knot,

and Turkey Rock Gardens, the latter so-named because of turkeys that roosted on it when *Green Hill* was operated as a farm.

The square design offered the option of further division into "knots," if desired, by the crossing of two axes. Wheelwright achieved this in one square, diversifying the planting with hosta, lily-of-the-valley and woods tulip. In a sixth rectangle there was a greenhouse constructed by Lord & Burnham, Irvington, New York, which also designed and built conservatories for a number of other du Pont estates in addition to the Rockefeller estate in Pocantico Hills, New York, the New York Botanical Garden, and Phipps Conservatory in Pittsburgh. Unfortunately, this was removed in 1999.

In 1938, the Garden Club of America celebrated its 25th Anniversary in Philadelphia and the meeting was reconvened in Wilmington with the *Hotel du Pont* as the headquarters. Eighteen Wilmington club members opened their gardens as a special feature, among them many with du Pont connections. *Goodstay* was featured as one of these with the following program notes:

> Century old box-bordered flower and vegetable garden, redesigned to relate to enlarged home in 1928. Truck patch redesigned as cutting garden in 1937, featuring a magnolia walk. The Park, a grove of old trees with tiny brook and naturalized spring bulbs and flowers. This, as well as flower arrangements in the garden, developed by the owner.

Though Wheelwright and Stevenson are listed as the landscape architects, Robert Wheelwright considered the input from his wife as a major reason for the garden's success. He wrote that, "Much of the charm of both house and garden is due to the unusual ability possessed by Mrs. Wheelwright to visualize plans and the fact that she has definite ideas of what she wants. ... She is a person who is fond of color and extremely sensitive to color combinations, consequently the planting of flowers has been largely under her personal care, and to her must go all credit for the subtle color relationships."

Wheelwright estimated that it took him about thirteen years to complete the garden's transition from its original state, when he began working on it, to its completed form. In designing the Magnolia Walk, he commented that he was fulfilling a girlhood dream of his wife's. The walk was defined by an allee of thirty-eight pink magnolias terminating at a circular reflection pool. Originally this featured only a jet of water, but was replaced by a sculpture of Venus by French sculptor Aristide Maillol. One of five hollow cast bronzes executed in France by the Rudier Foundry, it is now on display in the University's Old College Building in Newark.

In addition to horticulture, Ellen (Meeds) Wheelwright was keenly interested in fox hunting. Along with three friends, she was one of the four organizers of the Vicmead Hunt Club. Mrs. Victor du Pont was another, and from their two names the club's name, Vicmead, was adopted.

All of the Wheelwright furniture has been removed from the house, though the murals in the Chinese Room remain in place. Mrs. Wheelwright left the house and property to the University of Delaware at her death in 1968, and it is now operated by the university as a conference center and venue for social functions. The gardens are open to visitors daily without charge.

Goodstay

Owners: Andrew Lina, original
William Anderson
John Hirons
George McLane
William Pyle
Margaretta du Pont
Emma Paulina du Pont
T. Coleman du Pont

Ellen du Pont Meeds Wheelwright
University of Delaware, current
Constructed: c. 1740
Architect: Edmond Gilchrist (1924)
Landscape: Robert Wheelwright (from 1924)
Location: Pennsylvania Avenue
Wilmington, Delaware

The house underwent major expansion after the marriage of Ellen du Pont Meeds
to landscape architect Robert Wheelwright. Side entrance.

Gardens were important to the overall plan of *Goodstay*, first as a source of food, later as an integral part of the landscape. Photograph is taken from garden path looking towards former barn.

90

Constructed 1921-1923, *Granogue* is sited on 515 acres assembled from four contiguous farms.

GRANOGUE

A grand example of the American Country House Era

The Brandywine Valley is a living diorama of the du Pont dynasty. Sprawling mansions spread north, south, east, and west of Delaware Route 52, also known as Kennett Pike. Sequestered behind stone walls and split rail fences, they are often surrounded by open land trusts providing pastures for horses and sheep, and in at least one case exotic belted Galloway cattle. The largest and most imposing of these stately residences still lived in by a family member is *Granogue*, occupied by beloved patriarch Irénée du Pont, Jr., and his family.[1]

To make up the site for his estate, du Pont's father, great grandson of the founder of the DuPont Company, assembled four contiguous farms: the McCullough-Barksdale, Chandler-Rust, Harvey-Ely, and Donnelly farms. Collectively they represented over 515 acres. Having secured these, construction on the sixty-nine-room house began on August 21, 1921, and the move-in date was March 30, Good Friday, 1923. "With eight daughters and one son," Irénée, Jr., comments, "we pretty well filled the eleven bedrooms."

The rise in elevation from the road on which the house fronts is seventy-two feet, approximately the height of a seven-story building. It is an impressive and highly visible landmark reached by a driveway exactly one mile long, part of a nearly three-mile roadway system that winds through the property.

From the road the entrance to the estate is deceptive. To the right is a dammed pond, sometimes used as an unsanctioned swimming pool; further along is a magnificent barn, at one time the scene of *Granogue Farms* milk production (1917-1950), and now used for storing farm equipment and baled straw. Offices and a greenhouse are the next landmarks. At the end of the winding driveway, 362 feet above sea level, facing northwest over a glorious expanse of evergreens and open countryside stands *Granogue*.

A circular drive leads to the front entrance of the two-and-a-half-story Georgian house. Constructed of Germantown granite, it fairly sparkles in the sunlight due to the platelets of mica contained in the granite. "The stone was shipped from Germantown by train,"

Irénée explains, "off-loaded at the *Granogue* railroad station, then a stop on the Wilmington and Northern Railroad, weighed, and from there transported to the building site by wagons pulled by mules."

Granogue's formal entrance is a double doorway protected by an overhanging balcony with French doors. Above these is an arched Palladian window inset with clear glass panels of Gothic design and surmounted by a pediment. To the left and right of the entrance are two-story, forward facing wings. Family rooms are on the left and the wing on the right houses the dining room, breakfast room, service area, and accommodations for six live-in servants. The center part of the building has a hip roof while the wings are gabled. All roofs are slate and there are ten chimneys. On the top of the house is a cupola, "accessible by a very scary ladder," Mr. du Pont observes. From this perch Andrew Wyeth spent several weeks painting the surrounding Brandywine Valley.

Straight ahead at the end of the driveway, with the house to the right, is a two-bay garage—the main one is located down the hill and can accommodate twelve automobiles. In this garage, if the door is open, a visitor can see the first car Irénée, Jr., owned—a black 1936 Oldsmobile F-36 touring coupé. Though not used on a daily basis, the car is kept in perfect running order, is fully registered and insured, and is driven about 1,000 miles a year. There were six employee houses and stables for horses regularly ridden by the eight du Pont daughters.

Granogue was designed by Irénée, Sr.'s, fraternity brother (at Massachsetts Institute of Technology), Albert H. Spahr, who was the architect for many large residences in Grosse Pointe and Pittsburgh. General contractor was John W. Barnes from New York. The house is built on steel posts and beams, "like an office building," says Irénée, Jr.. There is crawl space under most of the house with a full basement only in the service wing. Floors are reinforced concrete covered with teak wood.

The front entrance leads into a foyer and three steps up to the main floor. On the right is a walnut staircase with a railing designed by master ironworker Samuel Yellin. A native of Poland, Yellin immigrated to the United States and became nationally known for his architectural ironwork. His firm grew to employ 200 workers with a client roster that included Yale and Harvard Universities, Washington Cathedral, and St. John the Divine in New York.

To the right of the twenty-five by seventy-five-foot front hall are the dining room with French doors leading to a solarium, the breakfast room, and service wing, mentioned above. To the left are the parlor, library, music room or living room, a small room that once housed Irénée's father's collection of minerals (now at the University of Delaware), and the Arch Porch (conservatory). There is also a first floor guest room. The basement, intended to be used for a billiard table, was instead set up as a laboratory for testing milk for *Granogue Farms*.

It is the oak-paneled music room that is the center of social activity and a showcase for a rare *in situ* example of an Aeolian pipe organ. Manufactured between 1880 and 1932, Aeolian organs were installed in the homes of some of America's most discriminating and wealthiest individuals. Among them, in addition to the du Ponts, were Andrew Carnegie, Frank W. Woolworth, and Louis Comfort Tiffany. Company records list the *Granogue* organ as Opus No. 1512. Of the 761 organs built by Aeolian from 1880 to 1932 just 250 are believed to still exist with many of these not in working condition.

More than seven thousand titles were available on pipe organ rolls. *Granogue's* collection included some 500 titles. The organ can now be played by computer through a system developed at Boston University, as Mr. du Pont demonstrated by pushing a button on his computer. Within moments music from Rudolf Friml's operetta *The Vagabond King* filled the room.

The organ is housed in the basement; however, the pipes are clearly visible from the living room level in a tone chute in back of a carved oak screen. The interior woodwork of the organ including the organ case is white oak and was fabricated by the Wilmington plant of the American Car & Foundry Co., later ACF Industries. Since its installation during construction of the house, the du Pont organ had not been maintained on a regular basis; however, it was completely restored in 1964-65, in 1970, and again in 1997.

Above the pipes and behind the screen is a Maxfield Parrish mural, the last commission accepted by the internationally acclaimed painter and illustrator. Irénée, Sr.'s older brother, Pierre, had known Parrish as a boy and it was hoped that his intercession would ease the path for Irénée to engage the artist. This was not to be at the outset, however, with Parrish responding that he was much too busy to consider the undertaking. A year later, Irénée approached him again and this time, perhaps as a result of a visit to *Granogue* to inspect the site for the projected mural, or perhaps because of the fee agreed upon, he accepted.

The mural was completed in 1933 and depicts a glorious mountain scene with large urns in the foreground, executed in the vibrant and luminous colors for which Parrish is known. It was done in three panels totaling 137 inches wide by eighty-seven inches high.

Unfortunately, as time passed the gesso began to crack and the paint curl. Parrish came to *Granogue* and attempted to repair the painting, but was not pleased with the result. He decided that the mural had not properly cured during the painting process and determined to repaint it in a more controlled heating environment. Twenty years after completing the first mural, at age eighty-three,

Parrish redid the entire work. After the new mural was installed, Irénée attempted to pay him for his additional work and effort, but Parrish refused. "There is an implied warranty that a commissioned work should last a lifetime," the artist responded. "There is no charge."

The suspended quatrefoil ceiling in this room is also a work of art. Fabricated in Italy, it is made up of sixty-eight panels: thirty flat panels, forty-six inches by fifty-one inches, and thirty-eight irregularly shaped cornice pieces. It is a perfect complement to the organ and mural. Above the fireplace is the widely copied, original, 1831 Rembrandt Peale portrait of founder of the DuPont Company, E.I. du Pont.

From the music room, French doors open to the solarium, known as the Arch Room because of the shape of its windows. Floor-to-ceiling windows offer dramatic views to the northwest, northeast, and southeast. At one time the solarium also looked over the tennis court, but this was moved to the south side of the house some years ago.

Du Pont houses are synonymous with du Pont gardens. This holds true of *Granogue* as well. When Irénée du Pont and his wife, Irene, lived on Rising Sun Lane, before moving to their new house, they had a Lord & Burnham greenhouse, built to their specifications. It was Gothic in design with dormer windows. Lord & Burnham's greenhouses were considered the gold standard for these structures and Mrs. du Pont was reluctant to leave it behind. As a result her husband had the structure dismantled, section by section, loaded onto a mule train and brought to its site on the new property. Orchids and gardenia plants came separately.

Unlike the owners of *Winterthur*, *Mt. Cuba*, *Owl's Nest*, and numerous other du Pont houses, Irene du Pont wished to design her own gardens rather than follow the plan of a professional landscape gardener. Her husband supported her in this and is quoted as answering a query by writing, "it seems desirable that Mrs. du Pont exercise her own artistic judgment in working up the planting plan of our new place and I have come to the conclusion that there would be more character and individuality resulting from her treatment than we could expect to buy from a professional."[2]

Mrs. du Pont sketched out her garden plans and worked with an engineer from the DuPont Co. in accomplishing her objectives. She was assisted by William Corbit Spruance, who was an advisor to the Wilmington Garden Club. The overall garden emphasis at *Granogue* was on spring bulbs, flowering trees, and in creating pastoral scenes that extended to pastures, crop fields, and lawns. The lower terrace was designed with walkways anchored by pyramid-shaped evergreens, and a formal garden was planted with roses, tulips, magnolias, and dogwood. The woodland garden featured native wildflowers. In the shrubbery garden, a special path was edged with ivy grown from cuttings brought from the first du Pont grave in Chevannes, France.

It was the rock garden, planted in 1924 on the southeast of side of the house, however, to which Mrs. du Pont gave special attention. She chose a more informal design and selected traditional species of plants including columbine, daisies, sweet William, and phlox. These bordered winding trails and paths, and the rock wall just above it.

The story is told that when designing the rock garden, inspired by a visit to the Philadelphia Flower Show, it was suggested that an underground watering system be installed. This was done at considerable expense; however, the first time it was used it completely drained the water tower supply. Some of the stones laid on top of the soil had punctured the pipes, with the result that her husband had no water for shaving. It was fixed the same day.

Special events have long been an important part of life at *Granogue*. The year after moving there, Irénée, Sr., and his brothers, Pierre and Lammot, put on a fireworks display to celebrate the fourth of July. One hundred and fifty guests were invited to a black tie dinner, a number that swelled to 5,000 when observers were included. After dinner, guests took straw mats and sat on the hillside as the three brothers, with jackets removed, proceeded to set off rockets to everyone's delight. The tradition lasted until 1957.

In 1987, Irénée, Jr., a motorcycle enthusiast, his son, and nine couples rode round-trip from *Granogue* to Michigan's Keweenaw Peninsula, the northern-most part of Michigan's Upper Peninsula that projects into Lake Superior Macinac Island—a distance of some 2800 miles. Irénée has now retired from riding himself, but maintains a keen interest in the sport and is host to the two-day Mid-Atlantic Super Series cyclo-cross race held annually at the estate. Some 1,000 cyclists and supporters attend from all over the United States.

Granogue

Owners:	Mr. and Mrs. Irénée du Pont, Sr.
	Mr. and Mrs. Irénée du Pont, Jr.
Constructed:	1921 - 1923
Architect:	Albert H. Spahr
Location:	Montchanin Road
	Granogue, Delaware

Notes

1. Personal anecdotes described in the *Granogue* chapter were recorded by the author in interviews with Mr. du Pont over a two-year period.

2. Hagley Museum & Library, Acc.228, File 226

Mrs. Irene du Pont was an avid gardener and designed the *Granogue* gardens herself. She was reluctant to leave the greenhouse behind at her former home on Rising Sun Lane, whereupon her husband had the greenhouse disassembled and brought to *Granogue* by mule train.

The living room at *Granogue* is characterized by an Aeolian pipe organ, one of 761 built between 1880 and 1932. In back of the organ screen there is a Maxfield Parrish mural,

The *Granogue* dining room is at the opposite end of the seventy-five-foot hall from the living room.
French doors open to a solarium and the breakfast room.

The morning room and library are across from one another and open off of the center hall.

Greenville House sits well back from the main road. It is approached by a curved driveway with entrances flanking a tenant house.

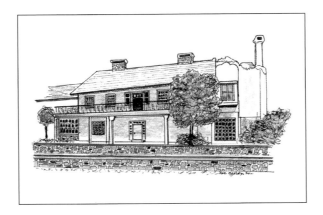

GREENVILLE HOUSE

Protected by a conservation easement with a stunning view of the water

Driving over the Hoopes Reservoir causeway, outside the town of Greenville, several family estates can be glimpsed across meadows or through century-old trees. One of these is *Greenville House* and it has been connected to the du Pont family since its construction more than seventy-five years ago.

Thirty-two of the United States have population centers with the name of Greenville, ranging in size from big to small. Greenville, South Carolina, has a population of some 450,000 while Greenville, Delaware's population is just 2500. Each is different, but Greenville, Delaware, is unique. The state's six most interesting places to visit as listed on the internet are all du Pont related and the DuPont Company is the state's largest non-government employer. Within the vicinity of the Delaware community there are more than one hundred named residences with du Pont connections. One of these is *Greenvile House.*

Situated on fifty-five acres overlooking Hoopes reservoir, the two-story house has design elements that were unique at the time it was built in 1935, and would still be considered innovative today. It isn't surprising, as owner, Francis Victor (Frank) du Pont, was an engineer who carefully reviewed the architectural plans drawn by his cousin, Victorine du Pont, and her husband Samuel Eldon Homsey,

Frank du Pont came by his engineering skills naturally. His father was T. Coleman du Pont, one of the three cousins who saved the DuPont Company from being sold to a competitor in 1902. He once vowed to "build a monument a hundred miles high and lay it on the ground." and fulfilled his promise by constructing the nation's first two-lane highway.[1] Frank followed in his father's footsteps, attending the Massachusetts Institute of Technology and later becoming Delaware Commissioner for the Bureau of Public Roads.

After graduation from MIT, he accepted a university position in the Aeronautical Division of its U.S. School of Military Aeronautics, obtaining his pilot's license in 1916 at the age of twenty-two. It was an interest that continued throughout his lifetime.

In that same year, he was an usher in his sister Ellen's wedding and a year later married one of the bridesmaids—Katherine Clark from Northampton, Massachusetts. Unfortunately neither wedding had a storybook ending and Frank was divorced in 1931. The following year he married Janet Gram, from Buffalo, New York, a cousin of Henry Belin du Pont, Jr., Lammot du Pont Copeland, and Reynolds du Pont. By this time Frank had relocated to Wilmington where he worked for the DuPont Company as a research engineer and the couple began planning their new Delaware home.

Greenville House is set well back on the property and has two entrances off of the main road, separated by a caretaker's house. From the driveway, steps lead down to a flagstone walk and a covered doorway framed in wrought iron with a climbing floral design. An iconic eagle door knocker, found on many du Pont front doors, is a reference to the schooner, *American Eagle*, which brought the du Pont family to America, landing in Newport, Rhode Island, on New Year's Day in 1800 after a tortuous ninety-one day crossing from France.

The two-story Colonial style residence has 9,000 square feet with seventeen rooms. The roof is wood shake and the exterior concrete block is clad with asbestos to look like brick. Construction of this type was not unusual for the time and insured an extra layer of protection against fire. A 1952 brick addition blends in with the asbestos so closely that it is not readily apparent that they are not of the same exterior material.

The spacious center hall has oak flooring, ten-foot ceilings, and elaborate crown molding. An additional architectural detail is the paneled arch between the front and back doors. To the right of the front door is a curved stairway to the second floor and on the left a passageway leads to the twenty by twenty-two-foot library paneled in knotty pine with built-in bookcases, a fireplace, and a bay window overlooking the gardens and reservoir.

At the end of the passageway two steps down lead to the east living room (twenty-eight feet by nineteen feet) with a marble fireplace. A second living room, known as the south living room, was added in 1952 and has the same square footage with a slightly different configuration. French doors open to a flagstone veranda that extends north and south across the length of the house with an expansive view of the gardens and water.

Beyond the hall stairway, the dining room with double doors is accessed through an archway complementing the one in the hall. On the dining room side a broken pediment frames a large pineapple, a symbol of hospitality. Mural wallpaper in an oriental design covers one wall of the twenty-two by eighteen-foot room. There is a bay window with a view similar to the one in the library.

Opposite the entrance is a fireplace and on either side are doors, one leading to the kitchen area and the other to a conservatory. Though small compared to most sun rooms, it would be a pleasant place to enjoy morning coffee or drinks before dinner. It is finished in brick with a marble fountain installed on an interior wall. The room would also be ideal for arranging flowers, as it has an outside entrance and the greenhouse, attached to the garage, is close by.

In 2009 the kitchen was completely renovated. Three former rooms were combined into one to provide a spacious open arrangement. In a previous rearrangement of staff rooms a former attached garage was enclosed to create a room for the cook. More recently, the servants' dining room was converted to a family room. The flagstone patio off of the kitchen was used for barbecues and informal dining.

Greenville House has eight bedrooms and nine-and-a-half bathrooms. In addition to the front stairway, they can be reached by the original elevator, still in use. It was installed by the Energy Elevator Company, a Philadelphia firm founded in 1929 that is no longer in business. The master bedroom is twenty by seventeen feet with a balcony facing the reservoir. Gold-plated fixtures in a dolphin design were installed in the master bathroom. Other bedrooms vary in size from the smallest, twelve by fifteen feet, to a guest bedroom the size of the master bedroom.

The basement level can also be reached by stairs or elevator. A bowling alley is unique in that it can be adapted for either ten-pin or duckpin bowling by opening a recessed gutter flush with the floor. When open, the gutter can accommodate the larger bowling balls used in ten-pin bowling. Another unusual feature in the basement is a fire door that divides the furnace room from the rest of the basement. Built like a barn door, it operates on an angled overhead steel track and is held in place by laundry-line type roping. In case of a fire in that area the rope would burn through, releasing and closing the door and isolating that area. In a further nod to safety, all door frames in *Greenville House* are fabricated from steel. Painted, they look like wood.

Formal tiered gardens take advantage of the view facing south to the mile and three-quarter Edgar Hoopes Reservoir. A primary source of stored water for the City of Wilmington, the reservoir has an average depth of one hundred feet and holds more than two billion gallons of fresh water. The reservoir project was begun in 1925 and dedicated in June 1932, about the time *Greenville House* was in the planning stage. Homsey Architects sited the house so that most of its rooms are able to take advantage of the extraordinary water view.

To the left of one driveway entrance there is an in-ground swimming pool and pool house with a tennis court nearby. On the right side of the other driveway there are two garage buildings, each with two bays. A tenant house is situated between the driveways. The greenhouse is attached to the garage closest to the house, while the other garage has a shop and is equipped with a hydraulic lift for working on cars.

Frank du Pont was a car enthusiast and had a Silver Dawn Rolls Royce built to his specifications. Silver sand in color, it had left-hand drive and was delivered in October 1952. The car was restored mechanically and in December 2011 sold at auction to a European buyer. It was considered in excellent condition and had just 59,600 miles on the clock at the time of the sale.[2]

Following Frank du Pont's death in 1962, *Greenville House* was sold, but remained in the family. It was purchased by Jonathan Bruce Bredin and his wife, Octavia Mary du Pont, the youngest daughter of Irénée and Irene S. du Pont. Known as Tibi, Octavia was a poet, artist, and writer and had an adventurous spirit.

Her interest in aviation matched that of her husband and she flew her own Stinson single-engine, fixed-wing airplane. She also rode horses bareback and owned an Indian motorcycle, manufactured in Springfield, Massachusetts, by her cousin, E. Paul du Pont. According to family lore, Tibi once got permission to climb the scaffolding of New York's St. Patrick's Cathedral in order to see the view from its highest window. Her free spirit was accompanied by an inquiring mind and keen intellect, and during World War II she worked at a hospital in New York doing cancer research.

Tibi's investigative and venturesome interests were matched by those of her husband. In 1972, he co-sponsored an expedition with the Smithsonian Institution to the Society and Tuamotu Islands, part of a chain of islands in French Polynesia. Previously he had supported work in southeastern Mexico with a 1960 expedition to the Yucatan Peninsula.

The Bredins were particularly interested in Ireland and purchased Donaghcumper House, a historic house in Celbridge, fourteen miles west of Dublin County Kildare, where they spent two months a year. Some of the Celbridge furniture was formerly owned by the Knight of Glin (Desmond Fitzgerald) and was purchased by them at Christie's London auction house. The couple also supported Winterthur Museum and joined eight cousins and others in purchasing for its collection a red and white oak joined chest that was made by Thomas Dennis in Ipswich, Massachusetts, in 1676.[3]

Greenville House is still in the Bredin-du Pont family and preservation of its fifty-five acres is insured by a conservation easement. Mrs. Bredin enacted the permanent legal deed restriction to protect the water resources of Hoopes Reservoir, while, at the same time, creating a wild life habitat and scenic open space.

Greenville House

Owners: Mr. and Mrs. Francis Victor du Pont, original
               Mr. and Mrs. J. Bruce Bredin
               Privately owned, current
Constructed: 1935
Architects: Victorine du Pont and Saumel Eldon Homsey
Location: Greenville, Delaware

Notes

1. Thomas Coleman du Pont was the great grandson of Eleuthere I. du Pont, founder of the DuPont Company. In 1911 he created the nation's first dual lane (super) highway, beginning in Sussex County and running the length of the state. It was dedicated and given to the citizens of Delaware in a ceremony held at the state capital July 2, 1924.

2. Silver Dawn models were introduced in 1949 and production was stopped in 1955. The model was the first car produced entirely by Rolls Royce Motors and was built primarily for the export market. The Silver Dawn was the smallest Rolls Royce ever built and was called a "sports saloon" because of its short wheelbase, low height and fast speed.

3. The Thomas Dennis joined chest is on display at *Winterthur* in the first floor galleries. The accession number is 1982.276.

Greenville House is surrounded by fifty-five acres overlooking Hoopes Reservoir and is protected by a conservation easement.

The house is covered with asbestos shingle imprinted to look like brick. A later brick addition looks almost identical to it.

Built as a summer retreat, *Hod House* was pre-fabricated by E.F. Hodgson Company, Bay City, Michigan, and shipped to Wilmington by train, off-loaded, trucked to its site, and assembled with a unique bolting system.

HOD HOUSE

A 1931 pre-fabricated summer house moves into the 21st century

The story of *Hod House* is one of evolution. It started as a vacation cottage surrounded by 500 acres of open country. Today the house, owned by Steven and Lisa Frankel, is a suburban residence on a tree-shaded lane in the heart of Centreville.

Before Montgomery Ward, there was Sears Roebuck. Before Sears Roebuck, there was the Aladdin Company, and before Aladdin, there was Hodgson Houses. A pioneer in the introduction of prefabricated buildings, Hodgson Houses was the company that first developed the idea of a portable building in 1892 with its Peep-o'-Day chicken coop that could be taken apart and moved. Next came poultry and brooder houses, which evolved into small houses that could be erected in a few hours using a unique key bolting system instead of nails.

But it was the Hodgson's Auto Stable, introduced in 1900, when automobiles were just beginning to become popular and few houses had a garage, that established the name of the company and paved the way for its success. In addition to houses, which included bungalows, cottages, and garages, Hodgson sold office buildings, schools, gymnasiums, playhouses, and pet houses.

By 1908, Sears Roebuck had entered the kit-house field and they soon dominated the market offering twenty-two different styles, a number later expanded to more than 350. Sears Roebuck sold houses that were pre-cut with separate numbered pieces, which were assembled on site and were accompanied by the necessary paint and stain. The average build time was three months. Hodgson Houses were completely prefabricated with windows, doors, and panels pre-painted, and hard pine floors stained and shellacked at the factory. By requiring only bolts to put them together they could be completed on average in three days. Buyers had a choice of using local labor to construct the house or opting for factory employees to do the assembling.

In their advertising Hodgson boasted that, "No matter where you go in this country, or in any country, you will find Hodgson Houses and satisfied customers." Backing up their claim was an impressive list of clients that included Astors, Belmonts, Goulds, Fields, Lowells, Morgans, Rockefellers, and Vanderbilts, as well as the du Ponts.

In Wilmington, the company had two du Pont clients. Margaretta Lammot du Pont, daughter of Irénée du Pont, Sr., and her husband Crawford Hallock Greenewalt, a brilliant chemist who later became president of the Du Pont Company, purchased a Hodgson House as a summer refuge from the heat of the city. It is this house that is now owned by the Frankels. Alfred I. duPont was also a Hodgson customer, purchasing one of the company's buildings, marketed under the name "Wigwarm," for use as a schoolhouse for the children of Nemours employees. This was later incorporated into the Wren's Nest cottage, a three-bedroom playhouse with an electrically equipped kitchen, where Alfred's stepdaughter, Alicia, entertained her dolls at tea parties.

In 1931, the Greenewalt house was shipped by train, as was the usual arrangement, and then trucked to its site outside the city on a 550 acre tract of land. Thanks to Hodgson's innovative key bolt system it was assembled there in just two days. The house is constructed of red cedar framing with redwood siding. It has double-wall construction and a waterproof fiber lining next to the cedar boarding; the roof is wood shingle. The inside walls, roof, and partitions were originally finished with beaver board, a mat-finished panel made of compressed wood fiber, also sold under the brand name Celotex.

Hod House has 4500 square feet and is on one floor. The front entrance opens to a center hall with the kitchen on the left and library to the right. Straight ahead is the dining room with a large picture window overlooking the attached Lord & Burnham greenhouse installed by a later owner. The library, formerly the dining room, opens to the eighteen by thirty-foot living room that forms the center section of the house.

There are fireplaces in the library and living room as well as in one of the bedrooms now used as a game room. A vintage sign over this fireplace advertises Buckley's Tavern, a Centreville watering hole established in 1951 by W.W. "Chick" Laird, whose mother was a sister of Pierre S. du Pont. Dennis Buckley was manager. The tavern is located in an 1817 building and is within walking distance of *Hod House.*

There are seven bedrooms and five-and-a-half bathrooms in the house. Bedrooms for the three children and staff were in one wing. The master bedroom and sitting room are located off of the library and a hallway from the living room leads to the six additional bedrooms. In one of the bedrooms the original dropped ceiling has been removed and is open to the roofline so that Hodgson's signature window is clearly visible—a two-by-three-foot window dominated by an H in the middle with a double crossbar. At the end of the hallway is a door to the three-bay garage. An open porch with access from the living room runs parallel to and the length of the hallway.

The Greenewalts used their house as a summer retreat, spending the rest of the year at their residence in the city. Following the du Pont custom of naming houses, but without giving it a grander name, which they thought would sound pretentious, they referred to their new house as *Hod House.* While living there, the house that would become their permanent home was being built nearby. When this was completed in 1935, the Greenewalts sold *Hod House* to friends, William and Elisabeth Prickett, who had it dismantled and trucked to a new location in Centreville, where it remains today resting on a pier and beam foundation.

During the period that the Pricketts owned *Hod House,* it metamorphosed from a summer cottage to a year-round house. Ceilings were raised to nine-and-a-half feet and modified to become tray ceilings, the kitchen was updated and the greenhouse added. The flagstone terrace off of the living room the Greenewalts had built was duplicated by the Pricketts and is accessible by French doors.

Other than the ceilings, the major change to the interior, at this time, was in the living room. William Prickett chanced to hear of a large one hundred-year-old Baltimore house that was being razed and he purchased all sixty of its doors. After the hardware was removed and the doorknob spaces were filled, the doors were refinished and painted white, and, then, installed as paneling on the walls of the living room. The effect is dramatic and, at the same time, adds additional sound-proofing to the core of the house.

The Frankels, who purchased *Hod House* in 2003, have made a number of changes to bring the eighty-year old house into this century. Central heating has taken the place of space heaters and central air conditioning has been installed, making it unnecessary to rely on cross breezes from open doors for cooling, though Lisa points out that this is still an effective way of cooling the house on all but the warmest days. Wall insulation has also been installed. "The footprint remains basically the same," Steven explains, "we just use the rooms for different purposes."

After purchasing *Hod House,* the Frankels explored their attic and found several items of interest related to former owners. A pencil sketch of Margaretta Lammot du Pont Greenewalt by Henriette Wyeth Hurd was one of their first discoveries. It was a preliminary drawing for an oil painting of Margaretta Greenewalt that the artist did in 1927 and had been left when the Greenewalts moved to their new house, Dripping Spigots, on Old Kennett Pike in 1939. Irénée du Pont, Jr., explains that the name Dripping Spigots was his daughter Margaretta's spoof on the name of Frank Lloyd Wright's architectural masterpiece, Fallingwater, built around the same time.

A second find was the passport document carried by William Prickett when he was an ambulance driver in World War I. As he drove from one country to another, it was necessary for him to clear customs at each border and the official paper, now creased and worn, bore the stamps of the countries as he entered and exited. The third article the Frankels came upon was a white dress carefully packed in tissue paper in a sturdy box. It was presumed to be the wedding dress belonging to Elisabeth Prickett. Steven and Lisa were able to track down the current relatives of both families who were surprised and pleased at their return.

The Frankels have had the kitchen completely remodeled to accommodate a husband and wife who both enjoy cooking and jointly preparing meals. To accomplish this, two interior walls were removed permitting direct access to the dining room and library.

Steven and Lisa have assembled an extensive art collection, inspired by paintings they had seen at the Barnes Foundation in Philadelphia, that focuses on local scenes and artists of The Eight and the Ashcan School. This movement grew out of an exhibit of paintings of The Eight Group held in Philadelphia in 1908. Five of these artists were also associated with the Ashcan School that included Edward Hopper, George Bellows and Maurice Prendergast.

William Glackens was closely associated with Dr. Barnes and often negotiated and purchased paintings on his behalf as well as being a recognized artist himself. In addition to a Glackens painting, the Frankels own paintings by other artists who were part of the movement including George Luks and Robert Henri. Despite the fact that the artists had different styles they were often motivated to paint urban and crowd scenes, frequently in poorer neighborhoods.

Brandywine artists represented in their collection include Carolyn Wyeth, Ann Wyeth McCoy, and Peter Hurd. Hurd, though born in New Mexico, studied under N.C. Wyeth and married his daughter, Henriette; Andrew Wyeth was his brother-in-law. The Frankels have recently acquired a painting Peter Hurd did for *Life Magazine* entitled *Air-Sea Rescue Practice,* which Hurd made from drawings made on the scene April 15, 1944.

A painting by American illustrator Frank Schoonover, who was commissioned by Irénée du Pont, Sr., to do two paintings for *Xanadu,* his Cuban retreat, hangs in the library. Another recent acquisition is a mixed media illustration of a western battle scene by Stanley Massey Arthurs. Arthurs studied with Howard Pyle and, when the artist died in 1911, he purchased Pyle's studio.

There is a third Hodgson House with du Pont family connections, one located on the grounds of Montpelier, President James Madison's house in Orange County, near Charlottesville, Virginia. William duPont, Sr., purchased Montpelier in 1901 while he lived in England and was preparing to return to the United States. In the 1930s, he purchased a seven-room Hodgson House clapboard cottage that was used for staff housing. When William died, he left Montpelier to his daughter, Marion duPont Scott, who named the cottage Bassett House for her horse trainer, Carroll K. Bassett, who had lived there and was also a skillful steeplechase jockey.

Bassett House is now the residence of the president of the Montpelier Foundation and his wife, and the association between Hodgson Houses and the du Ponts that began in the last century continues on into this one.

HOD HOUSE

Owners: Mr. and Mrs. Crawford H. Greenewalt, original
Mr. and Mrs. William Prickett
Mr. and Mrs. Steven L. Frankel, current
Constructed: 1931
Moved and reconstructed: 1935
Architect: Hodgson Company
Location: Centreville, Delaware

All Hod houses came with a signature window. While some homeowners replaced them,
it is a symbol of distinction among many of the owners.

When the Frankels bought *Hod House* it had no central heating or air conditioning. This has since been installed, though, with three fireplaces and cross breezes, they are often not needed.

The dining room has French doors to a terrace and at the far end is an attached Lord & Burnham greenhouse.

Hod House is a country vacation house that metamorphosed into a suburban dwelling. The library is conveniently located between the kitchen, master bedroom, and living room.

The *Hotel du Pont* celebrated its 100th anniversary in January 2013. It has been a symbol of hospitality and gathering place for the community ever since 1913. Credit: Courtesy of the Hotel du Pont

HOTEL DU PONT

The company-owned hotel celebrated its 100th anniversary in January 2013

Wilmington without the *Hotel du Pont* would be like New York without the Waldorf-Astoria. But, there is more to the analogy. Within seven years of the Wilmington hotel opening, the Waldorf-Astoria was controlled by one of the original planners of the *Hotel du Pon*t and his business partner.

The idea of the DuPont Company entering the hotel business was conceived by Pierre Samuel du Pont in concert with his close friend, former private secretary, and future DuPont Company treasurer John J. Raskob. Two other family members were also involved in the early planning—Pierre's brother-in-law, R.R.M. Carpenter, and his cousin, T. Coleman du Pont. Seven years after the *Hotel du Pont* opened, Coleman held controlling interest in the legendary Waldorf-Astoria along with Lucius Boomer.[1] Both hotels were centers of social events in their respective cities.

Following formal approval of the plan, construction of the hotel began at the corner of Eleventh and Market Streets overlooking Rodney Square, named for Caesar Rodney, a signer of the Declaration of Independence. Designed to be a part of the DuPont Company building, it was a situation as unique then as it would be today. Building was completed in the fall of 1912 after two-and-a-half years and the *Hotel du Pont* had its formal opening on January 15, 1913, Pierre's forty-fifth birthday.

It was a gala occasion with guests arriving in a parade of conveyances ranging from carriages with drivers in livery to puffing Stanley Steamers and elegant Pierce Arrows. Every room in the hotel had been booked for weeks in advance. Tours of the hotel were conducted according to rank and privilege, as was the custom of the day, and in the evening to celebrate the gala occasion a formal dinner for 295 invited guests was held in the hotel's eleventh floor ballroom.

The well-rehearsed staff had been assembled from well-known east-coast hotels. The general manager and executive housekeeper came from New York's Astor Hotel. The executive chef was from that city's Gotham Hotel. Coleman du Pont chose the front clerk from his Waldorf-Astoria staff and head cashiers arrived from Chattanooga's Hotel Patten and Philadelphia's Rittenhouse Hotel. Only the room manager position was filled by a local person, a former employee of the Clayton Hotel at the corner of Fifth and Market Streets. One year later that hotel was converted to the Queen Theatre.

Twenty-five thousand people were estimated to have visited the *Hotel du Pont* in its opening week. "Successful beyond expression," was the appraisal of the *Wilmington Morning News*. "At last the dreams of the people of Delaware have been realized, the reporter enthused, "and Wilmington has a fine up-to-date hotel of which any city might be proud." (January 16, 1913) The *Wilmington Every Evening* summed up the general feeling that, "The Hotel is a beautifully finished product of the architect and builder's art." (January 16, 1913).[2]

Built of granite block in an adaptation of Italian Renaissance design, the hotel was originally eleven stories high and had 150 rooms. Soon after opening, it became apparent that more rooms were needed and plans were drawn to add an additional twenty-five in 1916. Three years later ninety-four more rooms were built and, in 1937, the total rose to 300. In 1957, the twelfth and thirteenth floors were expanded at a cost of one-and-a-half-million dollars and the room count brought to the current total of 315.

From the outset, it was the goal of the hotel's managing group to create a hotel in Wilmington that would be considered world class, and no expense was spared to achieve this objective. Thirty-seven decorative window balconies adorned the Eleventh Street facade and the grand entrance was set off by a handcrafted ironwork and opalescent glass marquee.

Lobby floors, originally wood, were soon replaced by marble and mosaic made with colored Italian stones shipped in bags and created in situ by Italian craftsmen. They were then topped with tribal and nomadic Baluch rugs from Iran and Afghanistan. The walls were created from French Caen stone and, when the hotel first opened, wood-burning fireplaces were welcoming as well as warming. Coffered ceilings feature rosettes and scrolls.

The main dining room, later called the Green Room in deference to John Raskob's wife, Helen Green Raskob, is paneled in fumed oak. It is two-and-a-half stories high and was initially decorated in shades of brown, forest green, gold, and ivory, and complemented by six multi-tiered bronze chandeliers from Spain, each of which weighs 2500 pounds. The minstrel gallery in the northwest corner was often occupied by a trio that played at lunch and dinner. More recently a pianist is heard during Sunday brunch and at dinnertime.

The Green Room soon became known for its culinary skill, as it is today. It is often the setting for celebratory reunions, romantic liaisons and business luncheons requiring a discreet environment. A commonality that all diners share comes at the end of the meal when the hotel's legendary macaroons are served. The confection has appeared on Green Room tables for more than half a century and the hotel bakeshop produces upwards of a thousand a day. So popular are the macaroons that they have almost reached cult status.

Dana Robinson is the great nephew of William Raskob, who was John's brother. William was also a DuPont Company employee and regularly ate in the Green Room. Dana tells the story, now legendary, that his great uncle was so fond of the macaroons he asked that, when buried, one be placed in his jacket pocket. And it was.

The ballroom was originally located on the eleventh floor of the hotel. The room seated 500 and was distinguished by an arched ceiling and walls painted ivory and highlighted by gold. A small stage accommodated an orchestra for background music or for dancing during dinner and afterwards.

On the ground floor, the present-day Brandywine Room, then referred to as Peacock Alley, was originally a writing room, though in 1941 a twenty-six foot-long mahogany bar and a billiard table were installed and it became a popular cocktail lounge. Today's Christina Room was called the Club Room. Paneled in walnut, it was an inviting setting for enjoying afternoon tea or for reading. The new names for the rooms that connect at a right angle were chosen to be symbolic of the Christina River and Brandywine Creek that form a confluence near where the Christina River joins the Delaware River.

Pierre du Pont, Raskob, and Carpenter, three of the original four men who conceptualized the *Hotel du Pont,* remained in Wilmington, while Coleman, a city-boy at heart, promoted his business interests in New York[3]. Raskob was an avid theatre-goer, as was Pierre, who often ventured to Philadelphia to see plays, and he promoted the idea of building a legitimate theatre in Wilmington as an adjunct to the hotel. Open space at the rear of the DuPont Company building on Market Street between Tenth and Eleventh Streets, known as Pinkett's Court, was available and the three DuPont executives believed that it was a viable idea. Their willingness to underwrite any losses in the beginning was enough of an incentive to move the idea forward.

The Playhouse Company was incorporated on April 17, 1913, and the theatre was built in an astonishing 150 working days, with opening night held on October 15, 1913. The theatre originally had 1300 seats—600 in the orchestra, 500 in the balcony and gallery (now mezzanine and balcony) and 200 in raised box sections. The Playhouse opened with a production of *Bought and Paid For,* by English playwright George Broadhurst, for whom the New York theatre on West 44th Street is named.

In 1949, the theatre was redecorated and renovated with new seats, lighting, and supporting columns mirrored and wrapped in black and gold. Through the years the theatre has been leased to a number of impresarios and countless Broadway, Hollywood, and European stars have appeared on its stage. Among them were Maurice Chevalier, Mae West, Lena Horne, Carol Channing, Ingrid Bergman, Mary Martin, Alfred Lunt and Lynn Fontainne, Lawrence Olivier, and Rosalind Russell, who, when she entered the Green Room for dinner following a performance of *Auntie Mame,* received a spontaneous standing ovation.

A major renovation of the hotel took place in 1919. Much-needed additional sleeping rooms were added, the former Rose Room reserved for ladies became the new lobby, and the original lobby became the Soda Shop. The location of the main entrance was also moved and that space converted to a stylish ladies hat shop. But, the major change was the addition of the spectacular Gold Ballroom. The original eleventh floor ballroom was found to be too small for many of the city's functions and it presented logistical problems when fully occupied, with limited access by the elevators. There was also a safety factor to be considered.

The Gold Ballroom, located at the north end of the lobby, is a perfect complement to the Green Room at the south end of the building and is so well integrated with the original structure it looks as if it were part of the original design. Twelve-foot high American walnut doors, carved with images of peacocks and urns, are framed by the entry made of Italian rose-colored marble. Across the top there is a massive block of Caen stone, weighing one-and-a-half tons, with images of cornucopias filled with fruits and vegetables representing a bountiful harvest. When leaving, guests see industrious squirrels on the other side to indicate a return to the workaday world.

Immediately to the left upon entering, a curved stairway with an elaborate balustrade of bronze and polished steel leads to the Empire-style du Barry Room used for private functions, while wide marble stairs straight ahead lead down to the reception foyer of the Gold Ballroom. Considered one of the most beautiful hotel rooms on the east coast, the Louis XVI ballroom is eighty-eight feet long, forty-nine feet wide, and has ceilings twenty-nine feet high accentuated by two carved wood chandeliers from France. A unifying theme of "Love" is expressed in the ballroom's overall decoration.

The border of the ceiling has the figures of sweethearts Columbine and Pierrot, combined with blue rosettes. Cartouches over doors in each corner of the room represent courtship with depictions of two birds, two fish, two salamanders, the moon, and two stars. The mural paintings can also be interpreted as representing the four divisions of the universe.

In the ceiling spandrels there are medallions of twenty famous queens and courtesans including Agrippina (Roman Empress), Dido (Queen of Carthage), Catherine of Russia, Pocohantas, and Helen of Troy among others.

Large ornamental windows with decorative mirrors, slanted to reflect dancers' movements, extend the entire way around the room and are framed by Corinthian columns and scrolled broken pediments surmounted with urns. Those on Market Street were constructed so that the windows can be raised, leaving a space wide enough to drive a car through for automobile shows. In a room filled with allegory, the most distinctive feature is its sgraffito walls[4]. Thirty Italian workers, skilled in the technique, labored for over a year to produce the intricate romantic and classical designs.

The ballroom has been the setting for many celebratory and important events. Among them was a dinner party given in honor of Franklin Delano Roosevelt, Jr., and his bride-to-be, Ethel du Pont (see *Owl's Nest*). Their wedding was proclaimed by *Time Magazine* as wedding-of-the-year in its June 28, 1937, issue. Through the years hundreds of dignitaries and celebrities have visited the hotel, including eight U.S. presidents, Prince Rainier of Monaco, Queen Sylvia of Sweden, Douglas MacArthur, Charles Lindbergh, Amelia Earhart, Clarence Darrow, Oscar Hammerstein, Richard Rodgers, Bob Hope, Elizabeth Taylor, Katherine Hepburn, Gloria Swanson, Ethel Merman, and Bette Davis.

The years 1927 to 1933 might be called the Bowman years, when the hotel was under the management of Bowman-Biltmore Hotels Corp. and operated under the name *Hotel du Pont-Biltmore*. John McEntee Bowman was born in Canada and operated some of the most prestigious hotels and clubs in the world. He was responsible for building the Westchester Country Club in Rye, New York, as well as Biltmore Hotels in New York, Los Angeles, and Havana. His group operated Coleman's Waldorf-Astoria and Willard Hotels at the same time as they managed the *Hotel du Pont*. The hotel is now operated by the DuPont Company's General Services Department.

During the 1950s the *Hotel du Pont* went through a period of unfortunate modernization. Handcrafted and period furniture were replaced with artificial leather and contemporary pieces, oriental rugs disappeared and mosaic and parquet flooring were covered with broadloom carpet. Chrome fixtures and new lighting replaced traditional furnishings and the walnut reception desk was covered in plastic. At the same time the Eleventh Street balconies were removed and the traditional marquee gave way to a 127-foot steel and aluminum porte cochere.

The period feeling of the original hotel was later restored for the most part, though once again beneath the Renaissance Revival ceiling some contemporary furniture has been introduced into the otherwise period decor of the entrance lobby. Fortunately the 1918 grandfather clock, purchased by Herbert R. Stone during the Bowman era, with its cable-driven wound sound movement and nine-tube chime mechanism is still in place near the south entrance.

The hotel has original art in its public rooms that is worthy of a museum. Included in its collection of over 600 oil paintings and watercolors are three generations of Wyeths including N.C. (Newell Convers), Andrew Nathaniel and Andrew Newell Wyeth, Carolyn Wyeth, and Jamie Wyeth. Among other artists represented are Howard Pyle (*Conestoga Powder Wagon*), Frank Schoonover (*Sunflowers*), Edward Loper (*Elfreth's Alley*), Henry C. Meier (*Longwood* and *Fall at Winterthur*), William Dawson (*Red Clay Dawn*), and Frank Jefferis (*The Brandywine*), and landscapes by Italian painter Francesco Zuccarelli.

When the *Hotel du Pont* first opened, it accepted permanent as well as transient guests. The first person to book a suite of rooms was John Raskob, who planned on dividing his time between Wilmington and his winter residence. Pierre du Pont also booked a suite of rooms on the ninth floor that he maintained until his death. It has now been converted to office space.

Geoffrey Gamble, who works in the legal department of the DuPont Company, recalls as a small boy visiting what had been Pierre's apartment. "It was located on the ninth floor of the DuPont Building and became very important as evidence of Pierre's Delaware citizenship, and thus not subject to Pennsylvania estate taxes," he explains.

An often repeated story is that when confronted by Keystone State auditors and told to pay taxes on his Longwood property as a resident rather than a non-resident, Pierre threatened to uproot every tree on the property and move Longwood, "lock, stock and barrel," into Delaware. Wisely, the State of Pennsylvania accepted the *Hotel du Pont* as Pierre's legal residence.[5]

Hotel du Pont

Owner:	E. I. du Pont de Nemours and Company
Constructed:	1910-1913
Principal Architects:	Frederick Godley, J. Andre Fouilhoux and Joel Barber, New York

Notes

1. At this time, Coleman, along with L.M. Boomer & Associates, controlled not only New York's Waldorf-Astoria and McAlpin Hotels, but also the Bellevue-Stratford Hotel in Philadelphia and the Willard Hotel in Washington, D.C.

2. *Hotel du Pont Story*, Harry V. Ayres, Serendipity Press, 1981

3. Raskob later served as a vice-president of General Motors and afterward he and Coleman joined forces in constructing New York's monumental Empire State Building. In 1929 he and his partners purchased the property on which the first Waldorf-Astoria was located when the owners decided to build a new hotel on Park Avenue between 49th and 50th Streets. Raskob was able to purchase the site for approximately sixteen million dollars and immediately formulated plans to build the world's tallest building.

4. Sgraffito is a type of decoration in which thin layers of colored plaster are applied one on top of the other and then scratched through to reveal a color beneath, the depth of the scratch determining the design color.

5. In his biography of Pierre du Pont, George E. Thompson, Sr. said that the most immediate effect of Mrs. du Pont's death was action by the Commonwealth of Pennsylvania claiming that she was a Pennsylvania resident. Pierre reported that "all his lifetime he had publicly proclaimed he was a legal resident of the State of Delaware. ... Both had voted in Delaware and maintained an apartment at the *Hotel du Pont* to establish their residency in that state. At the time he purchased *Longwood gardens* he had given public notice to Delaware authorities that his ownership of the Pennsylvania property, "was not to be construed as a removal from Delaware."

The Green Room is redolent of a European hotel of the Belle Epoque era and its cuisine
has always been among the city's best. Credit: Courtesy of the Hotel du Pont

When opened, the hotel had 150 rooms. It has had two major expansions and now has 217 rooms. The lobby has been redecorated several times, but fortunately the Italian ceiling has remained in place. Credit: Courtesy of the Hotel du Pont

Wilmington's most prestigious events have always been held at the *Hotel du Pont* and the Gold Ballroom has been the setting for major social and business events including a dinner held in honor of the son of a U.S. President and his du Pont bride-to-be. *Credit:* Courtesy of the Hotel du Pont

LEGENDARY HOTEL DU PONT MACAROONS

Ingredients:
  1 pound almond paste (best quality)
  1 and 1/2 cups sugar
  5 egg whites
  1 tablespoon vanilla

Method:
  Mix almond paste, sugar and vanilla on slow speed with mixer until ingredients are crumbled. Add one egg white and mix until smooth. Repeat process until all egg whites are incorporated. The consistency should be soft but not runny. Preheat oven to 350 degrees. Bake fifteen minutes or until macaroons are golden brown. When cold, remove from pan. Macaroons should be eaten or put in airtight container and refrigerated. Makes sixty macaroons.

Krazy Kat's, the Inn's award-winning restaurant, located in the former blacksmith shop, was named for an eccentric former woman who lived there. She owned two dogs, but no cats. Photo credit: Courtesy of The Inn at Montchanin Village

The original Dilwyne Barn, the location of the Inn guest area and gathering room, dates back to 1850. It was originally a bank barn. Photo credit: Courtesy of The Inn at Montchanin Village

THE INN AT MONTCHANIN VILLAGE

A former DuPont workers' village is now a deluxe auberge

History and luxury go hand in hand at this inspired and unique adaptation of a village to an inn complex. Earliest maps of this area, dating to 1777, show the village to be situated on a triangular area of about 2.4 acres at the intersection of three roads, the principal one designated as Center Road. In 1935, the Highway Department assigned numbers to all state roads and it officially became Route 100. It has also been called Chadds Ford Road, West Chester Road, and, following the renaming of the train station by Col. Henry du Pont in 1879, Montchanin Road, a designation often used by local residents.

An official Delaware Historic Marker (No. 185), placed in 2008 on Route 100, just outside the Inn grounds, reads as follows:

VILLAGE OF MONTCHANIN

Settled at the triangular intersection of three roads in the early 19th century by workers from the nearby DuPont Black Powder Mills, this village consisted initially of only 2.4 acres. The Wilmington and Northern Railroad established tracks through the vicinity in 1869, leading to a period of sustained growth in population and area. The village, known as DuPont Station, became a major shipping point for the mills, and warehouses and rail sidings were built nearby to facilitate transport of the powder. In 1889, a new railroad station was constructed and a post office was established to serve the surrounding countryside. These signs of enduring settlement were commemorated with a new name for the village. Montchanin was chosen to honor Anne Alexandrine de Montchanin, who was the mother of Pierre Samuel du Pont de Nemours, the founder of the American du Pont dynasty. The range of architectural styles and the history of the hamlet were recognized when the Montchanin Historic District was added to the National Register of Historic Places in 1978.

In addition to Route 100, or Montchanin Road, the other roads referenced in the above marker are Kirk Road to the north and Rockland Road, once known as Wagon or Wagoner's Road, to the southwest. Through the years the land on which the village is located has passed through the hands of various related du Ponts, Carpenters, Drapers, and most recently to present owners, Nancy (Missy) and Dan Lickle. Mrs. Lickle is the great-great-great granddaughter of the founder of the DuPont Company, Eleuthere I. du Pont and sixth generation of Anne Alexandrine de Montchanin.

In 1991, when Missy Lickle inherited the property, which was once a part of the *Winterthur* estate, she and her husband thought it would be an interesting venture to convert the village into a country inn, a project they expected would take them several months to achieve. Five years later, on June 13, 1996, *The Inn at Montchanin Village* opened.

There are eleven restored buildings at the *Inn* dating from 1799 to 1910, most of which are constructed of stone, stucco, and wood in modified Gothic Revival style. In addition to the eight workers houses, now called cottages, there is a blacksmith shop, an 1890 stone schoolhouse, and a barn. While the majority of the inhabitants worked for the DuPont Mills, others worked in the textile mills along the Brandywine. Between 1870 and 1910, the period of greatest growth for Montchanin and related to development of the railroad, the village had some twenty-one buildings on about twenty acres. When the Lickles acquired the village, it was located on a four-acre plot; this has now been expanded to six-and-a-half acres.

There are a total of twenty-eight rooms located in the eight cottages, all named for family members or friends with the exception of Chase, named for a beloved pet dog. Each has been individually decorated by Mrs. Lickle and no two are exactly alike. Some rooms are equipped with fireplaces and all are furnished with period furniture and reproductions. Most have exquisite marble bathrooms that would be the envy of any world-class hotel. *The Inn at Montchanin* is, in fact, in just such company, having been singled out by *Travel + Leisure Magazine* as the world's best hotel for $250 or less, based on a readers' survey that had 500,000 respondents.

The *Inn's* great room, called the gathering room, was formerly the steer barn for *Dilwyne Farms*, the estate built in 1922 by Mrs. Lickle's grandparents, Robert Ruliph Morgan Carpenter, Sr., and his wife, Margaretta Lammot du Pont, a sister of Pierre du Pont who was the pivotal figure in reorganizing the company.

The barn dates back to 1850 and was built as a bank barn; during construction of the *Inn* the banks on both sides were removed. On the south bank side, the Lickles have had impressive steps built in its place, which lead to the *Inn's* reception area. On the north bank side they have creatively had a mammoth stone fireplace built of Brandywine granite. Hanging over the fireplace, and the focal point of the gathering room, is a portrait of Missy Lickle's grandmother painted when she was about age thirty.

The room is thirty-three feet by forty feet and has a cross-barred ceiling thirty feet high. In spite of its size, both privacy and warmth have been achieved by dividing the room into a number of individual seating groups. An honor bar adds to the inviting atmosphere, as does the secret-ingredients canape prepared nightly by the *Inn's* chef. Next to the gathering room is a conference room that can accommodate forty.

Across from the barn is the original farmstead dating back to 1799, the oldest structure on the property. The two-and-a-half story pink building has a gabled roof and cornice with brick corbels, and front and rear porches with stucco columns. It is now known as the Col. Henry A. du Pont cottage and houses the *Inn's* four premier suites.

Just down the hill from the Dilwyne barn, another original building on the property, the 1859 two-and-a-half story brick and stucco blacksmith shop, has been resurrected as Krazy Kat's, an award-winning restaurant. Its whimsical decor features ten feline and canine portraits that show the cats and dogs in full military uniform or formal finery.

The original forge used to heat horseshoes is still in place. In its role as a fireplace, it casts a warm glow over the intimate dining area. An adjoining sun porch offers a second dining option and a new bar has recently been installed. Above the restaurant, and accessible from its own entrance and parking lot, is the Crow's Nest, a private dining room. Another private room, the Board Room, is located in Carpenter House. The schoolhouse building is now used for private offices.

A row of former outhouses lines Privy Lane and have been converted to storage buildings for garden equipment. At the corner of Kirk Road and the drive down to Krazy Kat's, a well on the site has been covered over and a portico erected making it a convenient meeting point for guests.

In 2010, the Lickles opened a full service, 2,700 square-foot spa. To house the facility, an addition to the Dilwyne Barn was built on the site of the former dairy, with a separate entrance as well as one opening directly into the main building. The architecture and stone match the original structure, and the reception area has a welcoming fireplace. Special spa menus, featuring local fruits and organic vegetables, have been designed by Krazy Kat's Restaurant for delivery to the spa. These are served on individual tables in a charming setting that has a stone wall as a focal point.

The *Inn* grounds are professionally landscaped and overseen by a horticulturist. Two off-premises greenhouses supply flowers the year around for exquisite displays of seasonal flowers. In addition to the general landscaping, there are a number of individual gardens including one with its own ponds.

A unique addition to the landscape are garden signs posted at random intervals. The four-foot high iron signs offer tongue-in-cheek observations or sage advice such as "A person who aims at nothing has a target he can't miss" and "Minds are like parachutes, they only function when open," or "Cherish youth but trust old age." The property on which *The Inn at Montchanin* is built has been in the du Pont family for over one hundred years. From 1948 to 1952, it was briefly owned by a former Winterthur employee who purchased it from Henry Francis du Pont. He unfortunately suffered a massive heart attack and the property reverted to du Pont ownership when it was purchased by Margaretta L. du Pont Carpenter. She in turn left it to her daughter, Irene "Renee" Carpenter Draper from whom Missy Lickle inherited it.

Across Rockland Road is the former Wilmington and Northern Railroad two-story station built in 1889 in Shingle Style, popular from 1880 to 1910. It is characterized by overlapping fish scale shingles covering the irregularly shaped space, a second floor center gable, circular turret at one end, and multi-paned windows. The portico was originally designed to accommodate horses and carriages. An estimated 40,000 such stations were built in the United States between 1830 and 1950, with less than half still in existence.

Known as the DuPont Station when built, because of its closeness to the DuPont Powder Mills upper yards, it was later renamed Montchanin by Col. Henry A. du Pont. The current owner, however, has reverted to calling it by its original name.

The station achieved national recognition when it was the terminus for President Franklin D. Roosevelt, his wife, and mother, who arrived here in U.S. Car No. 1, on June 30, 1937. The gala occasion was the wedding of the Roosevelt's son, Franklin, Jr., to Ethel du Pont, daughter of Eugene H. du Pont, Jr., and his wife, Ethel Pyle du Pont. A temporary platform, festively decorated in red, white and blue bunting, was erected to exactly meet the height of the train's exit door. Today a freight train continues to use the rail line twice a day, though the station has been converted to offices.

Across the tracks, and in back of the station, are additional DuPont worker houses similar in style to those at the *Inn*. These have been rebuilt as condominiums and are known as Carpenters Row, a reference to the Carpenter family that once owned the property.

The *Inn* has hosted many celebrities, well-known politicians and corporate executives who no longer arrive by train, but by limousine or in their personal plane, sometimes accompanied by bodyguards who remain with them during their stay.

The Inn at Montchanin Village was added to the National Register of Historic Places on January 3, 1978.

The Inn at Montchanin Village

Owners: Individual owners prior to being acquired by the DuPont Company in the early 19th century. Mr. and Mrs. Daniel C. Lickle, current

Architect: Bernardon & Associates (for the Inn)

Location: Six miles north of Wilmington, Delaware, on Route 100 at Kirk and Rockland Roads. Montchanin, Delaware is 3,741 miles from Montchanin, France.

The north door of the original bank barn is now the location of the gathering room fireplace. Above it there is a portrait of Margaretta Lammot du Pont Carpenter, grandmother of the owner. Photo credit: Courtesy of The Inn at Montchanin Village

The Village of Montchanin has twenty-one buildings on it clustered along intersecting roadways. There are twenty-eight rooms located in eight cottages.
Photo credit: Courtesy of The Inn at Montchanin Village

Northeast view of *Louviers* facing the woods and private entrance drive from Rockland Road. The house was built of fieldstone and then stuccoed. It was originally painted yellow and is now apricot. Credit: Photograph by author

LOWER LOUVIERS

Across the Brandywine from the mills close by the Iron Bridge

Pierre Samuel du Pont de Nemours, founder of the American dynasty, emigrated to the United States in 1799 with his family that included sons, Eleuthere Irénée and Victor Marie. Eleuthere, the younger son, was by nature a more deliberate person. As it turned out, he was a determined businessman as well, forsaking his preferred profession as a botanist, as he identified himself on his passport, to develop the highly successful black powder business.

Eleuthere's two-year apprenticeship, working with Antoine-Laurent Lavoisier at the French government powder works (Regie des Poudres, Essonnes), provided the knowledge and training that led to his establishment of the DuPont Company in 1802 and production of its first barrel of gunpowder in May 1804.

Victor was more extroverted, adapting easily to his life as the French consul in Charleston, South Carolina, and later using his political skills to win a senate seat in the Delaware legislature. The contrast between the brothers was nowhere more apparent than in their command of English. Eleuthere never became fluent in English and was most comfortable when speaking his native language with inhabitants of the French community nearby. Victor, on the other hand, spoke English easily and fluently, but he was not successful in business.

The brothers' differences were apparent in architectural preference as well. Eleuthere chose a traditional Federal design for his house, *Eleutherian Mills*. Victor, while still engaged in the woolen business in Angelica, New York, prior to moving to Delaware, asked his brother to design a house for him that combined details of Federal and classical, i.e. Regency, architecture. It is testament to Eleuthere's desire to please his brother that he was able to accomplish this.

Victor's sophistication and love of entertaining is reflected in the design of *Louviers'* handsome south portico. Reminiscent of the piazzas on many of Charleston's single houses, to which Victor would have been invited during his time spent in that city, its terraced site overlooks the Brandywine in much the same way

as Charleston's Battery houses overlook the Ashley and Cooper Rivers.

Louviers faces north to woods bordering the half-mile private entrance drive, Blackgates Road, that leads to a carriage circle with the original carriage block and hitching post to the left of the entrance. Building was begun in 1810 and completed in March 1811, followed by a house warming thought to have been celebrated on July 4. *Louviers* was originally painted yellow to match the sand gravel used in paths leading to outbuildings and the gardens; it is now pale apricot. Construction was of fieldstone that was stuccoed, a popular exterior finish in France at the time, and one favored by Benjamin Latrobe, a British-born American architect (1764-1820), sometimes referred to as America's first professional architect.

Latrobe arrived in the United States about the same time as the du Ponts and was a friend of Thomas Jefferson, as were Pierre, Eleuthere, and Victor du Pont. It has been suggested that the neoclassical architect might have influenced Jefferson's design for the University of Virginia. It is quite possible then that Latrobe could also have had some influence on the design of *Louviers*, as family history records that plans for Victor's house were sent to Jefferson for his comments and he could very well have reviewed them with Latrobe.

Thomas Jefferson is reported to have commented favorably upon the innovative gravity-fed water system of the house, made possible by a spring up the hill that was high enough to produce piped water for both the first and second floors of *Louviers*. Carried underground in wooden pipes to the house, it was then distributed internally through lead pipes.

The gabled entrance of *Louviers* leads to the front door framed by sidelights with intersecting muntins. A fanlight has six bars radiating from the center, and above are three windows. The middle one, the width of the front door, has six panes while those on each side have additional arched panes at the top.

On either side of the front door, niches echo this same arched design. The two recessed openings, with curved backs and marble bases, are thirty-four inches wide, eighteen inches deep and seventy-five inches high. Originally these held images of Adonis and Venus. Mary Laird Silvia, who was brought up at *Louviers* and wrote an excellent book about the house entitled *The Other Side of the River*,[1] recalled that these were later replaced by urns of Chinese design. "The urns were about four feet tall and in shades of blue and green," she remembered. "Unfortunately these were stolen," Mrs. Silvia added, "One night we went to bed and they were there and the next morning they were gone."

The entrance hall (twelve by twenty feet) has a handsome staircase to the right that leads to a landing and then divides with stairways going to the left and right wings of the house. Decorative brackets are in scroll design. To the left of the entrance is the doorway opening to the dining room (fourteen by twenty-one feet). Directly across from the front door is the entrance to the living room, whose west end is in the shape of a half-octagon. The room is approximately twenty-by-twenty feet and also has an entrance to the dining room. Ceilings on the first floor are ten feet high.

French doors from the dining room, living room, and library open to the portico, or piazza in southern parlance, that overlooks a steep bank to the river. Eight chamfered columns of the Ionic order support the piazza. These were reportedly chosen by Jefferson, as their capitals are suggestive of the horns of the Merino sheep brought to Delaware in 1801 by Pierre Samuel du Pont to strengthen the wool industry. The balustrade that runs the length of the porch is in a tracery pattern.

From the living room, a door on the south side opens through a small vestibule to the fully paneled library. A fireplace is flanked by built-in bookcases, one of which swings open and, when closed, becomes a concealed door to the living room. The original telephone closet is still in place, located in the hallway between the entrance hall and library. Between the dining room and the new kitchen, added in 1934, there is a butler's pantry with access to the back stairway.

Many family members have lived at *Louviers*—some at the same time. Victor, for whom the house was built, moved there in 1811 with his wife, Gabrielle Josephine de la Fite de Pelleport (1770-1837), and their four children: Amelia (fifteen), Charles Irénée (fourteen), Samuel Francis (seven), and Julia Sophie (almost five). In 1824, Charles brought his bride, Dorcas Van Dyke, to live there. In addition to his parents, his sister Amelia and her child from a short-lived marriage were also residents. Victor died in 1827 and, in 1833, his younger son, Samuel, a career naval officer, moved to *Louviers* with his wife and first cousin, Sophie Madeleine. At one time there were said to be seventeen family members living there simultaneously.

Victor's widow decided that the newlyweds needed more room and proposed to the company, which at the time assigned housing on an as-needed basis, that she, daughter Amelia, and her daughter, Gabrielle, move to the house up the hill. Following completion of repairs and improvements, they made the move, and afterwards *Upper Louviers* began to be called by that name.

Several other family members occupied *Louviers* until 1882, when an explosion across the river made it uninhabitable. Windows and shutters were blown through the house and a large porch column nearly gave way. Following this the house was boarded up until

1897 when, after renovation, Henry Belin and his wife, Eleuthera du Pont Bradford, moved there. Henry died four years later, though his widow remained at *Louviers* for five more years. Between 1906 and 1914 the house was occupied by various company employees and used by the company for storage. Gardens were neglected and little attention was paid to the grounds.

During World War I, *Louviers* was occupied by soldiers who were assigned to duty at the DuPont Company to protect the powder mills. A high wooden fence with electrified barbed wire on top, believed to be the first in the country, was built between *Upper Louviers* and *Lower Louviers* and patrolled by foot soldiers. After the armistice, the mills no longer produced black powder and the house was not occupied, unfortunately providing an easy target for vandals and thieves who ravaged the house stealing mantels, doorknobs, radiators, window sashes, and doors.

With the "1921 Distribution" of property and assets the DuPont Company felt it no longer needed, *Louviers* was purchased by Mary A.B. du Pont Laird. She and her eleven year-old son, William Winder "Chick" Laird, Jr., spent hours investigating the nooks and crannies of the house and later clearing the land around the house of an overgrowth of weeds, vines, and a tangle of gnarled trees and saplings.

In 1934, in anticipation of his forthcoming marriage to Winnifred "Winnie" Moreton, Mary du Pont Laird gave *Louviers* to her son as a wedding present. A major renovation of the house was undertaken by him, working with architects Samuel Homsey and his wife Victorine du Pont, a relative of Chick's. It was at this time that a kitchen wing and pantry were added to the east side, replacing the original basement kitchen which had been at the north end of the house. The east chimney, one of two original to the house, was removed in order to make space for installation of an elevator serving all four floors that is still in use. A garage and gated wall were also added at this time, creating a service yard.

There are three bedrooms on the second floor and, during the 1934 renovation, the third floor was enlarged to accommodate a guest room, a playroom, and two maid's rooms. Dormer windows were added in each of the new rooms. A delightful chart, penciled on a wall in back of the master bedroom closet door, records the names, heights, and dates of the Laird children as they grew up at *Louviers*.

Mary Silvia wrote in her book that when her father assumed ownership of *Louviers*, the floors of the original house were so rotted that they needed to be replaced. In an early example of adaptive reuse, flooring from the nearby Hagley House (1814), uninhabitable due to damage from a 1915 mill explosion and facing demolition, was taken up and installed in various parts of *Louviers*.

Both Chick and Winnie Laird were enthusiastic gardeners and shared a common area to the south side of the house, on the former site of the property's original bank barn. This was divided into individual spaces indicated as Chick's Garden and Winnie's Garden and unified by a stone wall surrounding both gardens. Each had an entryway in the shape of half of an octagon. A yellow sand path led to Winnie's Garden and brightly colored flowers that changed with the seasons. At the end of the path was a pond surrounded by a walk leading to an open space called "The Ball Park," used for outdoor games. The gardens could also be entered from the riverside bank by steps built of Brandywine granite and flanked by handsome cast iron lions.

Chick's Garden was octagon-shaped, repeating the shape of the *Louviers* living room. Yellow sand paths within the octagon were edged in flowers similar to those in his wife's garden. In the center was an octagon-shaped grass area and at the end of the garden was a round patio comparable in size to Winnie's pond. It was a striking overall design that the couple planned together, evolving over time. At the end of "The Ball Park" was a walled area with a victory garden planted during the Second World War with vegetables, flowers for cutting, and raspberry bushes. Cold frames and a walkway were on the south side and nasturtiums were planted in front of the wall facing their joint gardens.

Chick Laird continued a *Louviers* practice of planting wedding trees when he and Winnie moved there. Family lore says the tradition was started by Charles du Pont, Victor du Pont's older son, when he brought his bride Dorcas to live there. Wedding trees have been planted by five generations of du Ponts.

Outlining the gardens, Mary Silvia reminisces, were American box bushes grown in sand by her father from Mt. Vernon cuttings taken by his mother who had been active in the estate's restoration. Black Gates Road extended around the garden and down to the privately owned Iron Bridge across Brandywine Creek.

Included in Mary du Pont Laird's purchase of *Louviers* were the tenant buildings across from it, known collectively as Chicken Alley. These were row houses used by DuPont mill workers. Originally there were multiple houses in the complex, later combined into two dwellings. Each house had a living room and kitchen on the first floor and two small rooms on the second floor. When built, they had no electricity and no running water; a pump for common usage was located outside and heat was provided by wood-burning cook stoves.

With Chick Laird's ownership of *Louviers,* Chicken Alley was completely renovated to add additional rooms, running water, and central heat. Mary Silvia remembers her father saying that, during the reconstruction to join the smaller houses together, it was discovered that the exterior walls were built as dry-laid walls. Heavy stucco had been applied to the exterior and the space in between filled with sand. When cutting into the walls to make doorways this was quickly discovered, and not so quickly remedied, with sand from above pouring down by the bucket full.

Following Chick and Winnie Laird's death their two gardens were combined, and a signpost now designates it as the Winnifred Moreton Laird Memorial Garden. A poignant poem is part of the marker. It reads:

> Our day of blue-blue sky is gone
> roll in sweet cloud
> covered in celestial blanket
> we hear the promise
> bluebird days to come

Louviers was added to the National Register of Historic Places on December 13, 1971, and followed by Chicken Alley on February 1, 1972.

Lower Louviers

Owners:	Victor Marie du Pont, original
	Mr. and Mrs. William W. Laird, Jr.
	Privately owned, current
Constructed:	1810-1811
	Addition: 1934
Architects:	Eleuthere I. du Pont and possibly other contributors, 1810; Samuel and Victorine du Pont Homsey, 1934
Location:	Wilmington, Delaware

Notes

1. *The Other Side of the River: A History of the Greater Louviers Property and Its Houses*, Mary Laird Silvia, 2006

Photograph of *Louviers* was taken prior to the 1934 restoration showing the east chimney (left) that was removed at that time. Credit: Hagley Museum and Library

The original *Louviers* barn was between the *Louviers* gardens and Chicken Alley. Razed. Credit: Hagley Museum and Library

Garden steps from the Brandywine bank led to Chick Laird's and Winnie Laird's gardens. Photograph by author

Row houses were built for DuPont Company workers in a number of areas close by the Brandywine. The houses, now referred to as Chicken Alley, were across from and to the left of *Lower Louviers*. Photograph by author

The southwest side of *Louviers* faces the Brandywine River. The architecture of *Louviers* has possible connections to Benjamin Latrobe and Thomas Jefferson. Credit: Photograph by author

Mt. Cuba was designed by Wilmington architects Victorine and Samuel Homsey in Colonial Revival style. The house has 29,000 square feet and is situated on top of a hill with sweeping views over the *Ashland Red Clay Creek* area.

MT. CUBA

A Colonial Revival mansion showcases the region's premier native plant garden

Set atop one of the state's highest hills, *Mt. Cuba* overlooks a sweeping expanse of lawn that falls away into a deep valley then rises to embrace a deciduous forest of tulip poplar and gingko trees. On a clear day you can see, if not forever, at least to the Delaware Memorial Bridge—eight miles in the distance. It's a stunning view.

Pamela Cunningham and Lammot du Pont Copeland met in Paris in 1929. She was a Juilliard School of Music student furthering her voice study; he was a great-great-grandson of Eleuthere Irénée du Pont, founder of the DuPont Company, celebrating his graduation from Harvard before joining the family business. The couple married one year later, settling in the new bride's native state of Connecticut, where Lammot worked as a chemist in DuPont's Fairfield plant.

In 1935, they relocated to Wilmington. As a site for their new home, they purchased 127 acres that included a 400-foot high hilltop reminiscent of Connecticut's rolling terrain. It was a perfect fit for the Virginia-style country estate the Copelands envisioned. Throughout the next fifty years, and into the 1990s, they added to their holdings until the property reached its present expanse of approximately 630 acres. Ground was broken for the house on St. Patrick's Day March 1936 and the Copelands moved to *Mt. Cuba* in July of the following year.

There is speculation as to the origin of the *Mt. Cuba* name, but the most popular belief is that it has an Irish derivation. In about 1730, the property on which the estate was built had belonged to Cornelius Hollahan who immigrated to the United States from County Kerry, Ireland, purchasing 250 acres along the Red Clay Creek from Letitia Penn, daughter of William Penn. He gave it the name of Cuba Rock, though it is not known why. At one time the Wilmington and Western Railroad ran a daily train from Wilmington to Landenberg, Pennsylvania, that stopped at what was then called Cuba Hill. In 1872, the railroad built a station there calling it *Mt. Cuba*, and the Copelands adopted this name for their property.

As architects for their Colonial Revival mansion, the couple selected Wilmington architects Victorine (a cousin of Lammot) and Samuel Homsey. The husband and wife architectural team incorporated classic Georgian details into their two-story design—rigid symmetry, geometrical proportions, hipped roof, gable ends and dormer windows. Handmade brick, laid in a Flemish bond pattern, was manufactured by C. H. Locker Co., of Glasgow, Virginia, the same company that supplied bricks for the 1935 reconstruction of Colonial Williamsburg's gaol.

The Homseys urged the Copelands to use period paneling for *Mt. Cuba's* principal rooms as a backdrop for the eighteenth century heirlooms and antiques the couple had begun to acquire. At the end of their search enough panelling was found in New England, Virginia, and the Carolinas to fully panel five rooms—the great room, living room, dining room, master bedroom, and a guest room. Pine flooring, mantels, and staircases were also brought from historic eighteenth century houses. The Wilmington plant of the American Car & Foundry Company (later ACF Industries), builders of Pullman carriages and custom yachts, was responsible for refurbishing and refinishing the paneling.

The *Mt. Cuba* floor plan is typical of Jamestown plantations and has a cross-axis design with intersecting hallways. From the forecourt, enclosed by serpentine brick walls, an entry door, the one most used by both family and guests, opens to a 189-foot hallway. Extending the full depth of the house, its walls are covered in late eighteenth century hand-painted Chinese wallpaper similar to that found at *Winterthur*. A door at the far end opens onto the front lawn. Living room paneling, removed from a 1744 Pasquotank County, North Carolina, house, has raised panels, a deep molded cornice with dentil detailing, and fluted pilasters with Ionic capitals.

The house has 29,000 square feet and, before its conversion to *Mt. Cuba Center*, included a formal living room, dining room, library, parlors, private studies, a conservatory, vaults for wine, silver and personal archival material, six bedroom suites, ten fireplaces, twelve bathrooms, four attics, and a servants' wing.

Only the conservatory remains as it was when the Copelands lived here. The orangerie served as a transition from the formality of *Mt. Cuba*'s eighteenth century interiors to the outdoors. In a departure from the rest of the downstairs, the floor is Greek Pentelic marble combined with Belgian black tile. The trompe l'oeil mural, executed by Robert Bushnell in 1953, depicts classical architecture and treillage with blue sky, vines, and treetops above the painted architecture. The furniture, chosen by Mrs. Copeland, is French provincial and is still in place.

In the basement, a pistol range kept Lammot's hunting skills in good form for duck-shooting parties on the Chesapeake Bay. Without venturing too far from home he was able to supervise Andelot, a 3,000-acre farm in Kent County, Maryland, where he bred cattle, though salmon fishing in Scotland took him further away. Both activities befitted Copeland's position as DuPont's largest individual shareholder and one of the richest men in America. He was also the last family member to hold the reins of E.I. du Pont de Nemours and Co. (1962-1967).

Paneling for the dining room was removed from a house in Stafford Country, Virginia, c. 1750-1775. Featured in Helen Comstock's 1958 book, *100 Most Beautiful Rooms in America,* the paneling is described as being painted yellow to harmonize with antique gold damask curtains. "Most of the furniture," Miss Comstock wrote, "was made in Philadelphia; the highboy with pierced finial represents the finest Philadelphia work, and the butler's chest of drawers is outstanding for the fretwork carving on the chamfered corners."[1]

In this handsome setting, the Copelands entertained friends and heads of state, including Presidents Carter and Reagan, the Crown Prince of Greece, and King Baudouin I of Belgium. John Gates, in his book, *The du Pont Family* (1959), describes this dinner: "the Copelands pulled out all the stops. Their chef (formerly in the employ of Lord Astor) and his staff worked overtime on the elegant meal, served on the finest export china. The service was gold, the wines vintage, the wine goblets the best crystal, and a footman stood behind each chair."[2]

Not all of the Copeland's entertaining was so formal. For her eightieth birthday celebration, Pamela Copeland was joined by her daughter, Louisa Duenling, and niece, Jean Shields, all of whom had birthdays within three weeks of one another. The three women collaborated on a twenty-five minute filmed spoof of Agatha Christie's *Miss Marple* crime series. Entitled *A Piece of Cake*, the stars were family members with Mrs. Copeland playing the lead role as Miss Marple and son, Gerret, cast as Rhett the butler. About 150 guests were on hand to enjoy the satire.

Upon Mrs. Copeland's death in January 2001, at the age of ninety-six, in accordance with the couple's plans for the future, the house and its property became *Mt. Cuba Center*, dedicated to focusing on the native plants of the Appalachian Piedmont Region. In preparation for the transition from private residence to charitable foundation, an auction was held at Sotheby's New York gallery a year after Mrs. Copeland's death. The 368 lots were sold in five hours for a total of $12,563,920, setting a record for an Americana auction.

In an unusual approach, Sotheby's held a preview of the sales contents at *Mt. Cuba*, inviting twenty-five known collectors of Americana to see the furniture and artifacts in their original setting prior to being shipped to New York for auction. The New York preview lasted ten days and attracted more than 3,000 persons—potential buyers and curiosity seekers alike. When the auction was held on January 19, 2002, bidding got off to a lively start. Rare eighteenth century candle stands that were expected to sell for between seven and nine thousand dollars each brought $75,000 and $87,000 respectively.

Most of the important furniture was sold at estimated prices or above, with the highest price being paid for a 1750 Philadelphia Queen Anne desk and bookcase, estimated to sell for between $400,000 and $600,000, that sold for $1,105,750. Among the rich and famous attending the auction were TV personalities Martha Stewart and antiques expert Leigh Keno, who was enlisted to advise a Boston couple on their purchases. It's interesting to conjecture that had such an event been considered twenty-five or more years before, it might not have taken place, as family members would doubtless have been keen to purchase the furniture for their own large houses then existent, a number of which have since been razed.

The Copelands shared an equal interest in gardening and called upon Philadelphia landscape architect Thomas W. Sears to plan the approach to their home, initial tree planting, and formal gardens around the house. In the 1950s, at the suggestion of Henry F. du Pont, a cousin and owner of *Winterthur*, the Copelands engaged the services of Marian Cruger Coffin, internationally known landscape gardener and a specialist in large estates, whose many wealthy clients included Childs Frick, Marshall Field and Frederick Vanderbilt, in addition to du Pont. One of her additions was the installation of the Round Garden (1951), close by the house, centered around a plunge pool in the shape of a Maltese cross. It now makes a charming reflection pool with crisscrossing water jets.

A planned swimming pool was never built. Tightly pruned Japanese holly form a perimeter around the pool and within are seasonal displays of blooming flowers that include tulips, lilies, delphiniums, roses, and chrysanthemums. From the Round Garden a grassy garden path leads to the Lilac Allee, fragrant and colorful in early May, and featuring twenty-five species of French hybrid lilacs. On the south side of the house, flanking a hand hewn brick wall, Coffin had a row of Ghent and Mollis azaleas installed to offer a spectrum of color ranging from pale pink to crimson.

When the Copelands acquired the property that became *Mt. Cuba,* it was a group of neglected corn fields devoid of any plantings. As the couple purchased additional tracts of land, they began focusing on plants indigenous to the Appalachian Piedmont Region. Stretching from New Jersey to Alabama, it is characterized by rolling hills, fertile soil, and plant diversity.

To guide their interest in achieving naturalistic gardens, the Copelands enlisted the aid of Seth Kelsey, a Harvard-trained landscape architect, who helped Mrs. Copeland select and arrange native plants in a series of informal settings she referred to as "bays." Kelsey also developed the winding path system connecting these areas that remains in place today.

Working with Lammot, Kelsey designed four ponds linked together in a sylvan setting with a high canopy of tulip trees and considered *Mt. Cuba*'s ultimate garden destination. The ponds rely on an elaborate re-circulating system for their source of water. Through placement of rills between ponds, the water sounds range from trickling to gushing, giving each pond its own personality.

Moisture-loving wildflowers, ferns, and native shrubs surround the area, home to a very contented family of turtles. A gazebo, positioned by a bridge at the lowest pond, provides a resting spot for today's visitors. Nearby is a mailbox in the shape of a schnauzer. In this canine container Mrs. Copeland kept clippers for instant pruning as well as a pad and pencil for making notes as to which plants she would like moved or changed. To care for the estate and follow landscape instructions, the Copelands employed a staff of fourteen gardeners.

Above the ponds is a three-acre site known as Meadow with a variety of grasses and herbaceous flowering plants. From Meadow the Dogwood Path wanders up the hill towards the main house. In addition to the many unnamed bays there are seven named areas within *Mt. Cuba*—South Terrace, Round Garden, Woods Path, West Slope Path, Dogwood Path, Meadow, and Water (Ponds)—each with its own identity and over one hundred species of Piedmont flora. The trillium, Mrs. Copeland's favorite flower, appears in many of these areas and is showcased on April garden tours.

Docent-led tours of *Mt. Cuba*'s gardens are open to the public, though reservations must be made in advance. *Mt. Cuba Center* uses the main house for its program of continuing education and offers a number of courses from March to October divided into three categories: *Native Plants and Gardening, Conservation and Habitat Protection,* and *Gardens in Art.*

Mt. Cuba was listed on the National Register of Historic Places April 2, 2003.

Mt. Cuba

Owners:	Mr. and Mrs. Lammot du P. Copeland
	Mt. Cuba Center, Inc.
Constructed:	1936-1937
Architects:	Victorine and Samuel Homsey
Landscape:	Thomas W. Sears, Marian Coffin, Seth Kelsey
Location:	Greenville, Delaware

Notes

1. *The Most Beautiful Rooms in America*, Helen Comstock, Bonanza Books, 1958

2. The du Pont Family, John D. Gates, Doubleday & Company, 1979

The Round Garden was designed by landscape architect Marian Cruger Coffim and features a pool in the shape of a Maltese cross with a crisscrossing fountain. Credit: Photograph by author

In a departure from the eighteenth century American antiques used to furnish the rest of the house, the orangery has French furniture. (opposite)

The Lilac Allee features twenty-five species of French hybrid lilacs.
Credit: Photograph by author

Moving water spills down a series of rills connecting four ponds, each with its own sound. The gazebo at
the edge of the water garden was moved to *Mt. Cuba* from *Old Nemours*. Credit: Photograph by author

The Dogwood Path leads from the house down to the ponds. A succession of different species provides changing vistas the year around.

NEMOURS

A Louis XVI chateau set in the middle of the Brandywine Valley

In 1902, Alfred Irénée duPont saved the DuPont Company in alliance with cousins Pierre Samuel and Thomas Coleman du Pont.[1] He saved it with a bold strategy executed by the three men whose elders were formulating a plan to sell the company to a rival powder manufacturer when faced with the sudden death of the president, Eugene, and no one to take his place. And he saved the company for future generations of du Ponts and, of course, for himself and his heirs.

Alfred was born in 1864, the great-great grandson of family patriarch Pierre Samuel du Pont de Nemours. A rugged individualist, at the age of thirteen he led the "fight" along with his two brothers and two sisters to stay at the family home, Swamp Hall, following the death of their parents within a month of one another. The orphans were determined to remain together in their own house, a plan approved by head of the du Pont clan and the children's great uncle, Col. Henry A. The arrangement succeeded with the retention of four servants and supervision by the oldest child, seventeen-year-old Anna and, from a distance in Louisville, the children's Uncle Fred (Alfred Victor).

A popular man among men, Alfred counted as friends during and immediately after his M.I.T. college days such diverse persons as pugilist John L. Sullivan, inventor Thomas A. Edison, and march king John Phillip Sousa. His closest associates were those he saw on a regular basis—men with whom he worked at the powder plant and the ones who played in the musical group he founded, the Tankopanicum Musical Club, the name coming from the Lenape Indian name for "rushing waters of the Brandywine." The group played for concerts and dances, and one of A.I.'s compositions, "Brandywine Belles," was included in Maestro Sousa's repertoire. Other compositions were "Louviers March" and "Henry Clay March." Alfred himself mastered the violin, piano, cornet, clarinet, flute, and bass.

Sadly, Alfred's home life did not keep pace with the success of his early DuPont career and his eighteen-year marriage to Bessie Gardner ended in a bitter divorce. His second marriage was to cousin Alicia Bradford Maddux, whom he had given in marriage to her first husband (Amory Maddux, 1902), one week after her divorce decree from him (October 8, 1907). It resulted not just in alienation from his children, with the exception of oldest daughter, Madeleine (Madie), but condemnation and ostracism by most of their relatives. Following a secret wedding ceremony held at New York's Plaza Hotel (October 15), the newlyweds returned to Wilmington and Alfred's Rock Manor (Rock Farms) estate[2] awaiting callers who, with few exceptions, never arrived.[3]

Shaped by these events and a desire to give Alicia anything she wanted, Alfred resolved to build the most opulent and luxurious mansion ever constructed in the Brandywine Valley. The setting for the country estate was a 400-acre property A.I owned at the top of Rockland Road (Wilmington) surrounded at the time by farmland and woods, a holding later expanded to over 1,500 acres.[4]

As architects for the palatial residence, du Pont chose Carrere & Hastings, whose seminal work, the New York Public Library, was a forerunner to a design portfolio that exceeded 600 buildings including houses for John D. and William Rockefeller, Andrew Carnegie, Henry Clay Frick, Henry Flagler, and J.P. Morgan. The firm was one of the foremost Beaux-Arts architectural firms in the United States and that, coupled with Alicia's passion for all things French, made it an ideal choice for design of the couple's new house. *Nemours* was selected for a name after the town in France that great, great grandfather Pierre represented in 1789 as a member of the Estates General, an advisory body to the king.

Having selected an architect, A.I. next turned his attention to a builder. Carrere & Hastings assumed they would have a part in the selection, but Alfred had already made up his mind. He chose James M. Smyth, a local builder-contractor with whom he had worked in his days at the mill. It was an inspired choice. Smyth knew A.I.'s disposition and expectations and, in turn, A.I. knew Smyth's capabilities. He accepted the undertaking with confidence and appreciation and remained on the job for ten years.

Restraint was used in the decoration of all rooms so that, while undeniably grand, there was no feeling
of ostentation as is indicated in the music room. A grand piano was finished in the same white and gold.
Credit: Courtesy The Nemours Foundation. (opposite)

Their agreement was sealed with a handshake and Smyth was told to work on a cost plus basis, to keep his own records, and one year after completion of the project to destroy them. As a consequence, no one can say with certainty what the cost was, though it is estimated that it was $2,000,000 in 1910 dollars, which would equal approximately $46,000,000 in 2010 dollars.

Construction of the Louis XVI chateau-style mansion took eighteen months. It was started in the summer of 1909 and Alfred and Alicia moved there in December of the following year. *Nemours* has 47,000 square feet, fully one acre under roof, and is the fourteenth largest private house built in the United States.[5] There are seventy-seven rooms, twenty-three fireplaces, and eighteen bedrooms, each with its own bath.

Nemours faces northwest and is built of Brandywine granite quarried on the estate and covered with stucco. The conservatory, however, is faced with Indiana limestone that is also used as trim for the house. Soon after construction began, a wood fence was built around the perimeter of the building site with guards posted and orders to admit no one other than authorized personnel, the exception being Alfred's former co-workers at the powder mill. After being rebuffed by family members, he is reported to have said, "I want a wall high enough to keep out all intruders, mainly those of the name of du Pont."[6]

The fence was later replaced by a nine-foot stone wall built around the 400 acres and topped with chards of colored glass. Though it was widely rumored that the jagged pieces of glass were placed there to keep out nosey relatives, at least one cousin, William W. "Chick" Laird, Jr., defended the act as a French tradition among chateau owners.[7] The basis for his argument was the medieval custom called *cheval de frise,* i.e. capping the tops of chateau walls with broken glass as a deterrent to intruders. Chick's more charitable explanation was that the sunlit shards reminded Alfred of butterflies of which he was fond. Whichever was the case, Chick recorded that anyone who brought a glass bottle to *Nemours* was paid for it. One penny each was the bounty for clear, brown, or green bottles, two cents for blue, and three cents for red. The practice, he said, provided a good contribution to Alfred's wall and created a financial windfall for the young entrepreneurs.

In the June 28, 1913, issue of *Town & Country* magazine an article about *Nemours* reported that, "It is a drive of more than a mile from the east lodge gates to the house itself, so that the mind and eye ... are in a mood to greet with enthusiasm the long, fine lines, the handsome exterior of the residence itself, which is one of the purest examples of French architecture to be found in this country." *The Architectural Record* of the same year described the *Nemours* entrance in a similar pleonastic style. "The detailing of the front elevation has also been well considered, and the columniation is at once dignified and gracious, and excellently adequate as a support for the entablature," the author wrote.

Not mentioned in the articles are the two pairs of gates flanking the front entrance at either end of the entry court that were added at a later date. The English gates are fifteen feet high and were built in 1488 for Wimbledon Manor House, now demolished, that once belonged to Henry VIII, who gave the estate to Catherine Parr, his sixth wife. The Russian Gates belonged to Catherine the Great's rococo palace in Tsaraskoya Selo, twenty-four kilometers (fifteen miles) southeast of St. Petersburg and now a World Heritage site. Acquired by A.I.'s future brother-in-law at auction, where he

disguised himself as a farmer, Alfred referred to them as "Kate's Gates." They are twenty feet-two inches high, including a six-foot-six-inch crest, and are an outstanding example of eighteenth century ornamental ironwork.

A.I. reviewed plans for the house with keen interest and made suggestions as he went along. One change was his insistence that there be a recess in the front entrance portico. This is framed by six Corinthian columns and leads to massive bronze front doors with an arched overdoor that open to a vestibule and the twenty-seven-foot by thirty-one-foot reception hall. It is impressive by any standard. The floor is covered in black and white marble laid in a diamond pattern and it has a coffered ceiling. This originally had a natural wood finish, but was later painted ivory and blue with gilded floral centers as the duPonts felt it was too dark. Walls are finished in creamy-yellow faux Caen (French) stone block and the fireplace in ivory and gold.

Of particular interest is the standing clock made about 1785 for Marie Antoinette. It was a collaborative effort by German cabinetmaker David Roentgen, known for his marquetry, and clockmaker Peter Kintzing. The recently restored clock has three cylinders, which produce music played on a dulcimer and pipe organ, and is in perfect working order. Above it is a portrait of patriarch Pierre Samuel du Pont done by American artist Gilbert Stuart.

Other paintings include a sixteenth century portrait of Queen Ellizabeth I and a seventeenth century portrait of the Madonna and Child attributed to Spanish artist Bartolome Esteban Murillo. The epigraph, *Aimer et Connaitre (*To Know and to Love), is carved on the fireplace and a portrait of Alfred painted by French artist Gabriel Ferrier hangs above. An interesting characteristic of Carrere & Hastings designs is that staircases are hidden from the entryway. At *Nemours* it is positioned off of the northeast corner of the reception hall.

Carrere & Hastings did a masterful job in placement and proportion of the first floor rooms, each of which can be reached by short hallways from the reception hall. The sequence of rooms from this point is the writing room, library, dining room, and service area off of the north hall, and the morning room, music room, drawing room, and conservatory entered from the south hall.

The two most important spaces, the dining room and drawing room, are positioned at opposite ends of the house with entrances in a direct line with one another. Each is approximately twenty-five feet by forty-two feet with two windows facing the front of the house. There are three arched windows facing west in the dining room while the drawing room has two windows facing east.

The drawing room is the most formal room at *Nemours* although its appointments are eclectic in design and origin. It is here that the duPonts and their guests would gather before dinner parties. The room is decorated in gold and cream with the cornice and ornate border below accented with gold leaf, as is the medallion above the French crystal chandelier. Drawing room furniture is largely of French origin, much of it selected by the duPonts at Parke Bernet in New York, Charles & Co. in London, or purchased by them on their travels. Accessories include a Tiffany Favrile vase from Tiffany Studios in New York, a Rosenthal ceramic puppy from Germany, and a nineteenth century porcelain plaque that is from Japan. Vases on the mantle above the carved marble fireplace are French and Belgian, and the paintings French, Italian, and English. Kulah prayer rugs in the corners were woven in Turkey.

From the drawing room, French doors open to the conservatory overlooking the pond. Approximately twenty-five by forty feet, it has a slight bow shape at the south end. There are eighteen doors in French door casements with eastern, western, and southern exposures opening to the east terrace, parterre, and southern gardens. The floor is white Italian marble with black inlay and walls are covered in elaborate chinoiserie treillage incorporating neoclassical designs. Just recently, the original background wall color, *eau de nil*, was discovered and restored. Birdcages are alive with chattering parakeets and finches, just as they were when the duPonts lived here. In each corner is a statue representing one of the four seasons. The ceiling fixture is white alabaster suspended by bronze rods.

The music room, next to the dining room with French doors to the east terrace, has now been restored to its original white and gold colors, and the grand piano refinished in the same white and gold. Overdoors incorporate a harp design, and sconces and fireplace andirons are in the shape of lyres. The Louis XVI settee and matching chairs are covered in Beauvais tapestry, also with a musical instrument motif.

Across from the music room the thirty-by-nineteen-foot morning room was also used for writing and reading. Three chairs are of historic importance. One from Mt. Vernon was part of a set of dining room chairs from the estate of President George Washington. Another was used in Congress Hall, Philadelphia, when that city was the nation's capital, as well as the social and geographical center of the original thirteen colonies. The third chair of special interest is a coronation chair used at Westminster Abbey on May 12, 1937, during the ceremony officially crowning George VI monarch of the United Kingdom.

The focal point of the dining room is the multi-tiered crystal chandelier believed to have originally hung in Schonbrunn Palace (Beautiful Spring), former summer residence of the Hapsburg monarchs in Vienna, where Marie Antoinette played as a child. The room is surrounded by elaborate plasterwork finished in gold leaf. A portrait of Louis XVI, over the fireplace, is an appropriate acknowledgement of *Nemours'* architectural heritage.

The dining room table can be extended to twenty-five feet. Following the 1932 wedding of Mrs. Jessie B. duPont's sister, Elsie, to Gen. Albert J. Bowley, seventy-two guests were seated in the dining room for a wedding feast. The duPonts owned more than 5,000 pieces of china and many complete sets. Of particular note is the china manufactured by Cauldon, established in 1774 and potter to Queen Victoria. The duPont set has more than 220 pieces.

Nemours' 7,000-volume library is approximately the same size as the morning room and paneled in oak from a seventeenth century English manor house, with heavily carved figures surmounting the soapstone fireplace. A portrait of an English family, painted by eighteenth century artist George Romney, considered the most fashionable artist of his day, hangs by the window. The bas-relief ceiling and paneling were installed after the house was completed, replacing wallpaper and a neoclassical plaster ceiling.

Having completed the decorating, and in some instances redecorating, of the house, and selecting much of the furniture and paintings, it is regrettable that Alicia did not live very long to enjoy them. Alfred was eleven years older than Alicia who was honest in telling him that, while she was grateful for having been rescued from her unfortunate first marriage, she could not return the love he had for her.

After *Nemours* was completed the endeavor that had been their common bond faded and the couple spent more and more time apart. An apartment in Paris became Alicia's choice of residence, but, with World War I approaching, she returned to Wilmington in 1914. To compensate for her absence from Paris, Alfred once again hired Carrere & Hastings to build Alicia another large house, this one in Wheatley Hills, Sand's Point, on Long Island's North Shore, far away from family members and close to New York, which substituted for Paris.[8] It was a happy diversion for her, as was anticipation of a trip to Charleston, South Carolina, to attend the St. Cecelia Ball, Charleston's major social event.

While she was in the southland, Alfred and his step-daughter, also named Alicia, went to California to renew acquaintance with the Ball family, Virginia friends who had relocated to California. In particular Alfred wished to see Jessie Ball, twenty years his junior, but with whom he had corresponded since their meeting fourteen years before when she was a young girl.

Upon checking in at the Del Coronado Hotel, across the bay from San Diego, Alfred was handed a telegram informing him of Alicia's unexpected death in Charleston, apparently from a heart attack (January 7, 1920). He returned to Delaware at once, but did not forget Jessie. Following a year of courtship by mail, they were married in California on January 22, 1921. After an extended wedding trip in California, the couple returned to Delaware and Jessie soon initiated a reconciliation with the family. At long last Alfred found the happiness in marriage that for so long had eluded him.

The stairway to the second floor at *Nemours* is accessed through an archway from the reception hall whose faux stone wall treatment continues to the second floor. The stair railing, originally wood, was replaced with a handsome bronze railing rescued from a French chateau. Beauvais, Gobelin, and Aubusson tapestries hang on the walls and on the northwestern exposure there is a stained glass window designed by A.I.'s son, Alfred Victor, and fabricated by D'Ascenzo Studios in Philadelphia. The window incorporates the du Pont family coat of arms and motto, *Rectitudine Sto*, translated as "Upright I Stand." The French crystal chandelier hanging over the staircase is said to have been owned by the Marquis de Lafayette.

Nemours has ten bedrooms on the second floor and eight on the third floor. Though decorated in good taste, they are not furnished with antiques as first floor rooms are. An interesting detail is that the door to the fire extinguisher on the second floor reads *Pompe d'Incendie*, a bow to Alicia's fondness for French phraseology. Hopefully, if ever needed, firemen could translate it.

Lou Ann Carter was a counselor, at Camp Lake Hubert in Minnesota, to Alicia's granddaughter by her adopted French daughter, Denise duPont (Zapffe).[9] As it was Jessie duPont's generosity that enabled Denise to attend camp, Lou Ann was obligated to write her weekly letters to report on the young camper's welfare. A formal acknowledgement was always forthcoming from Jessie's stenographer and signed, "Secretary to Mrs. duPont." Lou Ann also remembers Denise describing her visits to *Nemours* and the fact that she was always assigned to a bedroom on the third floor rather than one of the more formal second floor rooms.

In spite of all the grand trappings in the main part of the house, Alfred was probably most happy in the basement at *Nemours*, a preserve he had a free hand in designing and that appealed to his interests in mechanical, practical, and sporting pursuits. Two identical coal-burning furnaces to heat the house were installed in case one should fail. There is an ice-making room capable of manufacturing 30-pound blocks of ice, a back-up water heater, and a water bottling and carbonating system to convert spring water from the property to household use.

For entertainment there are two bowling alleys and a game room equipped with pocket-pool and billiard tables and a large shuffleboard table, where movies were also shown. The exercise room has a steam cabinet, and there is a gun closet for Alfred's favorite firearms as well as a bullet trap for target practice, indicating his continued interest in guns in spite of having lost an eye in a hunting accident. It is also on this level that Alfred kept his office and where rehearsals were held for the Tankopanicum Musical Club until he was no longer able to hear. Testament to A.I.'s engineering ability are the more than 200 patents he filed with the U.S. Patent Office, some used in the manufacture of the company's black powder.

Another great interest of Alfred's was automobiles. His first car was an 1897 Benz, and he added to his collection until his death in 1935 (April 29). During the years that the DuPont Company controlled one-third of General Motors stock, he was loyal to the company and drove only GM cars including two Cadillacs and a Buick that are still at *Nemours*.

After Alfred died, DuPont was directed to divest its interest in General Motors and, following the lead of several other family members, Jessie purchased a 1951 Silver Wraith Rolls Royce and, later, a 1960 Phantom V model. These automobiles are housed in the estate's five-bay garage that has a chauffeur's apartment and accommodations for the drivers of visiting guests. It isn't known for sure how many employees were employed at *Nemours*, but from payroll records it appears as though there were some fifteen in the household plus outside maintenance staff.

Almost as famous as the *Nemours* mansion are its exquisite gardens. Patterned after Versailles' Petit Trianon, the gardens extend one third of a mile from the front entrance of the estate and are the largest French formal gardens in North America. Special features include the Colonnade, Maze Garden, Reflecting Pool, Sunken Gardens, Boxwood Garden, Oriental Garden, English Rock Garden, and the Temple of Love.

The elaborate landscaping incorporates lakes, ponds, cascades, fountains and jets of water, several structures, various types of cast iron, bronze and marble sculpture, plus seasonal displays of foliage. Of particular note is the marble bowl in the Maze Garden that weighs fifteen tons and supports two life-size figures. Several greenhouses provided flowers for the house year round. It was the custom to welcome all visitors to *Nemours* with flowers, a tradition that continues to this day.

A.I.'s son, Albert Victor, a partner in the architectural firm, Massena and duPont, asked permission to submit a plan for the *Nemours* garden, and was told by Alfred, "Make it marvelous! Make it great!" Several of his ideas were incorporated under supervision by *Nemours* architect Thomas Hastings.

In addition to work on the garden, Massena and duPont designed the Carillon, located near the intersection of Rockland Road and Route 141. The 212-foot structure has thirty-one bells and was completed in 1936, a year after Alfred's death, and it is here that Alfred, Jessie, and Jessie's brother, Ed Ball, are interred.

The figurative likeness of Alfred on top of his sarcophagus has a small dog curled at his feet. Yip, A.I.'s constant canine companion, was an Airedale mongrel he found on a golf course. Three days after Alfred died, Yip followed his master, his death attributed to a broken heart.

The terms of Alfred's will stipulated that after bequests to the family and several employees were made, the residual should be used to create The Nemours Foundation. It was his desire that a hospital "for the care and treatment of crippled children" be established as part of the legacy and the Alfred I. duPont Institute was created for this purpose. It is regarded today as one of the preeminent children's hospitals in the world.

The *Nemours* mansion and gardens underwent a 38.6 million dollar renovation between 2007 and 2010. It is open for tours by advance reservation from May to December.

Nemours

Owners:	Alfred Irénée duPont, original
	Jessie B. duPont
	The Nemours Foundation. current
Constructed:	1909-1910
Architect:	Carrere & Hastings
Location:	Rockland Road & Route 141
	Wilmington, Delaware

Notes

1. There are several different spellings for du Pont. Alfred did not separate du and Pont with a space though most family members did.

2. Rock Manor is a 4,150 square-foot, thirteen-room Victorian stone house built in 1913 with eight bedrooms, three fireplaces and three-and-a-half bathrooms. It is located on property formerly owned by Alfred duPont and is still existent.

3. *Alfred I. duPont, The Family Rebel*, Marquis James, Pg. 208

4. *Town & Country*, June 28, 1913

5. Biltmore (1895), the George Vanderbilt house on 8,000 acres in the mountains of Asheville, North Carolina, is the largest with 135,000 square feet.

6. Alfred I. DuPont, *The Man & His Family*, Joseph Frazier Wall, Pg.199

7. *Tales Continued*, William W. "Chick" Laird, 1990

8. Alicia named her Long Island mansion White Eagle, perhaps believing it conveyed superiority over the name American Eagle so revered by the du Pont family, but it is also symbolic of peace and happiness which Alicia rarely achieved. White Eagle required a staff of twenty-nine to maintain. The estate was built in 1916 on 260 acres at a cost of $1,500,000 and was sold at auction a year after her death for $470,000 (New York Times, April 24, 1921). The name was changed to Roslyn Manor and later to Templeton. Purchased by the New York Institute of Technology in 1972, it is now known as the de Seversky Conference Center.

9. Alfred and Alicia adopted a French war orphan, naming her Adelaide Camile Denise du Pont. She married Dr. Carl A. Zapffe who became an internationally known engineer, chemist, and metalurgist. They had one son and seven daughters, one of whom they named Denise.

Architects, Carrere & Hastings, designed reception halls so that staircases were not in view as you entered a house. Credit: Courtesy The Nemours Foundation

The drawing room is the most formal of the public rooms. At large parties, guests gathered here for drinks before dinner. Credit: Courtesy The Nemours Foundation

Nemours is the second largest of the du Pont estates in Delaware's Brandywine Valley with 47,000 square feet. Only *Winterthur* is larger with 96,000 square feet. Credit: Courtesy The Nemours Foundation

The conservatory is much the same today as when the duPonts occupied the house. Parakeets and finches continue to chirp, and plants to thrive. Delicate treillage surrounds eighteen pairs of French doors. Credit: Courtesy The Nemours Foundation

The library has 7,000 volumes and is the same size as the morning room, twenty-five feet by forty-two feet.
Credit: Courtesy The Nemours Founation

The sculpture group, *Achievement*, was designed by Henri Crenier. Its base is a fifteen-ton marble bowl.
Credit: Courtesy The Nemours Foundation

Credit: Courtesy The Nemours Foundation

Aerial view of *Oberod* was taken by the Dallin Aerial Survey in 1938. Credit: Hagley Museum and Library

OBEROD

A Manor Monument on the property marks a boundary set by William Penn

With architecture inspired by farmhouses in Normandy and chateaux in the Loire Valley, and a setting amid rolling hills and a lush landscape, *Oberod* could easily be situated in the du Ponts' ancestral home of France. Considered one of the most important houses built by the du Ponts during the American Country House Era, *Oberod* is thought by some to have been the reason for this part of the Brandywine Valley being referred to as "Chateau Country."

Harry William Lunger and Mary Jane du Pont were married in 1934 and within a year of their marriage Mary Jane, known as Jane, had negotiated with her cousin, Lammot du Pont, for the purchase of a tract of land in northern New Castle County. The former Hollingsworth farm, it extends from Snuff Mill Road on the south to Burnt Mill Road on the north with Kennett Pike forming the eastern boundary. The price was ten dollars for 108 acres—less than ten cents an acre; the property was later expanded to 165 acres.

The Lungers selected DeArmond, Ashmead & Bickley, an architectural firm in Philadelphia, to design their 8,870 square-foot house. Ground was broken November 26, 1935, and the move-in date was in May 1937. *Oberod* is built in a U-shape with the front entrance at the bottom of the U. To the right of the front door is the family wing and to the left is the servant's wing. The style the Lungers chose came to be known as French Norman Revival and incorporated architectural elements that include a cobble and river stone gated forecourt, steep roofs, stone walls, dormers, oval windows at the back, and casement windows.

The 9,290 square-foot courtyard is impressive. Explanations for its size vary, from allowing room to turn a coach and four, to fulfilling Harry Lunger's wish to have an area large enough that he wouldn't have to back up his car when turning.

A three-story square tower with a peak roof is in the corner to the left of the front entrance and supporting outbuildings include a barn, a cottage, and a tenant house. The blue stone used for the main house was distressed to give it an aged appearance and a hint of whitewash added as a patina. While the Lungers lived here, Mrs. Lunger's favorite flower, wisteria, covered the courtyard walls. Honeysuckle climbed up the terrace wall at the back and a former guest tells of her delight in waking to its fragrant scent.

The main entrance to *Oberod* is from the west end of the courtyard. It has French doors with a finished flat stone surround, topped by a keystone of the same material and surmounted by a semi-circular arch. A wrought iron lantern light fixture is suspended from its center. The entrance hall floor is marble. Parquet floors in various patterns were installed in the rest of the house. The main staircase is made of walnut and there are two side stairways. Ceilings are twelve feet high.

To the left of the entrance hall is the dining room with French doors to the north terrace. Hand-painted silk wall covering depicts an oriental motif of long life and prosperity and is executed in a dominant shade of blue with beige bamboo and orange leaf accents. The Lungers enjoyed entertaining and to furnish the dining room Mrs. Lunger selected French Provincial chairs with cane backs and gray seat cushions to go with a cherry table seating sixteen. The fireplace has an Italian marble surround similar to the one in the living room. To the left is a plant room with its own outside entrance.

Also from the dining room is a door to the butler's pantry that has been completely done over by the new owner. Counter tops are quartz and the backsplash is white tile. Twenty-one china cabinets with glass-paned doors are above with an open wine rack for wines to be served at dinner. Off of the butler's pantry is the morning room with French doors to the side terrace. A Delft tile fireplace surround has scenes of castles, animals and birds.

In the south wing are the kitchen, laundry, servants quarters, and the garage. The generously sized kitchen has also been updated by the new owner and great care has been taken to ensure that both the butler's pantry and kitchen retain the period look of the rest of the house. The original servants callboard with twenty-seven connections is still operative.

To the right of the front entrance is the thirty-five-foot by twenty-seven-foot paneled living room. The Italian brown marble fireplace is decorated with a carved shell marble adornment in the center and three sets of French doors open to the terrace. A small hallway off of the living room leads to Mr. Lunger's study paneled in pearwood, which was fabricated and installed by the Bethlehem Steel Company. Beyond the study is the library, also with three sets of French doors to the terrace. An outside door from the study leads to a raised flagstone terrace that joins the living room terrace at a right angle and runs the length of the living room. Stairs lead down to the lawn from the middle and each end. There are also two bedrooms and two bathrooms in this wing.

At the west end of the terrace there was a Japanese teahouse designed by Victorine and Samuel Homsey Architects, a Wilmington firm that designed several du Pont houses. Plans were submitted in January 1958 and, following approval, it was built in October.

Mrs. Lunger entertained friends here as well as using it as a place of relaxation. The octagon-shaped teahouse has sliding glass doors, a flagstone floor, and a hand-split cedar shake roof. Lanterns hang from an extension of the roof on all sides. Simply designed wood furniture was chosen to complement the architecture.

Oberod has twenty-six rooms on two floors. On the second floor there are eight bedrooms including three staff rooms. The house has fourteen fireplaces, nine chimneys, ten bathrooms and five powder rooms. In one of the upstairs bathroom doorways the Lungers measured the height of each child on their birthday and marked it for comparison the following year. The new owner has kept this as a part of *Oberod's* history. In the first floor ladies room, tiles installed below a chair rail depict the creation of the martial arts. A separate men's room and cloak room is nearby.

In the tower, the Lunger's daughters had a third floor playroom where Annie Lunger Jones kept her collection of Madame Alexander dolls. Annie says that she received one of its Little Women dolls each year for Christmas, always saving it as her last and favorite present to open, though she preferred climbing trees and horseback riding to playing with dolls. "I was a tomboy," she comments. A brother's model airplanes hung from the ceiling. The third floor of the house was used for storage and in the basement there was a movie screening room, a billiard table, roulette wheel, and Harry Lunger's state-of-the-art woodworking shop.

Some time after signing off on the architectural plans for *Oberod*, and with construction underway, the Lungers sailed to France for vacation. They hadn't been there long before Mrs. Lunger discovered that in France casement windows open inwards, whereas the plans for *Oberod* specified that they open outwards. Undaunted, Mrs. Lunger cabled the architect with instructions to change all of the window sashes to conform to French design.

Jane Lunger loved horses from the time she was a child, though unfortunately she was allergic to them and unable to ride as a result of her allergy. In 1937, however, following the legalization of gambling in the state of Delaware, she decided to pursue her passion; she and Harry purchased their first racehorse. It was the beginning of a lifetime of racing and breeding thoroughbreds. The Lungers established Christiana Stables, named for the Delaware community, and adopted purple and yellow as their racing colors. During their careers they raced some forty-five stakes winners, a number of which they bred themselves, and their winning trophies were proudly displayed throughout the house.

Christiana Stables' most famous horse was Go For Wand, bred after the death of Mr. Lunger. The filly, born in 1987, was a result of the mating of Jane's mare, Obeah, to Deputy Minister. In 1989, Go For Wand was voted American Champion Two-Year-Old Filly and the next year was given the Eclipse Award for Outstanding Three-Year-Old Filly. Running in the 1990 Breeder's Cup race, the horse had a tragic accident when she stumbled coming down the home stretch and snapped her right front ankle. She was euthanized immediately and buried the next day at the Saratoga infield. In just three years, Go For Wand had earned more than four million dollars.

The filly's unusual name was chosen by Mrs. Lunger. It stemmed from a belief that a wand could offer protection from voodoo spirits. When an evil spirit appeared, natives would get a wand and wave it to chase them away. In another display of superstition at the track, Mrs. Lunger refused to clean the mud from the shoes she wore whenever Go For Wand was running. The horse was a striking foal with a narrow blaze (white stripe) on her face and was a special favorite. "She runs with such joy and abandon," Jane Lunger wrote in describing Go For Wand. Mrs. Lunger was involved in racing for sixty-five years and was often referred to as "a queen in the sport of kings."

On the northwest corner of the *Oberod* property there is a stone marker known as a Manor Monument. The monuments served as boundary points and this one is a reference to the east line of the Manor granted by William Penn to his daughter. The inscription on the marker reads. "This stone marks the site of the old hickory tree on the Delaware Pennsylvania Boundary, 1701, also a point in the east line of the Manor granted by William Penn in 1701 to his daughter Letitia." The land was part of Penn's holdings which included all of Pennsylvania and Delaware, given to Penn in 1682 by James, Duke of York, the future James II of England.

Nearly 2,000 feet of Burrows Run passes through *Oberod* property, bordering the 352-acre Burrows Run Preserve that is home to 179 bird and 115 wildflower species. The stream is a tributary of the Red Clay Creek, largest of the White Clay Creek tributaries. This is an important source of water for 100,000 residents of New Castle County and provides all of the water used at *Oberod*. As a consequence the whole estate is restricted (protected) from development by terms of a conservation easement that runs in perpetuity.

After Harry Lunger died (July 31, 1976), his widow continued to live at *Oberod* until 1978 when she gave the house to the Episcopal Diocese of Delaware to be used as a conference and prayer center. Mrs. Lunger then built a smaller house on the property designed by the Homsey firm. She named it *New Poems* and lived there until her death in 2001. After the house was completed, she had the Homsey teahouse moved from *Oberod* to *New Poems*.

Six years after Mrs. Lunger died, the Episcopal Diocese, citing increased competition from other conference centers and the high cost of maintenance, sold *Oberod* for three million dollars to a privately owned company to be used as a corporate retreat and training center. Second floor bedrooms have been adapted for corporate apartments and the basement level has been converted into a training area with a fully equipped lounge. Furniture of the period has been acquired through gifts and at auction.

In addition to the kitchen and butler's pantry the new owner has modernized the heating plant and completed exterior maintenance work to return *Oberod* to its original condition. Fortunately a diocesan plan to cover the courtyard with macadam and use it for parking never materialized. The original entrance to *Oberod* was from Kennett Pike; however, after being given to the Episcopal Diocese, the driveway entrance was relocated to Burnt Mill Road.

When the Lungers owned the estate, there were two buildings just inside the entrance, as there are now. The building to the right from the Kennett Pike entrance was a garage, since adapted as a dwelling, while the other was considered the gatehouse—dubbed *Harry's Gate*. A three-story white stuccoed house, it dates back to the eighteenth century. From 1929 to 1936 it was the residence of Daniel O. Hastings, a United States senator from Delaware.

Mary Jane Lunger was the daughter of Philip Francis du Pont and Elizabeth Braxton Horner. She was raised in Fairville, Pennsylvania, close by her future home. Several volumes of poetry were written by her father and from these came the names for both houses. *OBEROD: And Other Poems*[1] was published in 1919 and *NEW POEMS and A PLAY* was published in 1914.

Oberod

Owners: Mr. and Mrs. Harry W. Lunger, original
              The Episcopal Diocese of Delaware
              Vance V. Kershner, current
Constructed: 1935-1937
Architect: DeArmond, Ashmead & Bickley
Location: Centreville, Delaware

Notes

1. We lived in the land of Oberod,
   I and my wife and a little god,
   And we were as happy as we could be—
   as happy as mortals ever are—

The back terrace overlooks a broad expanse of lawn and mature trees. At the west end Mrs. Lunger had a tea house built that she moved to her new house.

Oberod was built between 1935 and 1937, the period in which the term "Chateau Country"
first appeared, and there are many who believe *Oberod* inspired the expression.

Silk wall covering in the dining room is hand-painted in an Oriental design that represents prosperity and long life.

The entrance hall is indicative of the formality of all of the rooms at *Oberod*, but Mrs. Lunger introduced warmth and personality by displaying her racing trophies in many of the public rooms.

French doors from the library open to the terrace and bring light to the paneled room. Floors throughout *Oberod* are parquet in varying patterns.

Owl's Nest was designed by architect Harrie T. Lindeberg, who was known for his
designs of houses that were both pastoral and sophisticated.

OWL'S NEST

Setting for a President's son and his du Pont bride's wedding reception

Of all the du Pont houses built in the Greenville area, *Owl's Nest* is perhaps the single example of a country house combining Tudor Revival with English Medieval style architecture.[1] Set well back from *Owl's Nest* Road, off of Kennett Pike, and screened by mature shrubs and trees, *Owl's Nest* was the 500-acre estate of Eugene H. du Pont, Jr. and his wife, Ethel Pyle du Pont.

As architect for their house, the du Ponts selected Harrie T. Lindeberg, a former associate of Stanford White and known as a designer of country houses for well-to-do clients including such prominent names as Pillsbury, Doubleday, Macy, and Armour. Lindeberg was an ideal choice as he preferred working with pastoral settings and was acclaimed for designing houses that looked as if they "rested on earth." And though his sense of scale was baronial (the house is 216 feet long), his houses were faultlessly scaled to make large interior spaces livable.

Owl's Nest is two-and-a-half stories high and is constructed of hand-burned skintled brick to form an irregular face and give the appearance of great age. The sculptured roof is made of one-inch thick slate slabs in shades of red, gray, and green that wave over bottom-hinged eyebrow windows. Each of its six chimneys is topped by a terra cotta chimney pot.

Lindeberg collaborated with noted landscape architect Ellen Biddle Shipman on the garden design. It was Shipman's strong belief that house and garden architects should work together and she encouraged clients to consult her before architectural plans were drawn, a concept with which Eugene du Pont agreed. In her thirty-two year career, she planned over 650 gardens for wealthy families throughout the United States matching Lindeberg's roster, among them Astors, Fords, and Dukes. Together she and Lindeberg were a perfect design team, dedicated to combining elegance with the pleasure of living comfortably.

A circular driveway at the front of the house, now the Greenville Country Club, surrounds a formally planted area complementing the Boxwood Garden entered on the left.[2] Over the gabled front entrance of *Owl's Nest* a lunette encases a copper arch featuring a spread eagle designed by German-born metal artist Oscar Bach. Considered one of the outstanding metal artists of the twentieth century, Bach's work is represented in the Vatican Museum, New York's Chrysler Building, Empire State Building, Radio City Music Hall, and Riverside Church.

The nearly four-foot wide front door, embellished with hand-forged faux strap handles, opens to a vestibule, the entryway to the two-story, thirty by forty-five-foot limed oak-paneled great hall with rough cast plaster and a beamed ceiling. On each side of the front door there is a large-scale window unit in nine sections of fifteen over fifteen casement windows. Each of the two windows has a total of 135 panes. Quartersawn, random width oak floors are pegged and secured by butterfly joints. A massive stone fireplace supports the carved overmantel frieze that incorporates the du Pont coat of arms as its focal point. Below it is a ribbon inscribed *"Rectitudine Sto,"* translated as "Upright I Stand." To the left of the crest is a castle with crenellated walls and to the right a schooner, a reference to the ship that first brought the du Pont family to America. In the center of the room is a sixteen-arm chandelier decorated with acanthus leaves.

Opposite the fireplace on the east wall a carved dog-leg staircase leads to the second floor; the entrance to Eugene du Pont's den is directly under the staircase. Running the length of the hall is an oak balcony, supported by square paneled and chamfered pillars, that has been used for orchestras, theatrical presentations, and as a perfect setting for beaming brides throwing bouquets to hopeful brides-to-be.

Though there are multiple rooms on the second floor, only the master bedroom and two others are indicated as bedrooms on Lindeberg's blueprints. Other designated rooms on the plans include Mr. and Mrs. du Pont's dressing rooms, a night nursery next to the master bedroom, a "child's room," sewing room, serving room and a sleeping porch. Additional second floor bedrooms, used by staff, are indicated by numbers one through five.

Daughter Aimee's bedroom was at the top of the stairs and to the left and is now the Greenville Country Club office. Her sister Ethel's room was across the hall next to the guest bedroom and is currently used as the club manager's office. Third floor bedrooms served various purposes, but according to accounts, sons Eugene III and Nicholas, whose bedrooms were connected by a shared bathroom, considered it their domain.

A reception area from the great room features an extraordinary strapwork ceiling divided into quarters by ribs stretching from the corners to a center medallion and decorated with flowers, fruits, and vines in shades of pink, salmon, green, blue, and yellow. From here entrances lead to a large living room on the left and the formal dining room on the right; straight ahead French doors open to the terrace.

Both the living room and dining room have fireplaces, among six on the first floor. Adjoining the dining room is an oval-shaped former breakfast room with a recessed ceiling. At one time a door on the south wall, since closed up, led to the kitchen. The twenty-five by forty-six-foot long living room has raised panels of walnut above and below the dado rail. A hand-carved sculptured encarpus of fruit and flowers encircles the fireplace.

At the south end of the living room, double doors on both sides lead to the brick-walled, glassed-in sun room, originally furnished with oversize wicker chairs and a settee. The floor is flagstone and eleven French doors with transoms open to the surrounding terrace. When the du Ponts lived here, a large carved spread eagle was mounted on the brickwork above the hood of the fieldstone fireplace.

Facing the sun room is the exceptional Boxwood Garden designed by Ellen Shipman in 1928, and selected by the Smithsonian Institution as one of only five gardens represented in their publication, *Archives of American Gardens*. The far end of the four-bed, axial garden is anchored by a teahouse, a favorite folly of Shipman. The teahouse has a slate terrace, twenty feet by seventy feet, and overlooks a reflecting pool with a charming fountain featuring bronze lotus flowers, leaves, and buds.

Shipman's plan for the garden specified that there should be four kinds of flowering trees—wisteria, crabapple, cherry, and laburnum. Some 10,000 bulbs were planted with over 170 varieties represented including narcissi, tulips, mertensias, hyacinths, primulas, and violas. These were massed in plantings of from ten to twenty up to two hundred, to provide a spectrum of color easily seen from the sun room. After 1938, landscape architect Marian Cruger Coffin, well-known in her own right and who worked with Henry F. du Pont on the design for the *Winterthur* gardens, acted as consultant.

While Eugene du Pont worked for the DuPont Company, his real interests were big-game hunting and agriculture. Legend has it that he was never happier than when puttering in his gardens, a hobby that earned him the good-humored nickname, "Dirty Gene."[3] Three farms spread over 523 acres were assembled to form the *Owl's Nest* estate, "more than sufficient to take care of my spare time," he wrote. The main farmhouse and barn, accessible from Old Kennett Pike, have been converted into private dwellings.

Other outbuildings included a gardener's cottage, an ice house, and a potting shed of similar brick and construction as the main house, three greenhouses, a pool house, dog kennels, and a hunting lodge. The four-bay garage with wash bay and chauffeur's quarters above and ice house are still existent.

Richard West came to the Greenville Country Club as a groundskeeper in 1979 and it seems safe to say he knows more about the house than anyone. In describing *Owl's Nest*'s du Pont days, he says that there were two 10,000 gallon water tanks under the driveway filled by gravity from a cistern that provided water for the house.

Additionally there was a 60,000 gallon water tank in the basement of the garage used to fill the swimming pool. "The pool held 50,000 gallons and there was no filter on it," Richard says, "when the pool water got dirty, Mr. du Pont just drained it." This was the pool originally used by the Greenville Country Club when it was formed in 1961. Lined with tiles imported from Holland, the entire swimming pool was buried on the property in 1964.

The fiftieth anniversary of *Owl's Nest*'s reincarnation as Greenville Country Club was celebrated in 2011. During this half century there have been many changes, not only in modernizing its physical plant, but also in additions to the building. Most significant of these is a seventy-five seat informal restaurant added in 1987, appropriately called the *Owl's Nest*, that offers club members an alternative to the formal dining room. Other changes include the building of a championship swimming pool, the installation of nine outdoor tennis courts and two indoor courts, and construction of four paddle tennis courts.

Owl's Nest was a perfect house for entertaining and the most famous of its gatherings took place on June 30, 1937. In 1936, President Franklin D. Roosevelt's son, Franklin, Jr., made frequent trips to Philadelphia, ostensibly to visit friends, but in reality to slip across the border to Delaware and visit *Owl's Nest* in order to see Eugene, Jr.'s daughter, Ethel, a striking brownette. In November, with FDR's election safely behind, their engagement was announced.

Beatrice Twer, a resident of nearby Rockland, Delaware, recalled driving to the Montchanin railroad station as a girl to witness President Roosevelt's arrival for the wedding. "Excitement filled the air," she wrote, "It seemed like a fairy tale, the merger of two such distinguished families. ... They had built a platform at the station and it was surrounded by secret service men. ... From the train and down the platform, with the help of a cane, came Franklin Delano Roosevelt, with his wife, Eleanor, close behind him. However, to me the greatest thrill, and what I recall most vividly, was a tall, distinguished gracious lady with blue white hair glistening in the midday sun—it was the president's mother, Sara Delano Roosevelt."

Their private railroad car, U.S. Car No. 1, remained on the siding of what was then the Wilmington and Northern Railroad, waiting to take the Roosevelts to Hyde Park after the festivities.

The wedding ceremony, described by *Time Magazine* as "wedding-of-the-year" (June 28, 1937, issue), was held at Christ Church Christiana Hundred, which in itself presented a problem. The church holds just 300, but the guest list exceeded 1000. Many of the du Ponts ended up sitting on the groom's side in order to be seated, though the situation was helped somewhat by the absence of some staunch Republican family members who shunned the wedding because of their antipathy to President Roosevelt. Three hundred and forty guests finally managed to squeeze into the church pews.

What had started as a beautiful day turned into a torrential downpour as the couple left the church, and many guests considered it a bad omen and portent of things to come. After the wedding, hundreds of cars clogged Kennett Pike as guests headed to *Owl's Nest*, four miles away, for the reception. A waterlogged carnival atmosphere prevailed, with souvenir, balloon, and hot dog vendors lining the route. Thousands of onlookers stood in the rain on the roadside hoping to catch sight of the just-married couple or President Roosevelt and his wife.

An often heard story is that the small elevator from the first to the second floor of the house was installed for the benefit of President Roosevelt. This seems unlikely as the president did not plan to spend the night at *Owl's Nest*. Another frequently repeated legend, also without documentation, is that the president, referring to the stormy weather, is said to have quipped, "This is a fine way to soak the rich."

Wedding gifts for the couple were displayed in two second floor rooms and the upstairs hallway. One room was set aside for crystal and silver, the other for linens, china, pottery, and miscellaneous household furnishings. Gifts of furniture were placed on the great hall gallery.

A press tent had been set up to accommodate fifty telegraph operators on hand to transmit reporters' copy to cities all over the world with details of the radiant bride's luminescent white tulle over white crepe gown, girdle of wax orange blossoms, bridal bouquet of butterfly orchids and lilies of the valley, and twelve-foot, three-layered veil (*Life Magazine*, July 12, 1937). It was also noted that she held a prayer book during the ceremony. Descriptions of what celebrities wore for the glittering wedding were relayed to all of the wire services. Sixty secret service men and state police and 350 soldiers, recruited from the 1st Regiment of Engineers from Fort DuPont and bivouacked on the du Pont estate, were on duty to provide security, but were pressed into service, utilizing tractors from the nearby du Pont farms, to free Packards, Cadillacs, Rolls Royces, and other mud-mired cars.

An anonymous du Pont scribe, who irregularly and irreverently published a newsletter, *Du Pont Dope*, for distribution to family members only, gave a humorous interpretation of the proceedings. "Christ Church," it was reported, was "overcrowded to a great degree, the small church taking on the semblance of a congenial inferno ... The only omission in the beautifully decorated church was the 'standing room only' sign which was not hung on the church door."

"The wedding over," the review continued, "the great migration started. Time stood still. Everything stood still—even America's foremost families. Several people suffered nervous frustration from the great delay and underwent treatment when they reached *Owl's Nest*. After a period of three hours, the guests arrived at the estate, which by then had become "Mud Mansion." H.B. du Pont slowed down to the point where he was only moving ten feet every five minutes on his way from the church to the house."

Uninvited guests were turned away by the hundreds and the driver of each car turning onto Owl's Nest Road was stopped and asked to show a pass. One neighbor, annoyed that she had not received an invitation, nevertheless, succeeded in making her presence known. In an act of celestial revenge, the lady, a private pilot, took to her aircraft and, with perfect timing, buzzed Christ Church just as the marriage vows were exchanged.

In spite of the mud and mire outside, inside *Owl's Nest* all was festive and sparkling. New York society band leader Meyer Davis and his orchestra played "Too Marvelous for Words," "Tea for Two," and other of the couple's favorites for dancing during the reception. Afterward forty special guests sat down for a wedding dinner. Following dessert, in timeless tradition, the newest member of the Roosevelt clan threw her wedding bouquet from the carved oak great hall gallery. The President and First Lady stayed until 11:30, an hour-and-a-half after the bride and groom had departed, and then boarded *U.S. Car No. 1* for the journey to Hyde Park.

Weather aside, it was a gala day and evening, but the soothsayers were right. Twelve years later the couple divorced.

Owl's Nest

Owners:	Eugene H. du Pont, Jr., original Greenville Country Club, current
Constructed:	1915 - 1920
Architect:	Harrie T. Lindeberg
Landscape:	Ellen Biddle Shipman, 1928-38; Marian Cruger Coffin, 1938
Location:	Owl's Nest Road Greenville, Delaware

Notes

1. The *Owl's Nest* name came from a tavern located at the intersection of Centreville and Old Kennett Roads. An owl nested in a nearby haystack and locals began using it as a point of reference for the tavern location.

2. In 1961 *Owl's Nest* was sold to developers and seventeen-and-a-half acres were acquired by the Greenville Country Club. Seven du Pont families were among the charter members. *Owl's Nest* was placed on the National Register of Historic Places August 30, 2010.

3. Eugene du Pont, Jr. was called "Dirty Gene" by family members. His cousin, Eugene E. du Pont, who lived in nearby Greenville at Dogwood, was referred to as "Clean Gene."

Lunette over the front door encases a copper arch created by Oscar Bach whose metalwork was used in the Empire State Bulding, Chrysler Building, and Radio City Music Hall. Credit: Photograph by author

Surrounding the fireplace is a carved wood encarpus with flowers, fruits, and flowers hanging from scallop shells in the upper corners and with cat-in-nine tails surrounded by palm leaves.

Teahouses were a favorite garden folly of Ellen Shipman's. The Boxwood Garden, in which this is located, is axial with boxwood-lined paths and a slate terrace in front of the teahouse.

Pierre du Pont purchased the Peirce house in 1906 and soon after began its renovation. The house had its beginnings in 1730, when Joshua Peirce built a simple farmhouse to replace a log cabin.

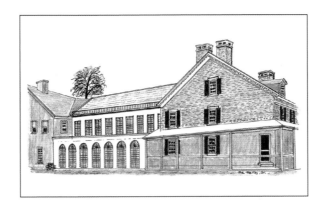

THE PEIRCE-DU PONT HOUSE
AND LONGWOOD GARDENS

A private park has evolved into one of the world's premier public gardens

Pierre S. du Pont was the great-grandson of Eleuthere Irénée du Pont, founder of E.I. du Pont de Nemours, and, though they never met, they shared a consuming interest in gardening. Eleuthere listed his profession as "Botaniste" on his passport. As an adult Pierre Samuel recalled his keen interest at the age of six in seeing the fountains at the 1876 Great Centennial Exposition in Philadelphia. Another childhood memory was his recollection of seeing the Matthias Baldwin greenhouse, also in Philadelphia, in full view of passers-by. He vowed at the time, prophetically, that if ever he was to have a greenhouse it would be open for the public to view from within and from without.[1]

Peirce's Park, some twelve miles from Wilmington across the Pennsylvania border, was a popular area for picnics and swimming. Originally the site of a Lenni Lenape (meaning True or Original People) Indian village, in 1700 it was included in a 400-acre land grant from William Penn to George Peirce. Peirce's great-grandsons, twins Joshua and Samuel, were particularly interested in the great variety of trees that existed. Author George Thompson reported that in the early nineteenth century Joshua and Samuel traveled by horseback through Pennsylvania, Maryland, Delaware, and New Jersey collecting seeds and saplings that they planted on their property, which became an arboretum known as Evergreen Glade.[2]

From 1899 to 1905, Peirce's Park changed hands four times with a contract finally made with a company interested only in cutting the specimen trees and converting them to lumber. When Pierre heard of the pending agreement, he contacted an attorney and gave her a check for twenty-five dollars asking that she put a ten-day option on the property to buy it. On July 20, 1906, he executed his option and purchased Peirce's Park for $15,500.[3] The property totaled 202 acres; today *Longwood Gardens* has 1,077 acres.

Pierre du Pont was thirty-six years old when he purchased Peirce's Park and was living at *St. Amour* with his mother. He had no need for another home; however, he was intrigued by the idea of renovating his newly acquired Pennsylvania farmhouse as a place to entertain family and friends and as a weekend retreat.

As early as 1829, there was a farm adjoining Peirce's Park owned by John Cox, who called it Longwood Farm. In the mid-1800s the Longwood Progressive Friends Meetinghouse used the name from the neighboring farm and in turn Pierre adopted the name for his property.

The *Peirce-du Pont House,* had its origin in 1730 when it was built by Joshua Peirce to replace a log cabin built in 1709. In 1764 a two-story addition was added at the east end of the house that included a new dining room, and in 1824 the house was doubled in size by the twins, with a two-story addition on the north side. Additional work done at the same time included raising the roof and reducing the size of the former dining room and a bedroom in order to make the line of the front of the house even.

The house is built of brick laid in a Flemish bond pattern created by alternating headers and stretchers in a single course. It is considered the most decorative brick pattern and at the *Peirce-du Pont House* the headers are dark glazed and the stretchers unglazed. The 1909 work on the house included adding a two-story wing and installation of electricity, plumbing and a heating system, collectively described by Pierre as "mighty changes."

The largest addition was made in 1914 with an addition that amounted to a mirror image of the original farmhouse and included a library and upstairs bedrooms (architects, Brown & Whiteside, Wilmington). The two wings were then connected by what is referred to as *Longwood's* first conservatory.[4] There are nine rooms on the first floor and eight on the second floor of the *Peirce-du Pont House* including six bedrooms.

The house is entered through the conservatory with the library to the left which has six pairs of French doors, four leading to the outside and two opening to the conservatory. Mr. du Pont's suite of rooms was directly above the library and has French doors and a French balcony overlooking the conservatory. To the right of the conservatory and up three steps was his office, a parlor, dining room, flower room, butler's pantry, kitchen, and pantry. This room included an electric warming oven as well as an innovative electric towel dryer and a walk-in silver safe.

Several innovations in the *Peirce-du Pont House* are unique even today. Below the floor of the library there is an electric rug roller. This device was designed to roll up a thirty-three by nineteen-foot oriental rug each spring and store it for the summer. Straw rugs were then put down in its place and the process reversed in the fall. Another innovative system is used in the conservatory, where Pierre used his engineering skill to design a system in which counterweighted windows slide down for storage in winter and screens are brought up from the basement for the summer.[5]

A fire protection system was installed in 1914 with sliding fireproof doors that can be closed to seal off rooms and hallways. In the basement a bowling alley was installed with a small glass-bottomed pool outside on the ground level providing natural light for bowlers.

In 1909, Pierre felt that enough work had been completed on the house that he could entertain. Accordingly, he sent out 500 invitations for a lawn party to be held on Monday, June 21, from five to ten o'clock.

Refreshments, prepared by Philadelphia caterer John Holland, included chicken salad and croquettes, deviled crabs, mayonnaise salmon with sauce, hams, assorted sandwiches, rasped (raised) rolls, ices, and cakes, plus claret punch, lemonade, and coffee. He was charged $1.50 per person including linens and service. Music was provided by the First Regiment Infantry Band of Wilmington and fireworks concluded the evening's entertainment.[6] The party was a great success and the following year 800 invitations were sent out. In making arrangements with the caterer, it was suggested that provision be made for one hundred chauffeurs rather than fifty.

By 1912, Mr. du Pont's garden parties were an established event and his brother-in-law, H. Rodney Sharp, who married Pierre's sister, Isabella, was helping to plan the events. For the following year Pierre hoped to have an outdoor theater installed for presenting the entertainment. It was built on the site of the original Peirce barn; however, because of his mother's illness the party was cancelled.

By 1914, the open-air theater had been completed and the party was described in detail by a reporter for Wilmington's newspaper, *Every Evening*. "Just after dark," he wrote, "electric lights were turned on ... and a spot light discovered four couples descending from the terrace above the stage to the classic strains of Beethoven's music. ... The finale was a frolic by the harlequins, who, much to the surprise of the guests, danced among them, throwing confetti and garden roses ... finally disappearing amid the trees. The audience might easily have imagined itself transported to the days of Marie Antoinette and the scene Versailles."[7]

Two weeks after this garden gala Pierre began experimenting with fountains for the theater stage and these were in place for the 1915 outdoor extravaganza. By this time the entertainment was in the hands of New York professionals. The parties were cancelled during the war years of 1917 and 1918, but by 1919 were back in full swing with 1000 guests attending. Following this celebration, the then-governor of Pennsylvania, William C. Sproul, wrote Pierre a letter of thanks (June 16, 1919) in which he said, "That party of yours on Saturday evening was the finest affair that I have ever seen."

The theater was redesigned from 1926-1927 with dressing rooms added and the seating area in the former barnyard area sloped for better sight lines of the stage. At this time the fountains were also augmented with 750 jets illuminated by 600 colored lights beneath the stage and a water curtain ten feet high installed at the front of the stage. The capacity of the theater is now 1500.

Plans for the *Longwood Conservatory* were formulated during World War I, but building was not able to get underway until 1918. Construction took three years and, in 1921, the Orangery and Exhibition Hall opened with adjoining greenhouses. The center sections of the Orangery are planted with carefully manicured grass while the perimeters feature a changing display of blooming flowers. The sunken floor of the Exhibition Hall is used for exhibits as well as for entertaining.

In a continuance of the annual garden parties, Paul Whiteman's Pavillion Royal Orchestra (later Palais Royal) played in 1923. Dinner was served at tables on the stage, the balconies, and in the new silk and walnut paneled Music Room Lounge, with dancing held on the lower level a few steps down. In 1924, a troupe of Russian gypsies performed with singers and dancers accompanied by a violin, accordion, and piano. The 1927 party was scheduled in September to allow time for completion of the fountain installation which by then was in perfect working order. Entertainment was divided into segments featuring water, dance and drama.

Colvin Randall quoted a local paper as reporting, "The thousand guests assembled ... sophisticated folk, who for the most part, simulate boredom as part of their code—gasped at the loveliness devised for their eyes." The final garden party was held in 1940, with an absence of several years because of problems on Wall Street and a looming war. It was attended by 1200 people. Pierre's parties had brought delightful, fun-filled evenings to hundreds of his friends in what was described by one attendee as "the most brilliant in the social history of the city." But, most importantly they established a pattern for entertainment at *Longwood Gardens* that would be enjoyed by the public for generations to come.

The first pipe organ at *Longwood* was installed in 1921 and was located in the northeast corner of the Exhibition Hall. It had sixty-three stops and 3,650 pipes, and the cost was $54,200; it was manufactured by the Aeolian Co., New York. The Azalea House was built in 1928. During the period of 1969-1973, the Azalea House was redesigned and again in 2003-2005. In 1982, it became known as the East Conservatory.

The 103-foot long by thirty-five-foot wide 1929 Ballroom, adjoining the Music Room (1923) and Azalea House, was principally designed to house a second pipe organ. It has 10,010 pipes divided into 146 ranks (sets), five thirty-two-foot pedal stops, and sixty-one combination pistons; it weighs fifty-five tons. The cost of the organ was $122,700. Two mammoth brass and crystal chandeliers hang from the ceiling, finished with 1,104 panes of pink etched glass, and the parquet floor, replaced in 2005, was fabricated to look like the original floor made from surplus World War I gunstock blocks.[8]

The second outdoor water feature at *Longwood* was the Italian Water Garden built between 1925 and 1927 near the estate's Large Lake and inspired by the Villa Gamberaia in the Tuscan hills overlooking the city of Florence.[9] Six hundred jets recirculate 4500 gallons of water per minute in eighteen pools. Though the four rectangular pools appear to be the same size, the two at the far end are fourteen feet longer in order to give the impression that they are the same when seen from the terrace.

Longwood's Main Fountain Garden was inspired by Pierre du Pont's visit to the 1893 Chicago World's Fair and, once again, excursions made to European gardens. The fountain garden was started in 1929, eight years after landscaping had been underway. It has 380 fountainheads, scuppers, and spouts and 10,000 gallons of water per minute are recirculated. The height of the fountains can reach 130 feet and the original pumps, installed in 1930, are still in use today. Plans are underway to rebuild the fountains, after which the pump house will be used as a museum. Trees used in the extensive landscaping were brought to *Longwood* from fourteen states.

To maintain the enormous volume of water required for operating the *Longwood* water features, du Pont had a 90,000 gallon underground reservoir built, which supplies a fifty-foot waterfall that empties into a basin. The complete system holds 675,000 gallons of water. Using field stone excavated from the nearby hills, a tower was constructed with chimes that could be activated from the *Peirce-du Pont House*. The chimes were replaced in 2001 with sixty-two cast bells, in essence converting the Chimes Tower to a Carillon.

In the nearly fifty-year period from 1908 to 1951, Mr. du Pont was also involved with a farming operation known as *Longwood Farms*. Though meticulous records were kept, activity was limited for the first four years. In 1912, it was set up as a division of the *Longwood* corporation, a new farm manager was employed, and the operation was expanded. Records show that, in 1932, Longwood Farms had seventy-nine steers, forty-one Guernseys, sixty Herefords, thirty-nine hogs, fourteen horses, fifty-six turkeys, twenty pheasants, thirty-one pairs of pigeons, sixty-three ducks, and 837 chickens.[10]

In a memo Pierre observed that the farm was not particularly successful financially, but served as a border between his gardens and his house. It also provided a more than sufficient supply of manure. Still, both he and Mrs. du Pont showed an interest in the farming operation. Pierre also took pleasure in chiding his cousin Henry (*Winterthur*) about the superiority in butterfat content of his Guernseys over Harry's Holsteins. After forty-three years, the farming operation ended in 1951.

With four-and-a-half acres of heated conservatories, *Longwood Gardens* is one of the world's largest horticultural display gardens. Its 1,077 acres include twenty outdoor and twenty indoor gardens with an amazing 11,000 species of plants and trees. In the conservatory alone there are 5,500 types of plants. The newest addition to the complex is the East Conservatory Plaza and the 4,072 square-foot Green Wall, a curved, glass-roofed corridor with 47,000 plants growing vertically on gently curving walls. Twenty-five species are represented and it is the largest installation of its type in North America.[11]

A million people visit the *Peirce-du Pont House* and *Longwood Gardens* annually to experience its combination of water features, botanical, musical, and historic attractions. When Pierre du Pont first owned *Longwood Gardens* and the *Peirce du Pont House,* he enjoyed inviting his friends for weekend visits. Later he opened the gardens to the general public and today, in accordance with his wishes, the house[12] and gardens are open every day of the year—destinations with a unique legacy that have brought pleasure and enjoyment to millions.

The Peirce-du Pont House and Longwood Gardens

Owners: Joshua Peirce, original
Pierre S. du Pont
Longwood Gardens, Inc., current

Location: near Kennett Square, Pennsylvania (3.5 miles)

Notes

1. *A Man And His Garden*, George E. Thompson, Sr., Longwood Gardens, 1976

2. *Ibid*

3. *Ibid*. An inventory of the Peirce Park included 202.75 acres of woodland and farmland, the main Peirce house (1730), two barns, a sheepfold, two ice houses, a water wheel, smokehouse, blacksmith shop, woodshed, two carriage houses, a summer house, washhouse and two tenant houses. The purchase price was $15,500.

4. *The Heritage of Longwood Gardens, Pierre S. du Pont and His Legacy*, Longwood Gardens, 1998

5. *Ibid*

6. *The Longwood Garden Parties*, Colvin L. Randall, Cedar Tree Press, 1975

7. *Ibid*

8. *The Heritage of Longwood Gardens, Pierre S. du Pont and His Legacy*, Longwood Gardens, 1998.

9. Mr. and Mrs. du Pont made eleven trips to Europe during which they concentrated on visiting gardens and chateaux in France and Italy. One of their favorite ships was the British Cunard liner, *RMS Mauretania*, launched September 20, 1906. In November 1907 the ship captured the Blue Riband for the fastest eastbound crossing of the Atlantic and in September 1909 the *Mauretania* won the Blue Riband for the fastest westbound crossing, a record that was to stand for more than twenty years.

10. *A Man And His Garden*, George E. Thompson, Sr., Longwood Gardens, 1976

11. *Longwood Chimes*, Issue 282, October-December 2010

12. During his lifetime Pierre du Pont referred to the *Peirce-du Pont House* as the residence or the farmhouse. Employees referred to it as the Mansion House or Big House. It was opened to the public in 1976 as the Peirce House and in 1979 it was renamed the *Peirce-du Pont House*.

Peirce-du Pont personal bookplate

Pierre du Pont had a wing built to match an existing one and between the two built what he referred to as Longwood's first conservatory.

Exit

Construction on the Longwood Conservatory was started in 1918 and it opened in 1921.

Longwood's Idea Garden is divided into eleven different plant groups including annuals and perennials, flowers, roses, vines, groundcovers, vegetables, herbs, fruits, ornamental grasses, and containers.

Longwood's Topiary Garden has more than fifty specimen yews in twenty shapes including a table, chairs, and birds.
They are trimmed every July and August.

The Conservatory has original marble floors and is often flooded with about three inches of water to create reflexions. It is used for seasonal displays and flower shows as well as private functions.

The Italian Water Garden was built between 1925-1927, There are six large and twelve small pools with 600 jets of water and a water staircase circulating 4500 gallons of water each minute.

Rokeby was built in 1836 as a wedding present for Gabrielle du Pont, following her engagement to William Breck.

ROKEBY

An imposing house with a past tied to the Brandywine

Silhouetted against the hillside, *Rokeby* is unlike any other of the du Pont houses in the Brandywine Valley. An integral part of the Henry Clay Village Historic District, the porticoed Greek Revival mansion was built in 1836 for Gabrielle du Pont, granddaughter of Victor du Pont, whose brother founded the DuPont Company. The house was a gift from Victor's son, Charles I. du Pont, when Gabrielle became engaged to William Breck.[1]

Family history records that Gabrielle wished for a house similar in design to *Upper Louviers*, where she had spent most of her childhood. Measurements were taken and the yellow stucco house built, with one major change—the architects measured *Louviers* from the inside. When the house was constructed, these measurements were mistakenly applied to its outside dimensions, with the result that *Rokeby* was considerably smaller than its model.[2]

In the past 175 years, the house has been lived in by a succession of du Pont family members who modified it, adding to the square footage and changing it to accommodate their needs. The current occupants, Gerret and Tatiana Copeland, have continued the practice and today *Rokeby* reflects their taste and personality. It is a stunning and unusual house with a distinguished lineage of du Ponts.

In 1835, William Breck and his partner, Joseph Dixon, purchased an existing cotton mill and grist mill located on the Brandywine. The cotton mill was renamed Breck's Mill while the grist mill retained its name of *Rokeby*. Both were converted to textile production. William and Gabrielle Breck, decided to use the same name for their house as was used for the former grist mill.[3]

Unfortunately the business venture was not a success and, in 1839, Breck and Dixon sold the mills to Charles I. du Pont, Jr., who had been living in Louisville, Kentucky, where he was in the paper business. The Brecks continued to live at *Rokeby* with their four children until relocating to Scranton, Pennsylvania, in 1859. In 1862, after his marriage to his cousin, Mary Sophie, Charles

purchased *Rokeby* (house), and he and his family lived there until he died.

Charles changed the entrance to the house from Barley Mill Lane to Center (Montchanin) Road and Victor du Pont, Jr., planted trees along the driveway on June 30, 1873, to commemorate his twenty-first birthday. The next du Pont to live at *Rokeby* was Mary Van Dyke du Pont, Charles, Jr.'s sister. On a table by a parlor window, the Copelands have a copy of the 1906 Jefferson David Chalfant pencil and crayon drawing showing Mary Van Dyke seated in front of this same window. Mary Van Dyke never married, but was active in a number of charities and was adored by her nieces and nephews; she died in 1909.

At that time, it was purchased by T. Coleman du Pont and rented by newlyweds, E. Paul du Pont and his wife, the former Jean Kane Foulke. E. Paul went on to develop the duPont automobile and rescued the Indian Motorcycle Manufacturing Co. from bankruptcy.

In 1911, Alice Hounsfield du Pont, a daughter of Coleman and Alice (Elsie) du Pont, moved to *Rokeby* and soon after enlarged the portico. The following year she married Paul Wilson, who was from New York. The elaborate wedding held at Trinity Episcopal Church in Wilmington was attended, according to the *New York Times*, by 1000 guests.[4] Unfortunately Paul Wilson died just four years later.

Alice Wilson continued to live at *Rokeby* until 1921, when she married Clayton Douglass Buck, Sr., in a considerably smaller ceremony held at what the *New York Times* grandly referred to as the Coleman du Pont summer home. In reality it was held at the Old Mill, described by William Winder "Chick" Laird as neither old nor a mill, but rather Coleman's "pleasure villa."[5] The newspaper reported that only immediate relatives were present, which would most certainly have been the case, as the size of the Old Mill would have dictated that. After their wedding, the Bucks moved to Buena Vista, his family home near New Castle, Delaware. Buck was later elected Governor of Delaware and, after that, U.S. Senator.

Henry Belin du Pont, Jr., and his first wife lived at *Rokeby*, from 1929 until July 1935, while waiting for their house, *Ashland Red Clay Creek*, to be built. Following their departure, Dorcas Van Dyke Buck, daughter of the former governor and his wife, lived there from 1943 until 1978 with her husband, Capt. Donald K. Farquhar. The Copelands have owned *Rokeby* since 1978.

The Henry Clay Village Historic District, named for the U.S. Senator and Secretary of State, is approximately three miles north of downtown Wilmington. Slightly less than one-half square mile in area, it was entered in the National Register of Historic Places January 1, 1988. It includes residences and buildings situated along the Brandywine River that were largely associated with workers employed by the mills and mill owners who built most of the houses for rental to their workers. At one time there were small stores, taverns, a church, a school and a post office. There are also a number of heavily wooded areas. An earlier name for the village, Rising Sun, is still in use today as a street name.

Rokeby is now approached from Brecks Lane, its third entrance location. A gently curving driveway climbing upwards frames the house surrounded by parkland and ends in a circle at the new and more formal front entrance put in place by the Copelands in 2009. The former glass-paneled exterior vestibule has been replaced by steps from each side ending on a balcony with a wrought iron railing. The front door was formerly the front door of Copeland House, Gerret's grandmother's house, razed in 1964. Above it the semi-circular window has bars radiating from the bottom that divide the solid glass background into separate panels.

The front hall floor, installed at the same time, is brown and white Italian marble laid in a diagonal pattern with the stairway to the left. On the right is the powder room designed by Mrs. Copeland with a one-of-a-kind sandblasted green glass pedestal and basin in a shell design finished from underneath in fourteen-karat gold.

From the stair hall a door leads to twin parlors with pocket doors similar to those at *Lower Louviers*. Each parlor has a slate fireplace that has been overlaid in goldleaf. The walls are covered in burgundy grasscloth. Doors from both parlors open to the veranda that was extended by the Copelands in the 1980s. Its supporting columns are thirty-three inches in diameter and twenty feet high and frame the dramatic gardens below that feature an abundance of color projected by more than 5,000 tulip bulbs that Tatiana had planted in 2012. Stone arches and walls, one supporting the sculpture of an eagle poised to take flight, separate the formal gardens from a backdrop of woods with the Brandywine Creek just beyond. Peony bushes and two dogwood trees were transplanted from *Mt. Cuba*, Gerret's boyhood home.

The second parlor leads into the less formal morning room with an art deco ambience accented by original Erté prints framed in gold and the art deco-design fireplace. The walls are pale gold grasscloth and the upholstered furniture is cream-colored cut velvet and linen. An anteroom separates the morning room and the library that is also used by Gerret as his home office. Focal points of the paneled room are a fireplace and a portrait of Gerret's father, Lammot du Pont Copeland, painted by Spanish surrealist artist Salvador Dali. The square Oriental rug is signed by the weaver in a small woven panel in the carpet fringe. Floor-to-ceiling windows look over the veranda and gardens beyond.

Rokeby was originally designed with the dining room and kitchen on the ground floor and the Copelands have kept to that floorplan. If the library is Gerret's lair, the dining room is Tatiana's. Mrs. Copeland has a Russian heritage and the dining room decor reflects these ancestral connections. Beige marble walls surround the fireplace and give the room a contemporary feeling. The octagonal dining room table was made by Vladimir Kagan, known for his sculptured designs in furniture.

The coat of arms of Tatiana's family is displayed by the dining room entrance. Hanging next to it, from a Russian fairy tale, is a mystical Firebird painting that Tatiana has had since she was a child. On another wall there is a charming painting done in petit pointe of a Russian Orthodox church. A painting, also of a Russian Orthodox church overlooking the Volga River, is above the sideboard.

From the dining room, French doors lead to the conservatory that also has a view of the gardens and the flagstone terrace. The swimming pool is in an idyllic setting with the woods in the background. The Copelands have recently had the kitchen remodeled with a skylight above a sitting area at one end and a door opening out to the terrace and across from the conservatory.

Steps and a walkway at the side of the house lead to the former *Rokeby* barn, now called *Bear Lodge*, which has been converted to a complex that combines facilities for entertaining, guest quarters, and, at the far end with a separate entrance, Tatiana's office. The great room is dominated by a massive stone fireplace that rises to the full height of the former barn in three setback stages resembling a stone skyscraper. It is surrounded by pine paneled walls and saltillo tile floors.

In back of the barn, the driveway leads to garages and a greenhouse. This part of the *Rokeby* property is less formally landscaped than the gardens surrounding the house. The western slope is banked with evergreens and flowering bushes that form an outdoor stage setting for a pageant of sculptures that includes five cranes, a rabbit, a frog, a panda, brought by the Copelands from China, and two self-confident pigs executed in bronze by local sculptor André Harvey.

Rokeby was added to the National Register of Historic Places January 1, 1988.

Rokeby

Owners:	Mr. and Mrs. William Breck, original
	Charles I. du Pont, Jr.
	T. Coleman du Pont
	Alice du Pont Wilson Buck
	Mr. and Mrs. Donald Farquhar
	Mr. and Mrs. Gerret van S. Copeland, current
Constructed:	1836
Location:	Greenville, Delaware

Notes

1. *Black Powder, White Lace*, Margaret M. Mulrooney, University of New Hampshire, 2002.

2. Family history relates that *Upper Louviers* was the model for *Rokeby* (also called *Rokeby Hall*); however, the twin parlors and portico are similar to those at *Lower Louviers*. As Gabrielle spent time at both houses, it would seem that she had features from each incorporated into the *Rokeby* plans.

3. About 1756, Joseph Gilpin built and operated a grist and saw mill at the bottom of Brecks Lane, where it meets the Brandywine Creek. In 1813, the property was acquired by new owners who

built a cotton spinning mill next to it calling the complex *Rokeby*, the name of a nearby mill community that had adopted its name from a poem written by Sir Walter Scott the year before (1812). In 1835, William Breck and Joseph Dixon purchased the mills and ninety-five acres and it became known as Breck's Mill. The original grist mill retained the name *Rokeby*.

In 1839, Breck and Dixon sold both mills to Charles du Pont, Jr. who converted them to woolen mills. The DuPont Company bought them in 1852. The *Rokeby* mill is significant for having been used as the company's first experimental station from 1903 until 1906, concentrating on developments in explosives and chemicals, until it was destroyed by fire.

In 1921, when the powder mills closed and the company sold much of its Brandywine properties, Breck's Mill was purchased by Mary du Pont Laird. After it was acquired by her son, W.W. "Chick" Laird, it was used as a theatre. It now houses two galleries and a post office.

4. *New York Times*, October 29, 1912.

5. *The Old Mill, Which was neither old nor a mill,* A reminiscence of William Winder Laird, 1974

The *Rokeby* barn, now called Bear Lodge, has been converted to an entertainment center, guest quarters, and offices. Credti: Photograph by author

The current owners of *Rokeby*, Gerret and Tatiana Copeland, have made a number of changes to the house that have personalized it for them, beginning at the front entrance. The front door had previously been the front door for Copeland House, which has been razed and replaced.

Rokeby has elements of both *Upper Louviers* and *Lower Louviers*. The twin parlors are similar to the ones at *Lower Louviers*. Fireplaces in these rooms are slate overlaid with gold.

Gerret Copeland's home office has floor-to-ceiling windows looking out over the veranda and gardens, many of them planted with some of the five thousand tulip bulbs Tatiana had planted in 2012.

The former *Rokeby* barn has been transformed into a combination guest house, entertainment center, and office for Tatiana. Now called Bear Lodge in recognition of Tatiana's heritage, it is a stunning complex.

In contrast to the formally planted gardens surrounding the house, the western slope is banked with evergreens and flowering bushes.

A stone archway separates two gardens from the woods just beyond. Dogwood trees were transplanted from *Mt. Cuba*, Gerret's boyhood home.

189

The aerial view of *Saint Amour* taken by Dallin Aerial Survey Company on October 31, 1927 shows the estate bordered by Kennett Pike on the west and Rising Sun Lane on the south. The estate was razed in 1978. Credit: Hagley Museum and Library

SAINT AMOUR

Home of three presidents of the DuPont Company

To celebrate the centennial anniversary of the arrival in America of Pierre Samuel du Pont de Nemours, 125 of his descendants from different parts of the country gathered for a commemorative breakfast on Monday, January 1, 1900. The site of the gala gathering was *Saint Amour,* the palatial residence of Mary Belin du Pont.

Lammot du Pont, a brilliant company chemist, who lived in Philadelphia with his wife, Mary, and their children was killed in a plant explosion in New Jersey in 1884. His bereaved widow, pregnant with their eleventh child, continued living there until six years later, when she decided to return to her native Wilmington, where she had lived until 1880, and build a new life and new house for herself and their children.

As architect for her ornate mansion, Mrs. du Pont selected Albert W. Dilks, well-known in the Philadelphia area as a designer of houses for wealthy patrons. Many of his clients lived in the city's main line suburbs in surroundings that would have been comparable to the ten-acre Wilmington location selected by Mrs. du Pont at Rising Sun Lane and Pennsylvania Avenue (Kennett Pike). It would also have been very convenient for her to see examples of his work at close range and, indeed, a number of his commissions were similar in size and style to the plans drawn for *Saint Amour*.

Dilks gravitated towards an elaborate and eclectic multi-textured Queen Anne style of architecture very much in vogue in England and the United States at the time. Characterized by a blend of Tudor Gothic and English Renaissance, it was well-suited to the needs of a household requiring multiple bedrooms for a large family and servants plus adequate space for entertaining.

The residence designed by Dilks could only have added to the area's repute as Chateau Country—a three-and-a-half story granite structure with forty rooms and more than 4,000 feet on the first floor alone. Castle-like in appearance, the imposing structure was distinguished by a crenellated courtyard, several chimneys, bays, turrets, and towers, some of which were attributed to the whims of the children, who were allowed to design their own rooms as

compensation for leaving their Philadelphia friends. Dilks was instructed to work their plans into his design.

Mrs. du Pont further encouraged the children to participate in the design of their future home by suggesting that each child carve a panel for the staircase of the dark, rich walnut interior. Only one daughter, Louisa d'Andelot, agreed with her mother and carved five panels in a floral motif, using many of the tools that had belonged to her grandfather, Alfred V. du Pont.

Located at 3001 Pennsylvania Avenue, *Saint Amour* was set on ten acres and was angled towards the corner. The entire acreage was heavily landscaped in several separate areas, including the property perimeters paralleling Pennsylvania Avenue and Rising Sun Lane. The gardens featured an extensive grape arbor supported by round concrete pillars, stone walls, paths, an octagon-shaped gazebo with a conical roof, and hothouses to provide flowers the year around. *Saint Amour*'s lawn and flower beds were laid out by John Campbell, a landscape engineer from Ardmore, Pennsylvania, whose first assignment was to plant 500 strawberry plants Mrs. du Pont had ordered from a Philadelphia nursery.

The estate's formal gardens were designed as a setting for outdoor social events. Beyond the gardens and greenhouses, at a right angle to the back of the house, is a still-existent, five-car garage with handsome herringbone brick floors and glazed white tile walls plus stables. Adjoining the garage are wings that once provided housing for the head gardener and chauffeur.

The family moved into *Saint Amour* in May of 1892: Mrs. du Pont, five sons (Pierre S., Henry Belin, William Kemble, Irénée, and Lammot, Jr.) and five daughters (Louisa d'Andelot, Sophie Madeleine, Mary Alletta, Isabella Mathieu, and Margaretta Lammot; a sixth daughter died in 1871). Pierre, the eldest, was attending Massachusets Institute of Technology, but living with his grandmother across the street at *Goodstay*, and kept a close eye on the house as it was under construction. During the period from 1907 to 1913, he lived at *Saint Amour*, paying his mother $130 per month for board. Pierre, and two of his brothers, Irénée and Lammot, were later to become presidents of DuPont.

Saint Amour, the name chosen by Mrs. du Pont for her residence, comes from a village in the eastern part of France near Andelot, the location of her ancestors. Local humorists, however, commented that the name, interpreted as Holy Love, was chosen because Mrs. du Pont had five daughters to marry off.

In describing the gala One Hundredth Anniversary celebration of the landing in America of Pierre Samuel du Pont de Nemours, the *Wilmington Evening Journal* reporter assigned to the event declared that it was, "More notable than any family reunion held in Delaware."

His account continues:

> To accommodate the attendees a fifty-foot by fifty-foot temporary structure, built of wood, was annexed to the house. Rough on the exterior, but furnished within as magnificently as if it were part of the residence, it had a special heating apparatus for the comfort of guests. Artists had transformed the bare walls of wood into panels of beauty for the occasion. Over all gracefully was draped bolts of cloth of white and pale blue alternately and streamers of the same tints were festooned at intervals along the walls. Electric lights studded the drapery, and to heighten the effect there were strings of evergreens, smilax and holly, the ceiling being adorned in the same pretty way.

> Standing along the floors and near the draped walls was such a wealth of flowers and tropical plants as had ever been seen at a private gathering in Delaware. There were forests of palms and ferns, and an abundance of orange and lemon trees, with luscious fruit dangling temptingly. There were begonias and roses in countless profusion all around the dining hall and throughout the residence. Massive pillars towered to support the roof of the dining hall, about which were entwined holly and greens ... arranged by a Philadelphia florist.

> On the tables roses and carnations were scattered loosely. In the dining hall of the residence, a special table was set for the children and twenty little ones, the girls in white costume. ... Lapitini's Orchestra of seven pieces from Philadelphia, behind a screen of verdure, gave a delightful concert which was continued throughout the afternoon. Seventeen waiters were in attendance. ... As the afternoon was drawing to a close Colonel Henry A. du Pont read the family history in which he traced the lineage of the family from more than two hundred years ago up to the present date.

Though the invitation specified that guests were invited to a breakfast, the *Evening Journal* described it as a dinner and noted that it was served at 1:30. Considering the menu and the time that appears to be a more accurate description. Johnny cakes and game pie were featured, symbolic of the first food eaten in the New World and aboard the ship, the *American Eagle*, that brought Pierre, his two sons, Victor and Eleuthere Irénée, and their families, to the United States. The youngest family member who ate in the main dining room was fifteen-year-old Maurice du Pont Lee. Younger children were served in the kitchen.

Everyone attending received an album of family photographs and at each person's place setting was a specially designed gold coin minted to commemorate the occasion. It was clearly a triumph with no effort or expense spared. Decorating costs, shared by the twenty-two grandchildren who issued the invitations, included:

200 carnations for large table	$ 4.00
100 roses for children's table	4.00
2065 yards cheese cloth @ 2 and 7/8 cents per yard	59.30
Renting 21,735 feet of lumber and paying for what was cut and not returned	162.74
Carpenter for putting up and taking down building	104.40
Renting plants	10.00

Upon Mrs. du Pont's death in 1913, her youngest son, Lammot, (the name Americanized from the French surname La Motte) acquired the property and moved with his family back to *Saint Amour* from Iris Brook, farther up Kennett Pike, where they had been living. Extensive renovations made at the time included removing a wooden porch that surrounded the house on all sides and replacing it with a stone terrace and adding an enclosed stone porch on the front of the house.

In 1918, working with prominent landscape architect, Marian Coffin, who also helped in designing *Winterthur*'s gardens, Lammot built the *St. Amour Garden*. It became a favorite family gathering place for teas, parties, and wedding receptions. Further modernization of the house took place in 1934 under the supervision of his cousin, Alfred V. du Pont, partner in the architectural firm Massena and duPont, and included adding a bowling alley in the basement.

During World War II, when gasoline rationing was in effect, Lammot contributed to the war effort by purchasing a bicycle and pedaling to and from his DuPont office. He got further exercise by chopping wood in a remote corner of the property for use in fireplaces.

Lammot, Jr., who served as president of the DuPont Company from 1926 until 1940, died in 1961 and his widow, Margaret Flett du Pont, lived in *Saint Amour* until her death in 1969. In 1970, Tower Hill School received title to *Saint Amour* and the house, having outlived its adaptability, was razed in 1972 to make way for athletic fields. Lammot, though he would have regretted the loss of the house, would have been pleased at its disposition, as he was one of the eleven founders of the school and served as a trustee from 1919 to 1952.

In 2004, the garden walls, paths, and fountain were restored through a grant from Rosa Laird Hayward McDonald in memory of her grandmother, Mary Belin du Pont. Landscaping for the restoration was the gift of the Tower Hill School Class of 2004. Once again the *Saint Amour Garden* has become a place of enjoyment for alumni, students, their families, and faculty who gather in the stone-walled enclosure for teas, parties and receptions.

Saint Amour

Owners: Mary Belin du Pont, original
Lammot du Pont
Tower Hill School, 1972
Constructed: 1891-92
Razed: 1972
Architect: Albert W. Dilks
Landscape: John Campbell, 1892. Marian Coffin, 1918
Location: 3001 Pennsylvania Ave. (Kennett Pike)
Wilmington, Delaware

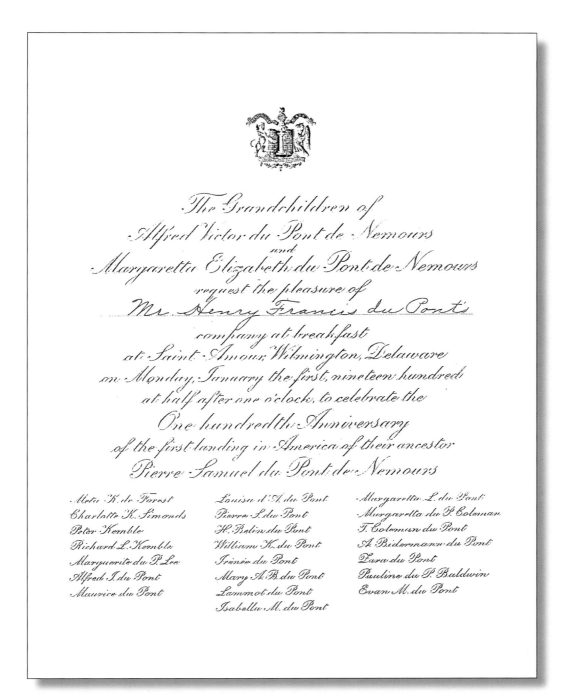

The invitation to a gala anniversary breakfast celebrating the arrival of the du Ponts in America held at *Saint Amour* on January 1, 1900. One hundred and twenty-five descendants attended. Credit: Hagley Museum and Library

Saint Amour was built on ten acres and the house designed by Philadelphia architect Albert W. Dilks. A permanent flagpole was built on the tower and a flag raised on July 4, 1902. Credit: Hagley Museum and Library

R. Brognard Okie was a Philadelphia architect who designed four du Pont houses and additions for several others. His first house in Wilmington was *Squirrel Run* designed for S. Hallock du Pont.
Credit: Photograph by Steve Boyden

SQUIRREL RUN

A classic Colonial Revival country house replaces a former worker village

Following World War I and the closing of its powder works along the Brandywine River, the DuPont Company sold off much of its land holdings to family members. Samuel Hallock du Pont, known as Hallock, was a director of Christiana Securities, the family holding company, and the son of William Kemble du Pont, a younger brother of Pierre, who was at the center of the company's 1907 reorganization. Hallock took advantage of the buying opportunity, acquiring 1300 acres that stretched along the Brandywine and included Squirrel Run Village and its former worker houses.

Considered a maverick by the family, in his youth Hallock kept a flock of Kent County Blue Hen fighting cocks, distinguished by their blue plumage and known for their ferocity and aggressiveness. Because of their behavior, the University of Delaware has used Blue Hens or Fighting Gamecocks for their team names since 1911. The breed is also responsible for one of the nicknames for Delaware, i.e. the "Blue Hen State."[1]

In 1925, Hallock, in anticipation of his forthcoming marriage, chose a prime site on his recently acquired property for building his house on the Brandywine. Following the du Pont custom of naming houses, he retained the name *Squirrel Run* that appeared on Delaware's earliest maps as Sqerrell Run. The stream initially provided the power for an early mill on the Brandywine—probably a cotton and wool factory.

Forty-eight families lived in the village of Squirrel Run, most were of Irish and Italian descent. According to William W. "Chick" Laird, Jr., writing in a booklet distributed to family members, due to the topography of the area, many of the houses were built in rows or "banks," with the first floor of the high side level with the second floor of the low side. Each of the houses had a garden, chicken yard, shed and an outhouse.

When Hallock was clearing the land for his house, all but a few of the houses were demolished. Nearly one hundred years later, following heavy storms, the current owners report finding shards of china from razed village houses still poking through the creek banks.

Hallock chose Richardson Brognard Okie, from Devon, Pennsylvania, as the architect for *Squirrel Run*. Okie was best known for designing houses in the Colonial Revival style and for his restoration work that included the Betsy Ross House in Philadelphia and the reconstruction of Pennsbury Manor, William Penn's estate.[2]

As a student Okie spent much of his free time driving through the back roads of Southeastern Pennsylvania and Northern Delaware, studying the architecture of eighteenth and nineteenth century farmhouses, measuring and writing down details of their construction, and making note of their relationship to the land. His designs were especially popular on Philadelphia's Main Line and other suburbs. Okie's style was well suited not only to the Brandywine Valley, but to Hallock's personality and his desire to have the house fit into its natural surroundings.

Squirrel Run was the first of five houses that Okie designed in Wilmington, as well as the largest, and each bears his trademark features: undressed fieldstone exteriors, three stories, prominent chimneys, spacious fireplaces, flat lintels, solid oak or cypress window and door frames, shutters and wrought iron details.

Hallock du Pont, with his first wife, Elizabeth Wrenn, then his second wife, Virginia Simmons, lived at *Squirrel Run* for nearly fifty years. In the succeeding years, several owners sub-divided and sold off parts of the original property. Present owners Steve Boyden and his wife Linda, an interior designer, have owned the property for ten years and have put their individual stamp on it to a much greater extent than any of the other three owners since the house was originally built.

In addition to reconfiguring much interior space, the Boydens have built a stunning outdoor complex that includes a swimming pool, pavilion with outdoor kitchen and bar, a lounging and relaxation area, outdoor fireplace, changing rooms, and a shower room. Their swimming pool replaces the original one, since filled in, that measured fifty by one hundred feet, was sixteen feet deep and had no filter system. Dirty water was drained and replaced with water from a well on the property. The re-location of the swimming pool required leveling of a sloping hill that has been banked with boulders moved from other locations on the estate, a project executed by Richard Lyon and Wallace Landscaping. New exteriors were painstakingly matched to the undressed blue stone of the original house.

The terrace of the lounge area is bordered by rectangular flagstones brought from the nearby Christ Church Parish House that had removed them to provide an even surface for its school. Three millstones, originally used at the DuPont powder works, were found in the woods and moved by the Boydens to *Squirrel Run*. One is embedded in the turning circle at the front of the house, two others have been creatively converted into fountains in the lily pond.

Squirrel Run is situated on twenty-two acres. The original house combined with the new outdoor complex increases its size from ten to 16,000 square feet. There are twenty-nine rooms including eight bedrooms, eight bathrooms, three powder rooms, nine fireplaces, and five chimneys.

The first floor reception hall, with random-width wood flooring, is seventeen feet wide and forty feet long with an elliptical stairway to the second floor and French doors at the east end opening to a terrace. The north-facing living room is twenty-four feet wide by thirty-five feet long and has a marble fireplace. The crown molding throughout the house, as well as all millwork, was done on the property in a purpose-built woodworking shop erected during construction of the house. Located next to the five-car open bay garage, it is the oldest building at *Squirrel Run*. There is also a two-car garage attached to the house.

The focal points of the dining room are a fireplace flanked by glass-paned china closets and large windows facing south and west. The Boydens completely remodeled the kitchen, converting the former staff living room-dining room into the family room and adding a fireplace, paneling, and a coffered ceiling. All bathrooms have been updated, but retain the original tile. The six-foot by eight-foot silver vault is still used for its original purpose as well as for storage of family documents.

Linda's design expertise was called into play with the Boydens' redesign of the sun porch and its conversion to a conservatory. A former outside window of the paneled library that opened to the porch has been replaced with a built-in bookshelf matching those on either side of the fireplace. Another window opened from the dining room onto the porch. Both original windows were relocated—one to a breakfast room and the other to a potting room. Glass fanlights, installed above the arched entrances from the stair hall opening to the living room, library, and dining room foyer are original.

The master bedroom on the second floor is located in the north wing. In addition to the bathroom, there are two dressing rooms, each with its own fireplace. Four additional en suite bedrooms are on this level. The servants wing had four bedrooms and two bathrooms. This has been reconfigured into a large guest suite, an office, and a laundry room. Additional staff rooms and a bathroom are on the third floor.

One of the Boydens' major design challenges required removal of an old chimney and installation of a support beam in order to create a standard staircase off the kitchen to the lower level. The previous stairway was narrow, winding, and somewhat dangerous.

Hallock's billiard table, now recovered with wine-colored baize, is still in place. The walk-in, temperature-controlled, wine cellar can hold up to 2100 bottles.

Other changes on this level made by Steve and Linda include converting the furnace room to a playroom and the original laundry room to an arts and crafts room. The room designated on blueprints as a gymnasium has been completely remodeled with the addition of floor-to-ceiling wall mirrors and state-of-the-art exercise equipment. A steam shower has been added in the full bathroom. New air conditioning and heating have been installed as well as new sound and security systems.

In addition to the garage and woodworking shop, other original outbuildings at *Squirrel Run* that were characteristic of large du Pont estates in the 1920s and 1930s are an ice house with a cupola topped with a squirrel weather vane (in recognition of the house name), a hexagonal stone smoke house with a cedar shake roof, a pump house, the former bathhouse—now a guest cottage, and the estate's gatehouse surrounded by stone walls. Beyond this there is an arched stone bridge over the run. An outdoor basketball court across from the pump house adds to recreational options.

Former owners added a tennis court and a paddle tennis court. Just below the paddle tennis court are the foundations of kennels that housed Hallock du Pont's prized Clumber Spaniels. The sporting dogs are distinguished by white coats, a long, low build, and a slow, rolling gait. The Clumber is one of the American Kennel Club's original nine breeds, registered in 1884, and is believed to have originated in France in the eighteenth century. Though Hallock raised several different breeds, including English cocker spaniels, Labrador retrievers, and greyhounds, his favorite was the friendly Clumbers that were also good hunters. Between 1935 and 1941, the Delaware Dog Gun Club ran their trial program at *Squirrel Run*. During those same years Hallock was president of the Wilmington Kennel Club that held a benched show at the estate.

Hallock du Pont was a great outdoorsman and had a keen interest in animal husbandry. In 1929, he purchased Whitely Farm, located in Mill Creek Hundred, from Arthur Whiteman, where he raised cattle and other livestock. This led to his contribution, over the years, to the University of Delaware's College of Agriculture and Natural Resources for research in cattle and swine diseases, and breeding and maintaining his favored Blue Hen Chickens.

Whitely Farm became Hallock's private game preserve. In its woods is a marker placed there in 1764 by surveyors Charles Mason and Jeremiah Dixon. From here the two men began their trip west that established the boundary line between Maryland, Pennsylvania, and Delaware. Mason and Dixon marked their line by milestones and by crownstones every five miles.

The farm was also the site of a visit by temperance advocate Carrie Nation in 1904, an event that reportedly drew a crowd of some 10,000. Whether Hallock was inspired by Mrs. Nation's visit and her habit of throwing hatchets at liquor bottles isn't recorded, however, he did practice throwing knives at *Squirrel Run*. After one such incident, in which he reportedly came too close for comfort, his first wife left that night, divorcing him soon after.

But, Hallock also had a softer side to his personality. Discovering a fine specimen of a weeping birch tree, one of the largest in the western hemisphere, across the border in Pennsylvania, he purchased the plot that the tree stood upon, fenced it in and gave it to his Uncle Pierre for his Longwood arboretum. He was also a major sponsor of the Pushmobile Derby (Soapbox Derby), that brought children aged eight to sixteen and policemen together in an annual race at a track he had built for the event at Whitely Farm.

In an act of compassion, Hallock set up a trust fund for World War I hero Sgt. Alvin York, who single-handedly breached enemy lines and captured 130 German soldiers. Hearing that the Congressional Medal of Honor awardee was destitute, du Pont established an endowment of $350 that was paid monthly for the rest of the former soldier's life.

Squirrel Run

Owners:	Samuel Hallock du Pont, original
	Richard S. du Pont
	Keith Stoltz
	Mr. and Mrs. C. Ronald Maroney
	Mr. and Mrs. Steve Boyden, current
Constructed:	1926-1927
Architect:	Richardson Brognard Okie
Location:	Greenville, Delaware

Notes

1. The official nickname for Delaware is "The First State" as it was the first of the original thirteen states to ratify the Constitution of the United States on December 7, 1787.

2. Richardson Brognard Okie's work was based on historical precedent rather than ostentation. In addition to Hallock du Pont, in the Wilmington area he was the architect for houses built for Nicholas du Pont, Henry B. du Pont, Jr., and Frances du Pont Morgan, as well as Thomas Edison. He also designed an addition to a house owned by Louisa du Pont d'Andelot Carpenter Jenney.

The ice house was one of the original buildings on the estate and was used to store ice, usually packed with straw. It would remain frozen this way, often lasting until the following winter. Photograph by Steve Boyden

The living room and dining room open off the stair hall. Millwork for the house was done on the property in a woodworking shop built expressly for that purpose. Credit: Photograph by Steve Boyden

The dining room fireplace is flanked by built-in china closets with carved shell back panels. French doors open to the east terrace. Photograph by Steve Boyden

The billiards room has Hallock du Pont's original billiard table, now recovered in wine-colored baize. There is also an exercise room and full bathroom with steam shower on the lower level. Photograph by Steve Boyden

The stair hall extends the full width of *Squirrel Run*. A door to the right of the stairway opens to the east terrace that has a circular boxwood garden as its focal point. Photograph by Steve Boyden

The Boydens have built an outdoor entertainment area that includes a bar, seating area, outdoor cooking range, dressing rooms and a new swimming pool. Photograph by Steve Boyden

Staglyn was constructed in 1934-1935 for Edith du Pont and her husband, Richard Riegel. It is built of fieldstone, but unlike most du Pont houses is in shades of ivory and brown rather than gray and blue. Its style is referred to as modified Colonial.

STAGLYN (FISKEKILL)

A northern Delaware estate has Swedish and French references

As the DuPont black powder business prospered, family houses extended northward, often clustered near the outlying stations of the Wilmington and Northern Railroad. Founded in 1866[1] as the Wilmington and Brandywine Railroad, it was reorganized in 1876 with Col. Henry A. du Pont serving as its president for the next two decades. Never a shy man, the colonel exercised his authority in this role to rename several of the stations, using local names as well as some with French connections in recognition of the du Pont heritage.

The 72.2 mile-long railroad began in Wilmington, operated five trains a day, and carried both passengers and freight. Delaware station stops included Lancaster Road, Greenville, Montchanin (DuPont), Winterthur, Guyencourt (Centre) and Smith's Bridge (Granogue), and in Pennsylvania Chadds Ford, Pocopson, and Birdsboro before ending at Reading, 9.1 miles away.[2] The name Guyencourt was chosen in recognition of Guyencourt, France, a small village of 250 inhabitants, seventy-five miles southwest of Paris, that was no doubt familiar territory to ancestors Pierre Samuel and Eleuthere du Pont.

Guyencourt, Delaware, is northeast of Wilmington between Kennett and Concord Pikes in New Castle County close to the Pennsylvania border. And though it shares a zip code with Greenville, residents often receive mail using Guyencourt as an address in the same way that some residents of Montchanin do.

This area, bucolic in the early 1930s, has kept much of its rural atmosphere. The train station has been converted to a private dwelling, but it is still very much an enclave of the landed gentry, hidden away from the flow of traffic on nearby Delaware State Road 92. It was this near-pastoral setting that appealed to Edith du Pont Riegel and her husband, Richard, when they chose a site for their country estate.

A daughter of Lammot and Natalie du Pont, Edith, nicknamed Skippy, was the great-great-great granddaughter of E.I. du Pont, founder of the DuPont Co. An attractive blonde, she was easily recognized around Wilmington, even by those who only knew of her. In 1996 *Forbes Magazine* named her as one of the four hundred wealthiest people in the United States.

For her twenty-first birthday, Skippy was given a Cadillac 452D V16 convertible sedan custom built for her. The model made its debut at the Chicago World's Fair of 1933. It was 240 inches long, the longest American car ever built, and weighed 6800 pounds. Coachwork was by Fleetwood and in the eleven years the model was offered just 4,076 were built. It could reach a speed of one hundred miles per hour. Base price of the 452D was $8150, equal to $104,000 in today's dollar, and it would now be worth an estimated $500,000 at auction.

The heiress would later buy a Chevrolet pickup truck for the sole purpose of plowing snow off the half-mile driveway from Guyencourt Road to her estate, a forty-two room mansion she and her husband built in 1934-35. They named their estate *Fiskekill* after a settlement along the Brandywine at the confluence of the Christina and Brandywine Rivers at Fort Christina.

The homesteaders included about sixty Swedes, Finns, and Dutch. These settlers are credited with introducing the log cabin to America. They called the creek "Fiskiekylen" or Fish Creek, using the Dutch word "kill" for stream and it was this name that the Riegels adapted for their mansion.

As architects, the couple selected Massena and duPont. The Wilmington firm also designed two houses for Pierre S. du Pont III, one in Westover Hills and a second one, *Bois des Fossés*, in Rockland, as well as the gatehouses for William duPont, Jr.'s *Bellevue Hall* and the Carillon Tower at *Nemours* for the young architect's father, A. I. duPont.

A curved driveway leads from Guyencourt Road to the estate's front entrance. On the left of the entrance a handsome bronze sculpture of a stag, cast by Unionville, Pennsylvania, sculptor Rikki Saunders, is in recognition of the change of name from *Fiskekill* to *Staglyn* made by new owners, Brock and Yvonne Vinton. Brock explains that they chose the name because of a stag frequently seen on the property as well as the numerous deer in the area. They have also placed an iron stag weather vane on the roof.

The three-story modified colonial house is built of fieldstone in shades that vary from ivory to dark brown, laid in a random pattern with quoined corners. Tile for the roof was supplied by Ludowicki Roof Tile in Lexington, Ohio, a firm founded in Rome in the seventeenth century and later moved to Germany before relocating to the United States. Meticulous records are kept by Ludowicki and they show that eighty-four squares of Georgian flat shingle tile were ordered for the *Fiskekill* project by Massena and du Pont on August 8, 1935, with an additional thirty-one squares ordered the next day for the garage roof. In later years the company supplied tile for the White House Promenade and the U.S. Air Force Academy.

Construction of the solidly built 16,000 square-foot house is steel frame with between eight and ten inches of concrete between each floor. It is positioned on a north to southwest axis. A vestibule at the front entrance was added by the Vintons that opens to the stair hall, seventeen by nineteen feet, with hardwood flooring laid in a herringbone pattern. To the right there are two steps down to a paneled office. Next to the office door an arched doorway opens to a service bar on the left and similarly two steps down to the living room.

The spacious living room, twenty-two by thirty feet, has a fireplace on the right with a wood mantle and black marble surround and hearth. The coffered ceiling was installed by Brock and Yvonne; floors are pegged, random width pine. French doors across from the fireplace open to a flagstone terrace overlooking the swimming pool and cabanas, and French doors on the southeast open to a solarium with a terrazzo floor. This room is flooded with light from windows that the Vintons have added on three exposures. From the solarium French doors open to a small terrace and balcony with steps down to a fountain and the open lawn.

The library is reached from the stair hall or by two steps up from the living room. Paneled in dark-stained pine, it has a fireplace and two windows facing the back lawn with built-in bookshelves on three walls. From the stair hall, an archway matching the living room entry leads to a passage with a barrel ceiling, from which French doors open to the dining room (twenty-six feet six inches by eighteen feet). There is a fireplace in the middle of the wall on the left and opposite it are French doors to the terrace. A pair of large crystal chandeliers hang over the dining room table, and to the right of the entrance, flanking a buffet, there are two built-in arched china closets with a shell design finished in silver leaf.

Walls of the stair hall, living room, dining room, breakfast room, and master bedroom were all hand painted by a team of three, headed by Brock Vinton's sister, Vicki Vinton, a professional painter specializing in decorative paint finishes. The project took six weeks to complete and there was no possibility of an extension of time, as *Staglyn* was the venue for the Vintons' wedding reception.

The living room walls were prepared with Venetian plaster in shades of butter yellow, then finished with a thin coat of polishing wax mixed with gold mica. In the dining room several coats of thinly troweled Venetian plaster were used in shades of gray and silver and finished with transparent gold plaster. Brock is an enthusiast of art from the Brandywine School and there are representative paintings in all of the major first floor rooms.

When *Fiskekill* was built, a butler's pantry separated it from the breakfast room. This has now been reconfigured as one large informal dining area with French doors that open to a patio and spacious grounds at the back of the house. The potting room and a large powder room with an ante room are still in place, though the kitchen has been completely redesigned and renovated to accommodate a contemporary lifestyle. The former servants' hall off of the kitchen is now used for informal gatherings. Its fireplace is one of four on the first floor.

There are fifteen bedrooms in the house and eleven-and-a-half bathrooms. During the renovation, master bedroom ceilings were raised two feet and additional windows and a balcony were added to take advantage of the morning sun. Walls of the master bedroom, once again hand-painted by the owner's sister, are glazed amber brown with a satin lacquer finish.

There is a full basement with a wine cellar, laundry room, cold storage room, mechanicals room, pool room, bar, and a recreation room that is of particular interest. The Riegels had a mural painted on all four walls of the recreation room depicting twenty-eight family members and friends in a western frontier setting. Figures are approximately three-quarters of full size. Five smaller figures decorate a passageway leading to the pool room.

On a wall near the entrance a painted "Wanted" poster features likenesses of two men identified as Paul Domville[3] and Jake Riegel. Beneath their portraits is the wording, "Wanted, at Wilmington, Delaware, For perpetrating a felony, Namely willfully, criminally and maliciously defiling the walls of the room in this residence, where you are now standing." Scenes on the walls of the room, all themed to the "wild-west," include a poker game, a group centered around a roulette wheel with stakes piled high, a bar scene complete with dance-hall girls, and an upright piano whose player is being watched with interest by another dance-hall hostess.

At the back of the house the swimming pool has separate cabanas for men and women. The greenhouse was constructed by Lord & Burnham, Irvington-on-Hudson, New York. The ten-car garage is built in a right angle that has four garages in one section and six in the other. Staff apartments are above.

One of the major additions by the Vintons was the building of a 3600 square-foot horse barn designed to match the house and garage. It includes a tack room and six stalls and is currently occupied by horses—Pierrot, "Finn" (Finneous P. McDust), "Niki" (Nekia), Rufus (Rufasa) and Bleu—and two pet donkeys.

Two annual events started by Brock and Yvonne are becoming traditions at *Staglyn*. A foxhunt takes place in October or November, with participation of between forty and fifty mounts and an equal number of guests. The colorful affair, held in association with the more than one hundred-year-old Radnor Hunt Club (Malvern, Pennsylvania), gets under way in early morning with the arrival of riders, horses, and hounds. Tracking begins about 11:00 in the morning and the chase lasts until somewhere around 3:00 in the afternoon. A traditional hunt club breakfast follows, though this can change. In a recent year the hosts chose "Burgers and Bordeaux" as a theme.

A second occasion, also involving horses, is a coach drive, usually held in April or May. The festive happening is organized by local artist, conservationist, and whip George "Frolic" Weymouth, internationally known for his collection of antique coaches and carriages. He initiated the coach parade at nearby *Winterthur* estate's Point-to-Point Steeplechase and has led it for thirty-three years. Between six and eight coaches join in the *Staglyn* parade, all brought from Weymouth's Big Bend farm.

When Brock and Yvonne Vinton bought *Fiskekill* it consisted of twenty-two acres; this has now been increased to forty-two acres. Included on the expanded property is a tenant building that brings *Fiskekill* and *Staglyn* full circle. The Riegels and the Swedes, who are credited with bringing the log cabin to this country, would be pleased to know that a log cabin dating back to 1840, brought from York, Pennsylvania, is now a prominent feature on the landscape.

Staglyn (Fiskekill)

Owners:	Mr. and Mrs. Richard E. Riegel, original
	Mr. and Mrs. Brock J. Vinton, current
Constructed:	1934-35
Architects:	Massena and duPont
Location:	Guyencourt, Delaware

Notes

1. *Delaware History,* Vol. XIX, Spring-Summer 1980, "Wilmington and Its Railroads: A Lasting Connection," Bruce E. Seely

2. Wilmington and Northern Railroad schedule, November 18, 1880

3. Paul Domville was a Canadian-born artist who received a degree in architecture at the University of Pennyslvania. He was known for the murals he painted in theaters, churches, banks, and private houses in the Philadelphia area. His collaborator, Jake Riegel, was the brother of *Fishekill*'s owner and an enthusiastic painter.

The Vintons are horseback riding enthusiasts and have four horses and two donkeys. To house them, they have built a horse barn with architecture matching the house and garage.

The spacious step-down living room has French doors opening onto a terrace that overlooks the swimming pool and cabanas. A door at the far end of the room leads to the conservatory.

The library has entrances from the living room and the stair hall. The richly paneled room has open library shelves on three walls and a fireplace. In most of the first floor rooms there are paintings representing the Brandywine School.

The dining room opens off a hallway next to the stair hall. The walls in the living room and dining room were decorated by Vicki Vinton, decorative finish specialist, a sister of the owner.

The lower level recreation room is unique. All walls are decorated with a mural portraying the original owners and their friends in a western setting.

The date on the west gable datestone of the original house is 1701. Additions were made in 1767, 1926, and 1986.

STRAND MILLIS

Oldest Delaware house west of the Brandywine River

A unique survival of William Penn's Quaker colony in the three lower counties on the Delaware, *Strand Millis* can trace its beginning back to 1685, nearly one hundred years before the country gained its independence. Originally the property was made up of 400 acres granted to William Gregg by Penn and was part of "Ye Manor of Rockland" in Christiana Hundred, a term meaning the land holdings of one hundred families. Gregg named his holding *Strand Millis*, translated as "Sweet Stream,"[1] probably because his property bordered the Brandywine Creek.

Gregg, who was born in Scotland, heard William Penn speak in Waterford, Ireland, in 1682 and converted to Quakerism. Later that same year, he emigrated from County Antrim, Ireland, to the Brandywine Valley with his wife, Ann, and their four children—Richard, John, Ann, and George. Three years later, after receiving his grant, he built a log cabin on the property, now destroyed, where according to William Gregg, his seventh generation grandson, "the only neighbors were rattlesnakes and Indians;" he lived there until his death in 1687.[2]

In 1694 his son, John, built the main house on the *Strand Millis* property, constructed of Brandywine granite found on or near the site. The design of the house follows the suggestion of a prototype in William Penn's prospectus for new settlers and is considered an important example of the Quaker style of building.

William Gregg, quoted above, goes on to say, "these men were called planters who owned their own plantations and with their slaves worked them profitably. Delaware was a slave state up to the Civil War. I remember my grandfather had two left, a mother and son. He freed them before his death."

Strand Millis was added to the National Register of Historic Places on July 16, 1973. According to that record, the Greggs were pioneers in milling and later in scientific agriculture. The document also mentions that members of the family owned mill seats at Strand Millis, Rockland, and Hagley.

The current owner, Dr. Ronald Finch, former Director of Historical and Cultural Affairs for the State of Delaware, thinks of *Strand Millis* as the Gregg house, even though through the years its ownership has passed through the hands of the DuPont Co., Henry A. du Pont, R.R.M. "Ruly" Carpenter (Knollwood Inc.), and Louisa d'Andelot du Pont Carpenter Jenney, before he acquired it. Dr. Finch's reasoning for keeping the original name lies in the fact that the Gregg family owned *Strand Millis* for over 200 years.

Being located within a half mile of the DuPont powder works meant the company was eager to acquire it as their business and land holdings increased. Despite repeated offers, the Gregg family refused until a major explosion damaged the house causing plaster on the walls and ceilings to crack, convincing them to leave. This was probably the explosion that occurred in the Upper Yard on October 7, 1890, the effects of which were felt two miles away. It was later estimated that as much as 150 tons of powder exploded and seven buildings destroyed. The Greggs are said to have accepted the DuPont offer the next day.

The *Strand Millis* property today is just short of thirteen acres (12.7) and there are four named buildings on it. These include the main house with approximately 5,000 square feet, the tenant house with 2,850 square feet, a bank barn, now called the gatehouse, with 1,535 square feet, and a four-stall stable with 1,000 feet.

The main house was completed in 1701 according to a datestone in place on the west gable. Additions were made in 1767, 1926, and 1986. The house is built on a north-south axis and backs up to the Brandywine Creek. It is two-and-a-half stories high with a wood shake shingle roof.

There are six dormer windows on the attic level—three at the front and three facing the river. Two bedrooms on the first floor of the original house were combined to form the living room. Originally there was a corner fireplace in each room, but these were removed by a previous owner and a fireplace of the period has replaced them. A previous owner had also installed casement windows that have been replaced with six over nine double hung windows.

The present dining room was at one time the kitchen and, while it has been completely renovated in keeping with the period in which the house was first built, electricity has not been installed in this room. On the second floor there are four bedrooms and three-and-a-half bathrooms.

At one time the east side of the house had been stuccoed. When Dr. Finch had this removed, the remnants of an original beehive oven were uncovered. This was reconstructed and is now fully functional. The trap door to the original root cellar is also still in place, though the original dirt floor has been replaced with hundred-year-old bricks originally used in downtown Wilmington sidewalks. Twenty-six foot-long rough hewn beams running the width of the 1701 house are still in place, some with original 312-year-old bark still on them.

The major structural change made by the Finches is the addition of a 900-square-foot great room that can be reached through an interior hallway or an outside door leading to this hallway. It is an extraordinary room with seven sliding glass doors that open to wrought iron balconies with southern, eastern, and western exposures; ceilings are twenty feet high. The centerpiece of the room is a walk-in fireplace built of stone salvaged from a Kent County, Delaware, bank barn. Embedded in the floor in front of the hearth area are two millstones made of French quartz from the Marne River Valley that had been used in mills on the Choptank River in Queen Anne County, Maryland.

During the time that R.R.M. Carpenter owned *Strand Millis* he gave it to his daughter, Louisa d'Andelot du Pont Carpenter as a wedding present when she married DuPont executive John King Jenney (July 20, 1929). Louisa hired main-line architect Richardson Brognard Okie to make a number of changes at *Strand Millis*. Well-known for his Colonial Revival style of architecture, Brognard designed five du Pont houses.

In the main house he designed a foyer that leads from the front door to the library on the left, the living room on the right, and a stairwell straight ahead. Brognard was also responsible for combining the two living rooms into one and added an enclosed porch on the west side of the house with steps leading to the driveway. The porch has since been reopened and the steps moved to the creek side of the house.

In addition to making changes in the main house Okie reconfigured the interior of the bank barn in order to convert it into a guest house, creating four guest bedrooms and four bathrooms. Dr. Finch has had this modified to create an apartment with two bedrooms, two-and-a-half bathrooms, a living room, kitchen, den, and laundry room.

Louisa du Pont Capenter Jenney was a free spirit and was in the vanguard of feminine liberation. She enjoyed pheasant hunting, horse breeding, and riding and was the first female master-of-the-hounds in the United States. She was also one of the first women to earn a pilot's license. But, it was her entertaining and the house guests who occupied her newly redecorated bank barn that provided the fodder for Brandywine cocktail chatter.

Among A-list celebrities who visited her were Tallulah Bankhead, Louise Brooks, Noel Coward, Greta Garbo, Clifton Webb, and Burl Ives. Closest of Louisa's friends was torch singer Libby Holman with whom she rented a ten-acre estate in Watch Hill, Rhode Island, a house in Palm Beach, and went sailing on the yacht owned by her mother, Margaretta du Pont Carpenter. Louisa was divorced from her husband in 1935. She died in 1976 in a crash of her private plane near Easton, Maryland, as she was preparing to land at the Wilmington airport.

The four-bedroom former tenant house is now occupied by Dr. and Mrs. Finch. Built c.1830, it has four bedrooms and three bathrooms, and was increased in size by the Finches, who had the former milk house connected to it that is now the library. It is also built of Brandywine granite and stucco. There are three dormer windows in the main part of the house and it has three chimneys and a hip roof with shake shingles.

In 2002, a Lenape Indian site was discovered on the property. Only four such sites have been identified in the Brandywine Valley in Delaware. With his keen interest in history, Dr. Finch reasoned that with the flat part of the property suitable for farming, its nearness to water and transportation, and with a natural spring nearby, it would have had an Indian site. Working with an archaeologist in an oval-shaped area 260 by 100 feet, over a period of several months he was able to determine that one had existed and uncovered a covey of arrowheads, now in the University of Delaware collection.

During the more than 200 years that *Strand Millis* was owned by the Gregg family, they purchased additional contiguous farms, increasing their acreage eastward to what was then the village of Rockland. More than 300 years after being established, the story of *Strand Millis* continues to unfold and enrich the history of the Brandywine Valley.

Strand Millis was added to the National Register of Historic Places July 16, 1973.

Strand Millis

Owners:	William Gregg, original
	John Gregg
	DuPont Company
	Henry A. du Pont
	R.R.M. Carpenter, Sr.
	Louisa d'Andelot Carpenter Jenney
	Dr. and Mrs. Ronald Finch, current
Constructed:	Log cabin, c. 1685
	Main house, 1694, completed 1701
Additions:	1767, 1926, 1986
Location:	Montchanin, Delaware

Notes

1. *Historical Notes on Old Belfast and Its Vicinity,* Edited with notes by Robert M. Young, Belfast 1896

2. *My Business Career*, William C. Gregg, 1933

The original fireplace is built of fieldstone found on the property. The duck decoys on the hearth are made of iron and weigh up to thirty pounds each. They were placed on the wings of sink boxes to keep them weighted down and at the surface of the water.

An allee of towering trees from the main road leads back to *Strand Millis*. The property backs up to the Brandywine and was at one time owned by the DuPont Company.

The four-bedroom tenant house was built about 1830. It has been extensively renovated and has been connected to the milk house with an addition. Other buildings on the property include a bank barn and stable.

The 1986 addition added 900-square-feet to the house that includes a twenty-foot high fireplace. In front of it are French quartz millstones from the Marne River Valley.

214

The collection of gunpowder and smokeless powder tins numbers about seventy-five. They date from the 1800s to the early 1900s and are decorated with ducks, dogs, and hunting scenes.

Upper Louviers was lived in by a succession of du Pont family members. In this photograph (taken between 1837 and 1865), Rear Admiral Samuel and Mrs. Du Pont are shown on the front porch. Credit: Hagley Museum and Library

The *Upper Louviers* tenant house and barn are still existent, situated between two holes of the DuPont Country Club. Credit: Photograph by author

UPPER LOUVIERS
(LOUVIERS UPPER HOUSE)

The house up the hill

The rutted lane leads off of Blackgates Road, flanked by golf holes eleven and thirteen on the left and twelve to the right, part of the DuPont Country Club's Nemours Course. Formerly a meticulously maintained driveway, it was the entrance to the gracious Greek Revival *Upper Louviers* mansion. Sadly the house was razed in 1978, though the cupola-topped tenant house and adjoining three-bay garage are still standing, paint peeling and in disrepair, a somnolent reminder of an era long gone. To the south white stakes and a stockade fence alert golfers that the remaining structure is out of bounds.

It wasn't always so. Originally a small thirty-five by thirty-two-foot stone farmhouse with a center hall and two rooms on each floor stood on the site. It was purchased by Eleuthere du Pont, probably in 1810 or 1811. At about the same time he was building a house for his brother, Victor, down the road and overlooking the Brandywine River, directly across from the company's powder mills. Victor chose the name *Louviers* for his house and lived there until his death in 1827; he also used the name for his woolen mill located below the house on the river's east bank just north of the Iron Bridge. Eventually the name was used for the surrounding area as well.

In its early years all housing was owned by the company and, following patriarchal practice, it decided where employees and their families should live according to their requirements. After Victor's death his widow, Gabrielle Josephine de la Fite de Pelleport du Pont, continued to live at *Lower Louviers* for six years, sharing the house with her son, Samuel Francis, her daughter, Amelia, and granddaughter, also named Gabrielle Josephine.

With the marriage of Samuel Francis to his first cousin Sophie, Eleuthere's daughter, Gabrielle believed that the newlyweds needed *Louviers* to themselves. With the company's blessing, she made plans to move to "the house up the hill," several hundred yards east towards Rockland Road, along with her daughter and granddaughter. To make her more comfortable the company made

a number of alterations to the farmhouse, including adding a two-story addition for a new kitchen, a dining room, a back hall, and additional bedrooms. The house also exchanged its colloquial name for the more formal *Upper Louviers.*

The name *Louviers* has been attributed to two sources. The printing shop operated by Victor's father faced the Ile Louviers and a small garden across the Seine. It was a sight Pierre and his sons saw frequently on their way to and from the shop and would have been indelible in their memory. The islet disappeared in 1849, when a channel was filled in, separating it from the mainland.

Another often-heard explanation is that as the town of Louviers, France, seventeen miles from Rouen, was a center of the wool industry with over forty mills and factories, that Victor thought this name would be appropriate for his woolen mill on the Brandywine.

Whichever story is correct, by having chosen to call his riverside mansion *Louviers*, Victor is credited for perpetuating the name in the Brandywine Valley.

Gabrielle died in 1887 and with DuPont's policy of moving families to houses on an as needed basis, several changes occurred. Gabrielle's daughter, Amelia, moved to *Rokeby* with her daughter (also named Gabrielle, who had married William Breck the year before). Samuel and his wife moved to *Upper Louviers* and brother Charles, also living at *Lower Louviers* with his wife, remained there while plans were drawn to increase the overall dimensions of *Upper Louviers*. It was during this period that the house metamorphosed from a simple dwelling into a distinguished residence.

The defining Greek Revival portico, supported by four Doric columns, was constructed at the circle drive entrance facing Blackgates Road. It had a sandstone floor cut in eighteen-inch squares set on a diagonal and edged in granite and was accessed by three steps that stretched between the two center columns. The double door entry was flanked by French doors on either side, leading to the parlor on the left and dining room on the right;

another set of French doors was installed on the west side leading to an open porch.

At the same time a third story was built with a flat gable roof. Ceilings were raised in the dining room, with decorative plasterwork and dado railing installed, and family bedrooms, a maid's bedroom, and two additional fireplaces with marble mantels were added.

Some time after 1837, Samuel Du Pont (in a departure from family tradition he capitalized the D), now a career naval officer, added two half-octagons at the back of the house overlooking the gardens, one for his study, later enlarged, and another for a pantry, the two connected by a conservatory. French doors were installed at this time opening from the stair hall to the conservatory. About 1850, a cast iron porch in the then popular grape vine design, topped with a pagoda roof, was built off of the kitchen and a water pump installed at the northwest corner of the porch.

The Du Ponts spent much of 1853 in New York, where Capt. Du Pont supervised construction of the New York Crystal Palace. The building was designed to house the Exhibition of the Industry of All Nations, considered to be the first World's Fair held in the United States. At 290 feet in height, it was the tallest building in New York City until it burned down one year after construction.

On a visit back to *Upper Louviers*, unaccompanied by his wife, who was ill in New York, Capt. Du Pont wrote her a letter extolling the beauties of the estate. So proliferous were the great variety of flowers in their blossoms and colors that it took him eight pages to describe them. "It is difficult to say what is the handsomest part of our grounds ... In the flower bed (at the front) is not one solitary inch of the ground to be seen, neither is there a weed in it. From the edge of the grass border to the top of the June roses, there presents itself an amphitheater closely packed with flowers of every hue, and of which no artistic gardener could improve," he enthused.

It is likely that Du Pont, with his and his wife's love of flowers, had the greenhouse built during this period. In front of it there was a bronze statue and marble bench that was placed there later, probably by Alfred I. du Pont for Alicia Maddox.

Samuel had a distinguished naval career and retired as a Rear Admiral. He was the first U.S. naval officer to command an armored ironclad ship—the USS *Montauk*, a single-turreted monitor; however, after a failed attack on Charleston, South Carolina, in 1863, he asked to be relieved of his command. He died in 1865, having lived at *Upper Louviers* for twenty-eight years. Dupont Circle, a traffic roundabout in Washington, D.C., is named for him. His widow, the last surviving child of E.I. du Pont, lived there alone for an additional twenty-three years, making a total of fifty-one years. The house was then occupied for six years by Captain Sidney Stuart, an army inspector for government-purchased black powder, until he was killed in a plant explosion in 1899.

More changes were made to *Upper Louviers* after 1901, when Mary Alicia Bradford, a great granddaughter of E.I. du Pont's, and George Maddox married and moved there. Second and third stories over the octagons were added, providing space for a bathroom, nursery, and bedroom on the second floor, and a sitting room, bathroom, and bedroom for the nurse on the third floor. Crystal chandeliers were hung in the parlor and entrance hall and carved wood mantels were installed above the fireplaces in these two rooms.

A decorative wrought iron gallery was added to the front porch at the second floor level and stone lions placed there by Alfred I. du Pont, who had intended to use them at *Nemours*, but changed his mind. A motto carved under the shields reads "Aimer et Connaitre," translated as "To Love and Understand." During this time the house was painted pink. Previously it was yellow similar to *Lower Louviers*, and during Admiral Du Pont's occupancy it had been white.

In 1914, with the threat of war looming, the DuPont Company expanded its operations across the river to the east side and a military unit was stationed at the plant. Soldiers were billeted in *Lower Louviers* to safeguard the black powder mills and a high wooden fence topped by barbed wire was constructed about half way between *Upper Louviers* and the lower house; it was patrolled on a regular basis. At the end of the war the soldiers departed immediately, the Brandywine powder mills were shut down, *Lower Louviers* was boarded up, and the fence removed.

After the Maddoxes divorced, Alicia moved to *Nemours* and Francis I. du Pont and his wife, Marianna Rhett du Pont, moved to *Upper Louviers* in 1918, living there until his death in 1942. Originally they used the house as a country retreat while maintaining their formal residence in Philadelphia. At a later date they lived at *Upper Louviers* the year round. Final alterations to the house were made by him in 1936 that included enlarging the octagonal study and adding a curved staircase.

A brick terrace at the back of the house was laid in 1959 at the direction of Mrs. du Pont, who remained in the house after her husband died. The bricks were antique and brought from New Castle pavements. Following her death in 1967, *Upper Louviers* was occupied by her son, Hubert, and daughter, Elise, until the 1970s. With their departure the house stood empty and unfortunately vandals began destroying the interior.

Elise du Pont Elrick, who wrote a detailed account of *Upper Louviers* in 1932 and revised it in 1970, described a railroad engine that Francis du Pont had installed at his former Wilmington house. "This is a proper engine with smoke stack, bell and cow catcher," she recalled. "It runs on a mining track, propelled by electric current in the rails, the throttle being in the cab to start and stop it." When Francis moved to Philadelphia he had the engine and track delivered to E. Paul du Pont on Buck Road for his children. After they were grown it was returned to Francis for his grandchildren's amusement and installed in a side yard at *Upper Louviers*.

Blackgates Road is a somewhat enigmatic street as it begins as a private road at the east bank of the Brandywine River and the Iron Bridge and becomes a public thoroughfare where it intersects with Rockland Road on the other side of two gate houses flanking the road. The address for *Upper Louviers* was simply Blackgates Road. At one time the entire area on the west side of Blackgates, extending to the woolen mill on the river, was referred to as Louviers and used as an address rather than Blackgates Road and a street number.

The *Upper Louviers* driveway entrance was on the left, approximately three-tenths of a mile west of Rockland Road towards the Brandywine. And, though the site is now surrounded by the DuPont Country Club golf course, some of the original oak, beech, and tulip trees are still in place, now grown into towering reminders of 200 years of family history.

The gatehouses on either side of the road are built of stone painted white and date back to the nineteenth century.[1] It is said that they were built at the direction of E. I. du Pont in order to give comfort to Victor du Pont's widow who felt isolated from her cousins across the river after she moved to *Upper Louviers*. They also provided some protection from strangers who might venture on to mill property. Each of the houses is eighteen feet square with a hip roof, originally wood shingle, and, when built, had dark green trim. On the Rockland Road side, they had centered round-headed windows set in an arch, but these have now been boarded over. Gateposts between the houses are also built of stone, stuccoed and painted white with dark green wooden caps. Treillage connected the houses with the gateposts.

The gates were made of wood and were originally painted either dark green, matching the trim on the houses, or black in reference to the Black Powder works; family lore supports each. In any case the gates no longer exist, though on the gateposts there are stern warnings against trespassing. At one time the houses had wood structures attached to the back side to increase the living space for its occupants. As the houses are no longer occupied, these were removed in 2010.

Mrs. Elrick ended her 1970 revised commentary about *Upper Louviers* with this plea: "Treat the house and all its memories with tenderness and respect." But, the supplication went unheeded and the house was torn down eight years later.

Upper Louviers

Owners:	Pierre Bauduy, original
	Eleuthere I. du Pont
	Gabrielle du Pont
	Admr. and Mrs. Samuel Francis Du Pont
	Mary Alicia Bradford and George A. Maddox
	Alfred I. duPont
	Mr. and Mrs. Francis I. du Pont
	Hubert and Elise du Pont Elrick
	DuPont Country Club, current
Constructed:	c.1802.
	Additions: 1833, 1837, 1901, 1936
	Razed 1978
Architects:	Alfred Victor du Pont and Charles du Pont
	Francis McIntire and Walter Carlson
Location:	Black Gates Road
	Rockland, Delaware

Notes

1. The gatehouses are considered to be on the National Historic Register of Historic Places as part of the Eleutherian Mills National Historic Landmark District. They are also listed on the *Historic American Buildings Survey, site DE-62.*

FRONT ELEVATION

LOUVIERS UPPER HOUSE

About 1850 a cast iron porch (right) was built off of the kitchen. It is likely that the decorative wrought iron railing over the front entrance was installed at the same time. Credit: Hagley Museum and Library

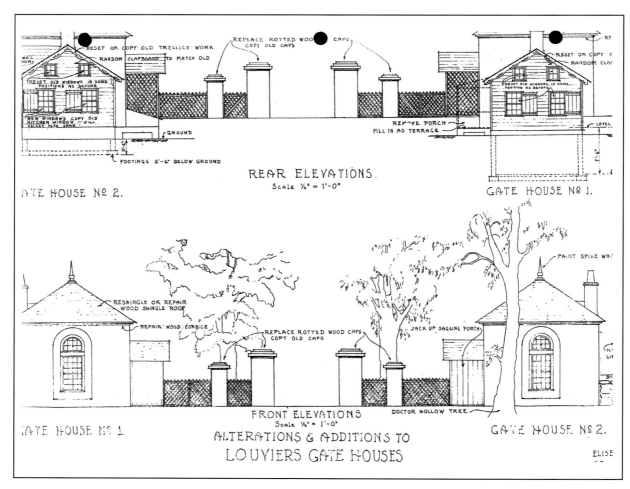

A detailed plan for rehabilitating the *Louviers* gatehouses was prepared by Elise du Pont Elrick c. 1970. Credit: Hagley Museum and Library

The *Louviers* gatehouses as they appeared in 2010. Photograph by author

Windmar is designed in Tudor Revival style, a popular style of architecture when it was built in 1906-1907.

WINDMAR

The only remaining house of seven neighboring du Pont estates

Approaching *Windmar*, a gently curving driveway lined with sixty-foot, round-shaped, scholar trees cautions drivers to slow down. But, there's another more visible warning: a roadside cutout of a blue mythical monster announces, "Dragon Crossing." Bemused double-takes are the usual reaction before proceeding onward; the explanation comes later.

Windmar is the sole survivor of a neighborhood once made up of seven du Pont estates bearing the legendary names—*St. Amour, Still Pond, Elton, Square House, Copeland House, Spanish House,* and *Windmar*. It was built in 1906-1907 by William Winder Laird and his wife, Mary Alletta Belin du Pont Laird. A successful banker and stock broker, Laird asked close friend L. Scott Townshend to join him in business. Three years later Townshend died, and afterward George Bissell and Hollyday Meeds joined the firm, known as Laird, Bissell and Meeds. It became one of the most prominent brokerage houses in the mid-Atlantic region.

Laird and his wife, who married in 1904, lived on nearby Kentmere Parkway while *Windmar* was under construction. The architect is somewhat uncertain. Blueprints for a later addition were drawn by Leon Wilde Crawford and hang in the entrance hall. The supposition is that his firm did the specifications for the original house as well; however, Mary Alletta was a talented designer and she may well have drawn the plans that were then supported by Crawford's technical expertise. Whichever is the case, *Windmar* is unique among du Pont houses. Its name comes from a contraction of Wind from Winder and mar from Mary.

David Craven, Laird's grandson, and now owner of the property, describes the architecture as modified English Tudor, commonly known as Tudor Revival, a style in great favor between the early 1900s and 1940. Typical of this style are centered arches, decorative half timbering and liberal use of diamond-paned windows, all of which are to be found at *Windmar*. Another often-found characteristic is an elaborate and large stacked chimney piece, prominently featured here above two dormer windows.

The house faces southeast and is finished in tan pebble stucco combined with hand-carved fish scale timbers that were originally brown. These have now been painted blue, the signature color of Winder Laird's daughter Wilhelmina (Mina) Laird Craven who lived at *Windmar* for her entire life of ninety-one years (1916-2008), inheriting the house from her parents.

As children Mina and her twin sister, Rosa, wore matching outfits—Mina in blue and Rosa in pink. Her preference for this color in everything from tennis court fencing to flowers to frocks, never changed. Known for her desire to have her own way about things, but also with a sense of humor, she was given the nickname, the Blue Dragon, hence the sign by the driveway, and she enjoyed having her grandchildren refer to her as "B.D."

Windmar has 13,000 square feet of living space. On the first floor are an entrance hall, living room, dining room, little living room, kitchen, butler's pantry, maid's dining room, porch room, and powder room. The porch room is so-called as it had been an open porch and was later enclosed for year around use. Walls downstairs have a stippled finish. There are seven fireplaces in the house and five chimneys. Floors downstairs are two-inch oak parquet over steel and the ceilings are ten-and-a-half feet high. All doors throughout the house have eight panels.

The term little living room is explained by the former library having been enlarged and converted to the present dining room, the former dining room being expanded and becoming the main living room and the former living room then being referred to as the little living room.

The new dining room was designed by Leon Wilde Crawford, mentioned above, and reflects other earmarks of Tudor Revival design—an asymmetrical floor plan and irregularly shaped rooms. *Windmar's* new dining room, positioned at an angle off of the little living room, faces northwest. It is a handsome space paneled in solid bookend walnut, unfortunately painted over by Mina who considered the room too dark. It is now off-white with her signature blue outlining the paneling, the diamond-paned window frames, and the brackets supporting the cornice, and covering the pilasters and baseboard.

The fireplace has a surround, possibly made of Mercer tiles, produced by the Moravian Pottery and Tile Works, Doylestown, Pennsylvania, that were at the height of their popularity at the time. The room could easily seat twenty-four at two tables. David Craven recalls his regular routine as a boy of arriving home from nearby Tower Hill School, going to his room to do homework, and afterward changing into jacket and tie for dinner.

There are seven bedrooms on the second floor and four on the third floor. A steel I-beam runs the length of the house and the three-inch by eight-inch cross beams are notched to fit into it. The house was originally heated by coal, but the heating system was upgraded to an oil furnace and later converted to gas. The basement laundry room had gas dryers so that laundry need not be carried upstairs to be hung outside, nor be seen.

Windmar's gardens were located behind a wall and off of the kitchen. They bore strong resemblances to the gardens at *Winterthur* and *Gibraltar* designed by Marian Coffin; however, there is no written reference to her having designed them. It is quite likely that Mrs. Laird, known as Aunt Mary by many in the family and Dookie (rhymes with bookie) by her immediate family, visited those gardens and adapted the designs that appealed to her for her gardens.

Mrs. Laird's gardens were laid out on two axes creating four quadrants with a fountain in the middle. The roof of the gazebo was made from rails that were originally part of the Wilmington and Northern Railroad spur line that ran from the Bancroft Mills, then the largest cotton finishing mill in the United States, to the Hagley Mills, part of the DuPont Company complex. David Craven recalls that his grandmother was particularly fond of roses, lilies of the valley, and gooseneck, a plant that produces a curved spike with white flowers. Though she had a full-time gardener, she liked to do much of the work herself. The Lairds had a chauffeur, but once again Dookie showed her independence and at times drove herself to *Louviers* on Blackgates Road where she tended the garden at Chicken Alley, having bought the two properties in "The 1921 Distribution."

And she was years ahead of her time with her automobile, an electric car with a handlebar for steering rather than a wheel; it had a maximum speed of fifteen to twenty miles per hour. A former handyman recalled that the Lairds always kept an extra battery charged up in the barn for Mrs. Laird. The barn, located in back of the house and now called the garage, had fourteen bays and was a combination barn and garage. Winder Laird's car had a license with the number 519, meaning that his was the 519th car to be licensed in the state at that time. When automobiles became more common, he obtained license plates for each child beginning with the number 130 and increasing sequentially.

The Lairds kept between fifteen and twenty cows. They grazed in the meadow between Brecks Lane and *Windmar* and were brought to the barn for milking. A trapdoor and winch are still reminders of a time when hay was lifted to the hayloft for storage and released to the dairy to feed the cattle. According to an oral history recorded by Mary Laird Silvia, the daughter of William "Chick" Laird, Jr., all employees who wanted milk could obtain it by going to the main house.

The garage has been modified to house very different automobiles than when it was built. David Craven has a collection of British automobiles that includes two Rolls Royces, a Jaguar, a Bentley, and an MG-TF sports car. They are all driven on a regular basis in order to maintain their charge and are available when needed. The garage is shared by his Bultaco Spanish racing motorcycle.

In addition to classic cars, David has maintained a keen interest in amphibious planes since his parents took him to Bermuda at the age of three and the plane splashed down for its landing in Hamilton Harbor. Following service as a pilot during the Vietnam War, he renewed his long ago infatuation with amphibians and purchased a Lake Aircraft LA4-180. During his ownership of the plane he flew the entire length of the U.S. east coast as well as from the Gulf of St. Lawrence to the Gulf of Mexico. Air controllers easily recognized his plane, comments David, by its "schoolbus yellow" color.

The Cravens raised English setters and Springer Spaniels, occasionally showing them. Though these are sporting breeds and can be used as gundogs, David says that they were raised as house dogs and that his father preferred Chesapeake Bay Retrievers for hunting. The kennels were located between the back of the house and the barn.

At the side of the *Windmar* garden is a gate leading to the property next door, *Still Pond*, the estate formerly belonging to Ethel Fleet du Pont, widow of William K. du Pont, younger brother of Pierre du Pont. *Still Pond*[1] was designed by architect Alfred Dilks and was reminiscent of *Nemour House (Old Nemours)*, William du Pont's boyhood home.

Mrs. du Pont was an enthusiastic gardener and specialized in raising iris, peonies, roses, dahlias, delphinium, and orchids. In 1926, she had a greenhouse built by Lord & Burnham especially for raising orchids and showed them in the Philadelphia, New York, Boston, and Washington flower shows. To transport her flowers, according to her daughter, Mrs. du Pont would borrow a horse trailer from one of her sons-in-law. The vans had to be well scrubbed to remove the smell of ammonia before she used one. Upon returning it, the sons-in-law would teasingly complain that the van smelled like flowers.

To showcase her orchids, Ethel du Pont had well-known ironsmith Samuel Yellin fabricate iron grill doors for the long living room windows at *Still Pond*. The Yellin Studio was preeminent in its field and at one time employed 250 workers and received commissions from Harvard and Yale Universities, the Metropolitan Museum of New York, and Washington National Cathedral in Washington, D.C. Brother-in-law Pierre was so impressed with the idea that it was later adopted by *Longwood Gardens* for displaying its orchids. Through the years other greenhouses were constructed for specific species and she was the first person in the United States to import tree peonies from Japan. Mrs. du Pont died in the Singapore Botanic Garden, which to her daughter was "a fitting end to a life of horticultural interest."

At 10:15 on the night of January 1, 1975, following New Year's Calling, a fire raged through *Still Pond*. It was believed to be caused by a broken gas line. There was a strong wind and though five fire companies in the Wilmington area battled the blaze, it could not be extinguished for two hours. Damage was put at over a million dollars and the twelve-bedroom stone house was completely destroyed and had to be demolished.

David Craven has since purchased the property. The greenhouses were given to a boy's school in Pennsylvania where they continue to be used for their intended purpose. The sole remaining feature of *Still Pond* is its handsome columned portico that stands in the shadows like a proud memorial to a time gone by, which it is.

Windmar

Owners: Mr. and Mrs. William Winder Laird, original
Wilhelmina Laird Craven
David L. Craven, current
Constructed: 1906-1907
Location: Greenville, Delaware

Notes

1. The name Still Pond, comes from a children's game, similar to Red Light, in which participants must remain in the position they are in when the leader calls out, "Still pond, no more moving."

Mrs. Wilhelmina Craven was the daughter of William Winder Laird and his wife, Mary Alletta du Pont Laird, and she lived at *Windmar* her entire life, ninety-one years. Her favorite color was blue, which was applied even to the dogs guarding her front door.

There are two living rooms at *Windmar* as a later addition brought about a re-arrangement of rooms.

When built, the dining room was paneled in bookend walnut. Following her preference for all things blue and believing it too dark, Mrs. Craven had the room painted off-white and the molding painted blue.

Known for her desire to have her own way about things, Mrs. Craven was given the nickname "the Blue Dragon," and encouraged her grandchildren to call her "B.D.," a name she found amusing. With this in mind she was given a doorstop with a blue dragon done in needlepoint.

Stillpond was the home of Mrs. William K. du Pont, sister-in-law of Pierre du Pont. During the night, after New Year's Calling in 1975, the house was completely destroyed by fire. Only the columned portico remains.

Winterthur was built in 1842 and was a private home to three generations of du Ponts before it became a museum and was opened to the public in 1951.

WINTERTHUR

An American country estate

Since 1951, *Winterthur* has been a museum housing an extraordinary collection of American antiques made between 1680 and 1840, rivaled, though not equaled, by the Metropolitan Museum of Art. But for 114 years, from 1837 until 1951 it was a home, albeit an extraordinary one, of three generations of the du Pont family.

The property on which *Winterthur* was built was at one time part of the farm operation of DuPont Company founder Eleuthere Irénée du Pont. His second-born daughter, Evelina (Lena) Gabrielle du Pont, married Jacques Antoine Bidermann in 1816 and they lived at Hagley House, originally built for a mill director. Bidermann was a business associate of du Pont's, and, when Eleuthere died in 1834, he acted as head of the company until his brother-in-law, Alfred Victor, became senior partner. Three years later four farms acquired by E.I. were put up for sale and in 1837 he and Evelina acquired 450 acres and began making plans for building their home.

As the site for their house the Bidermann's chose a part of the estate known as the Clenny Farm which had a small brook running through it called Clenny Run, named for William Clenny, who owned the property before it came into the du Pont family. The twelve-room house was Greek Revival in style, a square structure, three stories high with a window on each side of a porte cochere located on the north side and at the back a conservatory porch. It was built of brick with a stucco finish, popular in France at the time and used at both *Eleutherian Mills* and *Louviers*. Evelina and Antoine lived in a small farm house built for them while waiting for the main house to be constructed. When it was completed in 1842, they named it *Winterthur* (Door of Winter), for the Swiss town in which Antoine was born.

The Bidermanns lived happily at *Winterthur* for twenty-two years. Soon after moving there, they planted a kitchen garden and later a flower garden and orchard. In the years following, a gate house, greenhouse, carriage house, ice house, barn, dairy, and stables were added, as well as a water wheel and pumps to fill a reservoir.[1] Livestock included horses, cattle, pigs, and poultry—chickens, turkeys, and ducks. Over a period of time five small houses for employees and tenants were built. Evelina and Antoine died within two years of one another (1863 and 1865) and the property was inherited by their only child, James Irénée, who by then lived in France and was not interested in returning to the Brandywine.

Two years later, in 1867, James sold *Winterthur* to his uncle, Henry du Pont ("Boss Henry" or "Henry the Red," so-called because of his red beard) who lived at *Eleutherian Mills*. A West Point graduate and a partner in E.I. du Pont de Nemours & Co., Boss Henry was head of the firm for thirty-nine years, longer than anyone else in the company's history. His land holdings covered 1,135 acres and a later purchase of 800 more made him the state's largest landowner. Later acquisitions of some twenty farms increased the *Winterthur* holdings to 2,400 acres, or four square miles, including what is now Brandywine Creek State Park and the property of the Wilmington Country Club and Methodist Country House.

In 1874, Henry the Red made his only son, Colonel Henry Algernon du Pont, an autocratic Civil War hero, overseer of *Winterthur*. Soon after, he and his new wife, Mary Pauline Foster, took up residence. Henry and Pauline had two children who survived to adulthood, Louise, born August 3, 1877, and Henry Francis, born May 27, 1880.

Even before moving to *Winterthur*, Colonel du Pont had in mind several changes he wished to make. Among these were the addition of a second bathroom, relocation of a fireplace, and the creation of an archway in the hallway on the ground floor.[2] For suggestions as to how to accomplish the changes he engaged the services of his brother-in-law, Philadelphia architect, Theophilus P. Chandler, Jr., who designed Lammot du Pont's Philadelphia house and who also worked with Pierre du Pont at Longwood.

Ten years later further alterations dramatically changed the exterior appearance of *Winterthur*. A steep slate roof replaced the original flat roof, and an attic was added in addition to dormer windows and tall brick chimneys. Henry Algernon's final remodeling in 1902-03 altered the original house plan significantly, making it much more grand than its original owners could have envisioned. A new facade and porte cochere were added on the north side as part of a three-story addition and the entrance hall took on a stately appearance with the installation of an elegant marble staircase, later replaced by the 1822 Montmorenci circular staircase.

Other changes included the addition of a library on the second floor, a billiard room on the first floor, and a squash court in the basement. A new first-floor drawing room was built that combined the Colonel's office and the former parlor. Simultaneously, the dining room was enlarged by joining it with a small sitting room. Spanish tiles replaced the slate roof, wood cornices gave way to terra cotta ones, and new dormers were installed. To support the additional weight most of the original walls needed to be replaced.[3]

When Henry Francis's mother died, he was enrolled at Harvard's Bussey Institute which offered a curriculum based on horticulture and agriculture. Never a good student, he was tutored after graduating from Groton School in order to gain admission to Harvard. His chief interests at the time were flowers, music, and collections that included stamps and birds' eggs. Henry (Harry) was devastated by his mother's death and abandoned his plan of continuing on at Harvard to pursue graduate work.

Perhaps in an effort to continue his connection with his mother and with the approval of his father, who was by now serving in the U.S. Senate and spending most of his time in Washington, Harry took over his mother's household duties: supervising the staff, approving menus, ordering uniforms and special foodstuffs, determining changes in decoration, and managing the gardens. It was this latter activity that brought him closest to her as he redesigned Pauline's rose garden, rebuilt the greenhouse and added two more. At the same time he was experimenting with different species and planted fifty varieties of daffodils.

On annual trips to Europe with his father, Harry visited numerous gardens and museums, all the while increasing his knowledge of interior and garden design. His daughter, Ruth Lord, recounted in her book, *A Daughter's Portrait*,[4] that it was on these trips that her father "stepped up his horticultural pursuits ... (showing) ... the beginnings of real scholarship, fueled by growing excitement in the field." In the early 1900s, he began to order plants in huge numbers from such sources as Kew Gardens in England. One thousand Golden Spur daffodils and 500 tulips of two varieties are examples Lord cites.

The Colonel began to recognize Harry's ability in this direction, prompting him to place his son in charge of all of *Winterthur's* grounds. "Harry responded," Ruth Lord writes, "with a dramatic surge of activity ... he began to plant 'the March Bank,' for which he ordered an astounding 29,000 bulbs ... the next year he ordered 39,000 more bulbs."

At the same time as Harry was developing as a horticulturist, he was also increasing his interest in a young female acquaintance named Ruth Wales. In 1912, she attended seven house parties at *Winterthur*, but it was not a whirlwind courtship. Harry did not propose to Ruth until May 5, 1915. A year later, on June 24, 1916, the couple was married in Hyde Park, New York, and departed on a three-month-long, cross-country wedding trip. Harry was thirty-six and Ruth twenty-seven.

The *Winterthur* farm operation, begun under the Bidermann ownership, had declined over the years as politics took over the Colonel's interest. By 1914, in recognition of Harry's outstanding job of managing the estate gardens, he also turned over the responsibility of *Winterthur Farms* to his son. It was a wise decision and one Harry accepted with enthusiasm, giving him the opportunity of combining his interests in horticulture and agriculture fostered by his studies at the Bussey Institute.

"With his father's blessing, he began an intensive search ... for the best specimens of Holstein stock available."[5] And, on the way home from their honeymoon, he arranged to visit herds in Nebraska, Minnesota, and Illinois. As manager of the agricultural activities at *Winterthur*, Harry was determined to produce the finest specimens of livestock available. Accordingly, he established farms specializing in one specie, i.e. sheep, hogs, beef cattle, horses, turkeys, and one for 2,000 chickens.

His primary interest, however, was in his quest for Holsteins that could deliver milk with the highest butterfat content. In order to increase this, Harry raised Jersey and Guernsey cattle that had a much higher butterfat content and mixed their milk with the Holstein milk. The Colonel supported his son's endeavor and is supposed to have remarked, "Well, it won't cost as much as a yacht and it might do something for humanity." His cows set records for milk production, producing more than 1,000 pounds each on a monthly basis.

Cows were sensitive to the men who milked them and it was important that the same workers milk the same cows every day, otherwise they might hold back some of their milk. A few of the *Winterthur* cows were so productive that they needed milking four times a day. The men wore uniforms and were instructed to shower daily, then an unusual practice.[6] At one time seventeen men were employed exclusively for milking. In 1931 milking machines were installed.

Because of a split in the Republican party, a Democrat was elected in 1916 and Colonel du Pont's term in Washington ended, resulting in his increased involvement in estate affairs and greater interest in Harry's farm operation. Blacksmith, carpenter, paint, and butcher shops were added, in addition to separate barns for calves, heifers, and steers. Six barns were built for wintering young stock. In 1917, an enormous dairy barn, 319 feet by forty feet, was built and, by 1923, at the peak of production, there were 450 in the herd.[7]

A commercial operation was put into place with deliveries to individuals as well as the *Hotel du Pont*. Harry's sister, Louise, left a standing order when she was in residence at *Eleutherian Mills*. It consisted of five quarts of milk per day, one-and-a-half pints of cream per day, five pounds of butter every third day, and one pound of sweet butter per week.[8]

All food consumed at *Winterthur* was raised there with the exception of spices, coffee, tea, and similar items. The orchards grew apples, peaches, and cherries, and the vegetable garden covered five acres. During winter, ice was harvested from the duck pond and stored in ice wells lined with straw. After ice machines were invented the duck pond became a social gathering place for workers who lived at *Winterthur*. On Farm Hill there was a club house with a stage where parties and theatricals were held by employees. There was also a farm band and an employee baseball team.

In 1923, Harry and Ruth visited the home of Electra Havemeyer Webb in Shelburne, Vermont. The trip was planned to study the cattle-breeding operation of her father-in-law, but the couple made an impromptu visit to see Electra's collection of American

The swimming pool, now converted to a reflection pool for insurance purposes, was the setting for the debut party of Harry and Ruth du Pont's daughter, Pauline Louise. Credit: Photograph by author

On Saturdays in spring and summer, classic cars are parked at the front entrance of *Winterthur*, evoking times when the du Ponts invited guests to their home for weekend festivities. Credit: Photograph by author

Magnolia Bend includes many species. Sargent cherry trees, lavender in varying shades, viburnum, and roses are all represented.

Spring at *Winterthur* begins when thousands of daffodils begin to bloom, some yellow, some white. They are a harbinger of spring and as fleeting as the season itself – gone before the advent of summer. Credit: Photograph by Steve Boyden

decorative arts. On the same trip, they made a side visit to interior designer Henry Davis Sleeper's summer house where they saw rooms decorated with doors, windows, fireplaces, and paneling rescued from American houses being demolished. The two visits changed the du Ponts' lives.

Three years later, Harry and Ruth built a fifty-room Georgian Colonial house on 6.2 acres on Meadow Lane in Southampton, New York, and Harry decided the couple should complete the interiors in the same way Sleeper had. To this end Harry started buying old houses, several of them, from the eastern shore of Maryland, and salvaging their interiors, some of which he used in the Meadow Lane residence that he named *Chestertown House*. To furnish the house he began filling it with 18th century antiques, some 1,900 over a two-year period, including furniture, china, textiles, and paneling.[9] On December 31, 1926, the Colonel died. Harry, who had spent his entire life at *Winterthur*, and who considered *Chestertown House* a summer retreat, was now master of the Delaware estate. It was a liberating and challenging time for him, but not one for which he was unprepared.

Harry and Ruth had discussed the idea of making *Chestertown House* into a museum of early American antiques, not during their lifetime, but after they died. With the Colonel's death, Harry realized that *Winterthur* would be a more suitable location for the interiors he was collecting. The years after his father died were devoted to planning, remodeling, and building, described by Ruth Lord as "an explosion of activity."

Having watched his father rebuild and substantially increase the size of *Winterthur* when he was in his early twenties, Harry was undaunted about doing the same thing. He hired architect Albert Ely Ives to design a nine-story, 130-room addition that increased the size of the house to 175 rooms. Five hundred workmen labored from 1929 to 1930 to accomplish the feat. European-style details incorporated into the 1902 renovation gave way to Palladian windows, Federal facades, and Colonial cornices to more accurately complement Harry's collection of American antiques.

E. McClung Fleming describes the major changes to the former house as being removal of the former conservatory and construction of a new one, relocation of the main entrance and replacement of the Spanish roof tiles with more simple ones and the dormers with a more traditional design. Changes were also made in landscaping close by the house including stairways, retaining walls, terraces, walks and construction of a large swimming pool flanked by two bath houses.[10]

In 1929, du Pont purchased all of the quoins, stone window sills, and interior woodwork from the 1762 Port Royal house in Frankford, Pennsylvania. These were installed in what became the entrance, parlor, and a bedroom of the new wing. Henry was so pleased with the results that, from this point on, his collection became an obsession and complete interiors, furniture, and fixtures were gathered from east coast houses scheduled to be razed. Acquisitions were made from Massachusetts to Delaware, Virginia to South Carolina.

New room installations and additions to the building were ongoing between 1931 and 1951, and Fleming says that by 1946 fifty-six new period rooms and hallways had been completed. With plans firmly in place for *Winterthur* to become a museum, twenty-two final room installations were made. Today there are a total of 175 named period rooms and spaces with architectural settings that provide a context for the collections of paneling, furniture, paintings, rugs, wall coverings, china, glassware, metalwork, needlework, furnishings, and artifacts.

The rooms represent every period of American antiques beginning with the 17th century and continuing through the William and Mary (1700-1725), Queen Anne (1725-1760), Chippendale (1760-1790), Federal (1785-1840), and Empire (1815-1840) periods. Soon the collection outranked the American Wing of New York's Metropolitan Museum and buyers at Americana auctions knew they needed deep pockets if Henry du Pont was in the bidding gallery.

As period rooms were completed, the family used them just as any family would their own rooms. And while thoughts of making the house into a museum no doubt had their genesis at *Chestertown House*, no room was considered "off limits." Harry and his wife, especially the latter, took the value of the collection more or less in stride, though their daughter Ruth Lord tellingly recalls that at *Chestertown House* canopied beds and quilted bedspreads "were never to be sat on." She also recounts the story of a guest breaking a valued glass bottle, with Harry hastening to assure the guest that it didn't matter and then promptly fainting.

Harry and Ruth led a structured life at *Winterthur*, though it was not organized in a way familiar to many people. Their life was luxurious, lavish, and sophisticated. Everything was planned and carefully staged. Ruth Lord commented in her book that her parents had a lot in common and "moved heaven and earth to guard against uncertainty. Order and orderliness were crucial to their lives," she said.

When guests arrived, they often brought their own staff and all plans were made before their visit. Arrivals, activities, all meals, and entertainment—music, bridge, recitals, movies, monologues, bowling, swimming, tennis, golf, croquet, badminton, squash, walking, skeet shooting, farm visits, riding—were planned in advance. Golf was played on Harry's private nine-hole course (now expanded and called Bidermann Golf Course).[11]

Weekend house guests could number thirty or more with arrivals scheduled about tea time. For the evening meal, guests assembled for cocktails before dinner, then joined their host and hostess, who at dinner sat across from one another in the middle rather than at the ends of the table.[12] Flower arrangements were purposely designed so that conversation across the table was difficult. Guests were expected to talk with persons on their left and right, following Ruth's example of first chatting with the person to her left, then turning to the person on her right. A favorite number for dinner, often black-tie, was twenty-two and a footman in white tie stood behind each guest chair to serve and be of assistance.

Both Ruth and Harry were passionate bridge players and it was a favorite after-dinner activity. First-run films, shown in the badminton court adapted as a movie theatre, were also popular. All guest breakfasts were ordered the night before from cards placed on their beds and served in their rooms the next morning.

When the du Pont's daughter Pauline Louise made her debut June 26, 1935, 125 guests were invited for dinner around the pool at eight-thirty, with other guests invited later for dancing. The party ended at four-thirty in the morning. Fifty employees from the estate helped with parking cars, and guests were announced as they descended the steps from the terrace to the pool. It was a beautiful clear and starry night, but a striped and decorated tent had been set up along Clenny Run in case of rain. Three hundred gladioli decorated the pool area with colored lights and balloons in the trees.

Dinner started with jellied bouillon and fairy toast (white bread, trimmed, toasted, spread with butter and decorated with colored sprinkles), followed by cold salmon, followed by creamed chicken and fresh mushrooms, new peas, and rice croquettes, with ice cream and assorted cakes and petits fours for dessert. Swimming was encouraged with bathing suits in various colors and sizes available in the bathhouses whose Art Deco interiors Ruth Lord described as "splendidly garish"—shiny chrome and magenta porcelain for the ladies', chartreuse and black for the men's. A diving act provided entertainment before supper served at midnight. Harry was an opera buff and classical music was regularly played through speakers built into the wall between the bathhouses.

Ruth Ellen's debut party in September 1939 was on a smaller scale, as war threatened; the caterer was warned that in case of war the party would be canceled. Still, 400 were invited for a dinner dance. Guests entered the Port Royal Hall where they were received by Ruth Wales and Ruth Ellen, then ushered to the conservatory. The dining tent was decorated in green and white with masses of flowers banked around poles, while the dancing tent was pale pink with a fuchsia dance floor and pink and blue streamers fluttering from the poles. The walk from the conservatory to the dancing tent was lined with pale blue silk and twenty fruit-bearing peach trees. Harry described it as "really quite ravishing."

The three most important things in life to Harry were his house, his farm, and his gardens, and they all intertwined. With the March Bank, Harry delved into the realm of progressive blooming, a theory of gardening practiced by British landscape gardener Gertrude Jekyll, in which flowers bloom in succession during the year. At *Winterthur* this begins in January with snowdrops, continuing into April when the daffodils ordered from England start to bloom.

After the March Bank, Azalea Woods is the best-known of the *Winterthur* gardens, begun when a blight destroyed the chestnut trees first planted there. White, pink, red, and salmon azaleas are complemented by white flowering dogwood with rhododendron near by. Other themed gardens are Magnolia Bend, Winterhazel Walk, the Sundial Garden, Sycamore Hill, the Pinetum (planned by Harry and his father together), Enchanted Woods, a children's garden, the Reflecting Pool (former swimming pool) Garden, and the Glade Garden. The last garden Harry planned was the Quarry Garden, situated in an abandoned quarry that had supplied the stone used in building *Winterthur's* walls.

At one time there were 450 employees (including thirty-four household servants) and ninety houses and residences at *Winterthur*. These are now all painted tan and numbered. Dormitory arrangements were made for single men and women and married couples all had individual houses. Single men ate in a dining hall at night with food prepared by wives of employees. The men were charged for the number of meals they ate during the month and the money was then distributed to the women who prepared the meals.

The original gatehouse and entrance to the estate from Kennett Pike was just past the entrance to the Wilmington Country Club going north. The gate was operated by a turning wheel in the gatehouse similar to a ship's wheel. In 1867, when Henry's father was president of the Wilmington and Northern Railroad, a railroad station was built on the property and a post office opened in the same building. A post office still operates on the property, though in a different location. *Winterthur* has ten miles of paved roads.

During the period that the DuPont Company controlled General Motors, most of the family owned cars it manufactured. Ruth drove a Buick, Harry owned a sixteen-cylinder Cadillac with the du Pont crest emblazoned on the rear door. After DuPont's divestiture of General Motors stock, Harry bought himself a Rolls Royce though he never learned how to drive.

As Harry had planned, in 1951, *Winterthur* took on its new role as a museum open to the public. The bowling alley was reconfigured as a lane of shop fronts and the squash court was adapted as a village square. He and and Ruth then moved to the *Winterthur Cottage* they built across from the museum. Though the house was considerably smaller, the family's routine of Summer in Southampton, Autumn weekends in New York, Winter in Florida, and Spring at *Winterthur* never changed. And until he died on April 11, 1969 Harry coveted his title as "Head Gardener."

Winterthur

Owners:	Jacques Antoine and Evilina Bidermann, original
	Henry du Pont
	Henry A. du Pont
	Henry F. du Pont
	Winterthur Museum & Country Estate, current
Constructed:	1839
Additions:	1902, 1929-31
Location:	Kennett Pike
	Winterthur, Delaware

Notes

1. *History of the Winterthur Estate*, E. McClung Fleming, *Winterthur Portfolio*, Vol. 1, 1964

2. *The Architectural Development of Winterthur House*, Jonathan L. Fairbanks, *Winterthur Portfolio*, Vol. 1, 1964

3. *The Building of Winterthur Museum*, Henry F. du Pont, *Winterthur Illustrated*, 1963

4. *Henry F. du Pont and Winterthur, A Daughter's Portrait*, Ruth Lord, 1999

5. *Ibid*

6. Tom Maddux, *Winterthur* guide, June 29, 2011

7. *Discover the Winterthur Estate,* Pauline Eversmann with Kathryn H. Head, the Henry Francis du Pont Winterthur Museum, Inc., 1998

8. *Winterthur Farms* order confirmation dated October 6, 1925, Hagley Museum and Library

9. *Chestertown House* was kept until Henry du Pont's death in 1969. Contents of the house not sent to *Winterthur* were auctioned off. The house was sold to Baby Jane Holzer, who defaulted on the mortgage, and finally in 2003 to Calvin Klein who had it demolished in 2009.

10. *History of the Winterthur Estate*, Fleming.

11. The course opened officially in 1929 at a family gathering. Spread over eighty acres, the course consisted of nine holes and 6,480 yards of fairways. It took a staff of seven men to care for the course in summer. Devereaux Emmet was the golf course architect. *Discover the Winterthur Estate,* Eversmann and Head.

12. Henry du Pont kept detailed records for sixty years of the menus served at *Winterthur* and on which of the fifty-eight sets of china the meals were served.

Henry A. du Pont, Henry Francis's father, decided to establish a Pinetum as a source of changing colors the year around, from spring blossoms to dense evergreens.(opposite)

English Regency was selected as an architectural style for the cottage in order to separate it from *Winterthur* and its collections of American furniture.

WINTERTHUR COTTAGE

A past preserved

Henry Francis and Ruth Wales du Pont left *Winterthur* in January 1951, and their new house across from the museum was ready for them in October. "There were not too many backward glances, for life in the evolving museum had become increasingly difficult," daughter Ruth Lord recalled.[1] Her mother confirmed this in a letter to a cousin, Montgomery Hawks (November 3, 1951). "I think once we get organized we shall be much more peaceful than in such a big place as we were previously," she wrote.

The du Ponts' sentiment was expressed 140 years before by Robert Ferrars in Jane Austen's 1811 novel, *Sense and Sensibility*. "I am extremely fond of a cottage;" he said, "there is always so much comfort, so much elegance about them." It summed up Henry Francis's (Harry's) credo exactly, and he left the museum with a feeling of pride and accomplishment. The museum was officially opened to the public October 30, 1951, with an appropriate ceremony.

To design the new house Harry consulted a longtime friend, Thomas Tileston Waterman. An architectural historian as well as architect, Waterman established his national reputation through his work at Williamsburg and he and Harry had worked together since 1932. *Winterthur Cottage* was designed in the period between July 1 and August 15, 1950. As its site Waterman and du Pont chose the spot that had first been occupied by the Antoine Bidermann farmhouse overlooking Clenny Run.

The architectural style selected for the *Cottage* was English Regency as it was to be decorated and furnished, in a complete departure from *Winterthur*, with European antiques. From the du Ponts' New York apartment, French and English furniture that had been in storage for years was put into place in the new dwelling and was described by Ruth Lord as seeming, "very much at home."

After living in the 175-room *Winterthur* mansion, almost any house would seem considerably smaller, though its description, made by Harry's wife, Ruth Wales, to another correspondent as "sweet and not too big," might seem a bit strange to most homeowners. The *Cottage* has fifty rooms, is ninety-four feet six inches wide by 127 feet six inches long, and has 21,345 square feet on three levels with two elevators. Exterior construction is stone and stucco.

The new house was located directly across from the *Winterthur Museum*. The entry floor is black and white marble and immediately to the left of the front door are a powder room and cloakroom. Facing the front door is a centered staircase constructed by Savery & Cooke, a Wilmington iron fabricating shop. The railing is natural mahogany and bannisters are painted white. Six steps lead up to a spacious entrance hall twenty-seven feet wide and fifty-four feet long painted pale gray to set off the English and French antique furniture and oriental carpets brought from New York.

At the far end is a double-wide entrance that led to the dining room which had a mirror on each side of the doorway. On the right side of the hall is the entrance to the conservatory flanked by pairs of Tuscan order columns topped with Ionic order capitals. The conservatory floors are verdigris marble veined with white, and an outside door opens to a flagstone terrace. When Henry and Ruth Wales lived here, the southern exposure was heavily planted with year-round greenery, and rattan furniture was used to create an informal atmosphere.

At the top of the stairs and to the left, a twelve foot by twenty-four foot passage leads to the former drawing room. An elevator is on the left as you enter the hallway and just beyond are steps down to the cloakroom. Two large bow windows in the drawing room overlook Clenny Run; beside them a double-hung window also looks over the stream. At the east end of the room two windows face the museum. Furniture was from the Louis XVI period (1774-92) and included a pair of arched-back sofas purchased in the 1920s for the couple's New York apartment.

The fireplace on the wall across from the bow windows has a white wood surround with tiles showing figures in oriental dress; above the fireplace there was a mirror framed in gold leaf. The hearth is white marble. Framed murals of country scenes were on three walls, one with a cottage by a river, another with two houses in a rural setting, and a third of a forest scene with a bridge across a stream. Each evening cocktails and canapes were served in the drawing room by two footmen.

A double-wide doorway opens to the Green Parlor, or family room, that can also be reached from a doorway in the entrance hall where it was flanked by torcheres and a pair of side chairs covered in antique needlepoint. A table with an iron stretcher was laden with coffee table type books and a pair of Chinese vases. Above the table was a large tapestry depicting a French chateau.

The family room (thirty by fifty feet) had walls covered with multiple coats of dark green lacquer, Henry's favorite color. Bow windows match those in the former drawing room. A pair of antique vases and a clock were on the mantle and over the fireplace was a portrait of Ruth Wales and elder daughter, Pauline. On the wall opposite there was a Steinway grand piano above which was a portrait of Henry Francis, now hanging in the museum. Ruth Wales was an accomplished pianist and composer, who could play by ear or from sheet music and could entertain guests according to her daughter by "belting out songs music hall fashion."[2] A card table, with French, straight-back chairs, upholstered in a floral fabric, was set for a game of bridge. Both Henry and Ruth were avid bridge players and score-pads were kept at the ready.

The dining room, overlooking Clenny Run, is twenty-seven feet wide by forty-two feet long and is at the far end of the entrance opposite the stairway. An adjoining flagstone terrace is reached by a door from the dining room. Framed French tapestries, woven at the royal factory at Aubusson about 1770, depicted courtiers in tête-à-têtes and whispered conversations. A set of eighteen Thomas Chippendale chairs were made for the first Lord Melbourne in 1773; other furniture was primarily Louis XVI.

The doorhead carving and molding surrounding the doorway on the dining room side are the most elaborate in the *Cottage*. For dinner parties a footman stood behind every other chair to assist with serving. A staff of eighteen was employed in the household. Following the death of Ruth Wales, the table was always set for four even though Harry often dined alone, and he continued to dress for dinner.

Twenty sets of china were rotated for daily use. Table settings were planned around what flowers were available from the greenhouse with china matched to the flowers. At times there were as many as five arrangements on the table. The du Ponts had one hundred sets of place mats with matching napkins and successful combinations cross-referenced by flower type and china pattern were recorded in notebooks kept by Harry's secretary.

Favorite foods remained much the same as at *Winterthur* with luxury fare that included caviar, lobster, and terrapin. Unlike at the big house, terrapins were not kept in the basement. Food supplied from the collective *Winterthur Farms* included dairy products, beef, poultry from the farms, fruit from the orchards, vegetables from the gardens, and grapes, oranges, and figs grown in one of the estate's twenty-seven greenhouses.

A stairway from the entrance hall leads up seven steps to a landing and what was called the mezzanine level with a bedroom suite, and continues twelve more steps to the third floor bedrooms. On the basement or lower level there was a children's recreation room with pine floors, a brick-floored room used for entertaining, a wine cellar, silver polishing room, laundry, china storage room, work shop, and a room for the heating system.

In February 1961, First Lady Jacqueline Kennedy invited Henry Francis to head the twelve-member Fine Arts Committee charged with redecoration of the White House. Mrs. Kennedy considered the project to be one of restoration and by placing Henry du Pont, a recognized authority on American antiques, as head of the committee, she felt that its decisions could be made without challenge. At the same time she relied on New York decorator Sister Parish and French interior designer Stephane Boudin for advice. Mrs. Kennedy was particularly impressed by Boudin's treatment of the Red and Blue Rooms in the presidential mansion and gave him increasing control over the project, though credit was often given to the committee.[3]

While Henry du Pont acquired hundreds of important antiques for the White House and was always asked for his opinion, it is believed that it was Boudin whose opinion the first lady most valued. It is also reported that du Pont was allowed to arrange furniture in the rooms undergoing restoration as he wished, but that upon his departure the head usher was told to reposition it as it was.

Henry and Ruth Wales loved to entertain, both at *Winterthur* and the *Cottage*. Other notable guests at the *Cottage*, indicating the du Pont's broad spectrum of interests, included Prince Ranier of Monaco, philanthropist and socialite Brooke Astor, Brandywine artist Andrew Wyeth, and in May 1961, Jacqueline Kennedy, who flew to *Winterthur* in the Kennedy private plane for lunch and an early dinner with two members of the Fine Arts Committee. The du Ponts' first party in the new house was held in the conservatory on October 30, 1951, the evening of the museum opening.

Once settled into the *Cottage,* Harry continued planning for the future. A large piece of property was sold to the Wilmington Country Club and across from the entrance gatehouse other acreage was sold to the Methodist Country House, a retirement home.

In 1963 one hundred and forty-one acres were leased to form the Bidermann Golf Club that incorporated the *Winterthur* course in its plan. A major tract of land extending from Rockland Road on the south to Thompson Bridge Road on the north was given to the state of Delaware to create Brandywine Creek State Park. These transactions reduced the *Winterthur* holdings from 2400 acres to nine hundred and eighty-three.[4]

Ruth died in 1967 and Harry continued his life as a country squire, maintaining his interest in the Holstein cattle that had won so many awards, making notes about garden changes, and, in one instance, approving the purchase of a Georgia interior to complete representation at *Winterthur* of rooms from the thirteen original colonies.

In 1968, at the age of eighty-eight, Harry planned a trip to the United Kingdom and Ireland with longtime friend, Joseph Sweeney, curator emeritus of *Winterthur Museum*. It was du Pont's first flight and he prepared for it by having his luggage packed six weeks in advance, and one of his two Rolls Royces sent ahead with his chauffeur so they would be at London's Heathrow Airport to meet him.

At the Pan American Clipper Club at Kennedy Airport, Harry created considerable interest by having his longtime footman, Louis, serve him breakfast from the buffet. To make certain that nothing would go wrong, he and Sweeney traveled to New York in his smaller Rolls Royce the day before the flight, followed by another car with Louis in case there should be a problem on the road.

Upon arrival in England, du Pont had Sweeney fill out his debarkation card as he was having trouble with his eyes. When asked whether to put down "Industrialist" as his occupation, Harry replied, "No, I'm a farmer." A four-room suite had been reserved at Claridge's: separate bedrooms for du Pont and Sweeney, one for the butler and chauffeur, and a sitting room.

The two men traveled to Belfast, Bodnant Gardens, and Portmerion in Wales, the Royal Horticultural Gardens at Wisley, Winchester, Bath, Sezincote House in the Cottswolds, and Kew Gardens in London. In Ireland they had lunch with Wilmington friends, Bruce Bredin and his wife, Tibi (Octavia du Pont), at their house in Celbridge in County Kildare, and in Dublin they attended the Dublin Horse Show several times. Upon his return Harry declared the trip a great success and said, "Flying is the only way to go to London."

Winters were spent in Florida and in April 1969 he became ill while at his home in Boca Grande. Concerned that it might become a final illness, a friend flew him back to Delaware. Unsure of his surroundings, he asked his longtime butler, Maurice Gilliand, if he was at *Winterthur.* Assured that he was, he died peacefully the next day (April 10). When asked what du Pont's life at the *Cottage* was like, Maurice answered with what could have been Harry's epitaph, "He lived like a Sun King," he proclaimed.

A four-day auction of furnishings from the *Cottage* was held by Samuel T. Freeman, Philadelphia auctioneers, November 11 to 14, 1974. The sale total was $343,093. Twenty years later on October 14, 1994, 265 lots from the *Cottage* were sold by Christie's Auction House in New York in a one-day sale that totaled over two million dollars. The *Cottage* is now the location for the museum store, plant store, and offices.

Winterthur Cottage

Owners:	Mr. and Mrs. Henry F. du Pont, original
	Winterthur Museum & Country Estate, current
Architect:	Thomas T. Waterman
Constructed:	1951
Location:	Kennett Pike
	Winterthur, Delaware

Notes

1. *Henry F. du Pont and Winterthur, A Daughter's Portrait,* Ruth Lord, Yale University Press, 1999

2. *Ibid.* Pg. 98

3. *New York Times,* January 21, 2009

4. *Discover the Winterthur Estate,* Pauline K. Eversmann with Kathryn H. Head, the Henry Francis du Pont Winterthur Museum, Inc., 1998

Principal rooms of the cottage were accessed from the entrance hall. The Green Room
was to the left, the dining room straight ahead and the conservatory to the right of the
stairway. Credit: Courtesy, The Winterthur Library: Winterthur Archives

The Green Room, also called the living room, was the center of social activity. It was painted this color and given this name because it was Henry Francis's favorite color. Credit: Courtesy, The Winterthur Library: Winterthur Archives

The dining room overlooked Clenny Run. It was decorated with Aubussson tapestries woven at the factory.
Credit: Courtesy, The Winterthur Library: Winterthur Archives

The Conservatory was just off the entrance hallway, where it could easily be seen. It was always filled with plants in full bloom grown in the estate greenhouses. Credit: Courtesy, The Winterthur Library: Winterthur Archives

Xanadu is situated on the Hicacos Peninsula of Cuba. When Irénée du Pont, Sr. purchased 180 hectares of property, it was undeveloped, but had five miles of pristine beach. Credit: Hagley Museum and Library

XANADU

Paradise found: a du Pont mansion on Cuba's Hicacos Peninsula

When Irénée du Pont, Sr., reached the age of forty-nine, he decided to retire as president of the DuPont Company and divide his time between his Delaware estate and a warm weather destination. Rather than head to Florida as many of his relatives did, he chose a place ninety miles southeast of Key West and eighty-seven miles east of Havana: Varadero Beach, Cuba, on the northern coast of Matanzas Province.

Today Varadero is an international destination for Canadians and Europeans, though vacationing in Cuba remains difficult for most Americans. In 1927, when du Pont visited there, it was an undeveloped jungle ringing the rocky Hicacos Peninsula on Cuba's north shore. His purchase of 180 hectares on the peninsula included five miles of beach-front property, but instead of building a house there, he selected a site on the San Bernardino crags looking over the sea, albeit with the convenience of an elevator installed later to reach the soft, white sand.

The peninsula had no water, roads, or electricity when du Pont arrived there, but with his engineering background and the expertise and bilingual attributes of Cuban architects Covarrocas and Giovantes, the mansion was soon deserving of the name he bestowed upon it: *Xanadu*. The appellation was inspired by the opening line of Samuel Taylor Coleridge's "Kubla Khan" poem: "In Xanadu did Kubla Khan a stately pleasure-dome decree."

Xanadu was designed to have all of the comforts of home—meaning Granogue, Delaware. Surrounded by a stone wall and entered through an iron gate, a two-lane road leads to the twenty-room mansion. *Xanadu* is three-and-a-half stories high with eleven bedrooms and adjoining bathrooms, has three large terraces, seven balconies, and a private dock that accommodated guests' yachts. There was also an extensive wine cellar. Rocking chairs and wicker chaises longues on the verandas invited guests to relax before and after dinner.

Mahogany for the beamed ceilings, paneling, stair rails, and columns was brought 400 miles from Santiago de Cuba, in the southeastern part of the island, and marble for floors and bathrooms was from Italy, Spain, and Cuba. Furniture and fixtures included stunning chandeliers and Spanish period furniture with a number of custom-made pieces. Carved woodwork in the ceilings and balconies, geometric patterns in the floors, and arched doorways were among the decorative features.

Du Pont was especially fond of his music room (living room) at *Granogue* and wanted a room with a similar atmosphere at his Varadero Beach house. Accordingly, he ordered an Aeolian organ for installation in the living room at *Xanadu* that was reputedly the most expensive organ in Latin America. Music was piped through two shafts to the altana (covered roof garden) from the organ's basement location. At mealtime, guests could listen to favorite international selections. After dinner in the mansion's coffered ceilinged altana, there was lively dancing to the Cuban *son*, from which the salsa was derived.

At *Granogue* international artist and illustrator Maxfield Parrish had created a mural that was placed in back of the carved organ screen. Du Pont was so pleased with this that he decided to install similar artwork in the salon at *Xanadu*. Frank Schoonover was a part of the Brandywine School of Art, just as Maxfield Parrish was, and both had studied with Howard Pyle at Philadelphia's Drexel Institute. Schoonover's illustrative technique was similar to Parrish's and du Pont believed that his work would fit in perfectly at his new hacienda.

On March 24,1931, after *Xanadu* had been finished, Irénée wrote to Schoonover saying, "I have considerable wall space on the south side of the Living Room of my house in Cuba which should have a large picture hung on it. I think it would be particularly appropriate were this picture to represent a sea fight involving

Spanish Galleons or Pirates because the site of the house was an old rendezvous for Pirates two hundred years ago. ... I imagine the size of the painting would be five by eight feet."[1] Later that year, du Pont invited the artist to sail with him to Cuba on the *SS Moro Castle* to see the estate. In an oral interview, Schoonover later said that he believed it was the ship's last crossing from New York to Havana before it burned on September 8, 1931.[2]

As a result of their meeting, Schoonover accepted a commission for two paintings. Du Pont confirmed their agreement in a letter dated December 29, 1931.[3] He wrote that one painting was to be placed in the living room over the fireplace and to be the same size as the organ grill opposite, for the sum of $1,000. The other painting ordered for the "wall behind the piano" was to cost $2,000.

The artist worked in his studio in Wilmington for two years to complete them. Schoonover numbered all of his paintings. *Capture of the Galleon* was No. 2001 and measures 66.75 inches high by 108.5 inches wide. *Pirates Picnic Ashore* was No. 2000 and is 108.5 inches high by 66.75 inches wide. Schoonover's oral history identifies the painting as *The Party Ashore* or *Pirates Picnic Ashore*. This painting depicts pirates on the Island of Mindanao (Philippines, Land of Promise) being entertained by a continuous feast and dancing girls on a sailcloth, one from the Sargasso Sea. As a thank you to du Pont for his hospitality while in Cuba, Schoonover painted a water color of *Xanadu*, No. 1886, eight inches by seventeen inches.

Du Pont was delighted with the paintings and they were installed at *Xanadu* in 1934. His pleasure was also evidenced by the fact that for a Christmas card he had the *Pirates Picnic Ashore* painting reproduced as a jigsaw puzzle with "Merry Christmas from Granogue" imprinted across the image.

It took a staff of 150 to maintain *Xanadu* and the capital investment of the property was estimated at two million dollars. In 1963, it was valued at three million dollars. The cost to run it annually was $125,000, or in today's dollars about $1,250,000. Irénée referred to it as his "most expensive indulgence."

The *Xanadu* gardens were planted with tropical flowers, vegetables, and papaya, avocado, coconut, and banana trees. On a visit in January a friend from Delaware wrote a card saying, "My room looks out on the garden and," she exclaimed, "we had fresh okra for lunch!"

Irénée du Pont's chef at *Xanadu* was Johannes J. Wintels, who began working at *Xanadu* in the mid-1930s and remained there until the estate was taken over by the Castro regime in 1959. He and du Pont enjoyed a warm relationship and Irénée referred to him as "El Maestro." Wintels' granddaughter, Maggie Littleton, says that among favorite foods he prepared for his employer were sea-grape jelly made from sea-grapes grown on the estate, mango chutney, and liver pate with truffles. "El Maestro" was famous for his pastries and surprised Mr. du Pont every day with a special dessert. After Fidel Castro took possession of *Xanadu*, Maggie relates that du Pont moved the Wintels family to Wilmington for several years, and that he established a trust fund for his former chef that lasted until his death.

Another story Maggie Littleton shares further shows Irénée's compassionate nature. Along the water's edge at *Xanadu* there were caves and in one of them a reclusive man dwelled in solitude. Called "El Grillo Gallego" (the free-loading cricket) by the household staff, du Pont had no problem with his being there,

and from time to time would take food from the kitchen to the old man. Dressed in his favorite old shorts and tattered shoes, du Pont could almost have been mistaken for a cave-dweller himself. In another cave, near the seventh hole green of the *Xanadu* golf course, he provided nourishment of a different sort. When his house-guests were playing a round of golf, Irénée made sure that a secreted ice chest was filled with La Tropical Cerveza to quench their thirst.

A common sight and source of entertainment for guests were Irénée's pets, described as "an armada" of iguanas, that seemed to have free rein. According to an account written in 1951 by Gerald Street[4] a friend of Irénée du Pont's, "They lived in caves along the golf course and vary in size from a little over a foot long to slightly over four feet from nose to tail. ... They recognize food by color, preferring yellow food." The largest of the iguanas was a male, mistakenly named Bouncing Betty, who was taught to jump when food was held at shoulder height, keeping just the tip of his tail on the ground. "There are," Street wrote, "about twenty iguanas around the golf course, about five near the house, and an equal number in the garden."

The property grew in size to about 1,325 acres. A private landing field was added to the property and an eighteen-hole golf course designed by English-born golf course architect Herbert Strong, considered one of the best golf architects in the United States. The course was completed in 1931, but after being hit by a hurricane two years later that swept away greens and fairways, it was re-designed as a nine-hole course.

Irénée, Sr., greatly enjoyed entertaining friends and relatives at his Cuban estate, including his son, daughters, sons-in-law and DuPont Co. executives. Son Irénée, Jr., recalls bringing friends during a spring break from Dartmouth College. Nor were celebrities ignored. Ernest Hemingway, Cary Grant, Esther Williams, and Ava Gardner were among those who visited and sunned themselves on the Varadero beach, then, mojito in hand, sought the shade of its towering palms. In the 1930s and into the pre-Castro days, Havana was known as "the Paris of the Caribbean" and Varadero was its "St. Tropez."

Du Pont spent about four months a year at *Xanadu*. His last visit was in March 1957. Fidel Castro came to power in 1959 and in 1961 it was confiscated by his government.[5] Today the estate operates as Varadero Golf Club. Hotel reservations are accepted at *Xanadu* for the six rooms now available and meals are also served to outside guests.

"Kubla Khan" ends with the lines. "For he on honey-dew hath fed, And drunk the milk of paradise." At du Pont's *Xanadu*, the milk seemed to be in endless supply.

Xanadu

Owners:	Irénée du Pont, Sr. original
	Republic of Cuba (Republica de Cuba), current
Constructed:	1928-1930
Architects:	Covarrocas and Giovantes
Location:	Varadero Beach, Republic of Cuba

Notes

1. Letter dated March 24, 1931, Irénée du Pont to Frank E. Schoonover

2. Oral History between Frank Schoonover and his son, Courtland Schoonover. Delaware Art Museum Manuscript Collection

3. Letter dated December 29, 1931, Irénée du Pont to Frank E. Schoonover

4. *Recent Observations of the Iguanas, Xanadu, Cuba,* by Gerald B. Street, 1951

5. After Fidel Castro took power, several former *Xanadu* employees fled to Florida and Sophie du Pont May, oldest daughter of Irénée du Pont, Sr., provided them with pensions.

Irénée du Pont hired Frank Schoonover to paint a mural for the south side of the *Xanadu* living room.
As a thank you for the commission and du Pont's hospitality in Cuba, Schoonover gave him a painting
of *Xanadu*. Credit: Courtesy The Frank E. Schoonover Fund, Inc.

Xanadu was sited on the San Bernardino crags with its veranda looking over the sea, a perfect place for reading and relaxing.
Credit: Hagley Museum and Library

The richly paneled entrance hall had a coffered ceiling, marble floor and custom-built furniture.
Credit: Hagley Museum and Library

Irénée du Pont was fond of entertaining and his diversified guest list included his son's friends from Dartmouth College, corporate friends from the DuPont Company, Ernest Hemingway, and Cary Grant.
Credit: Hagley Museum and Library

Frank Schoonover's mural painting, *Pirates Picnic Ashore*, measured five feet by eight feet and dominated the south side of the living room. Credit: The Frank E. Schoonover Fund, Inc.

EX LIBRIS

XANADU

Irénée duPont

In addition to his painting of *Xanadu*, Frank Schoonover designed a bookplate for du Pont. Credit: Hagley Museum and Library

Appendix 1

THE SIEGE OF GUYENCOURT

When thunder cracks the summer sky,
With lightning's savage light:
Though safe abed, the children dread,
Such terror in the night.

From ballads sung to calm the young,
Wise mothers oft resort,
To one they know from long ago,
"The Siege of Guyencourt."

This day of doom has dawned in gloom,
Its skies foreboding ill;
When through the pall, a trumpet's call,
Now echoes, hill to hill.

Those castle bound too hear the sound,
Alarums rouse the fort;
As brave men ring the battlements,
To stand for GUYENCOURT.[1]

The outposts go before the foe,
And now the die is cast;
As DOGWOOD, DOGGONE, LETDOWN fall,
Defended to the last.

A signal lights on CUBA'S heights,
Relief is on the way!
Can LONGWOOD, HAGLEY, and GRANOGUE,
With RENCOURT, save the day?

To GUYENCOURT its allies march,
Full sworn to raise the siege;
As each man vows, if fate allows,
To honor lord and liege.

WAGONERS ROW and DILWYNE,
Join ROCK SPRING'S grenadiers;
And now contend, in waves on end,
The bridge below LOUVIERS.

From GOODSTAY and GIBALTAR ride,
To shouts of "Au secours!"
A fresh brigade, with ELTON'S aid,
To VALMY and NEMOURS.

FAIR HILL, RIDGELY, ROKEBY, all
With FOXWOOD now combine:
As one they halt each new assault,
Amid the bullets' whine.

Now CROOKED BILLET, OBEROD,
BOHEMIA MANOR too;
Advance their way to RANDALEA,
To gain the rendezvous.

On they charge, through each barrage,
To ELEUTHERIAN MILLS;
From ST. AMOUR and WINTERTHUR,
From HEXTON, TULIP HILL.[2]

POINT LOOKOUT now and FISKEKILL
Greet CALMAR'S musketeers;
As LIMERICK, at double-quick,
Joins FAIRTHORNE'S fusiliers.

Has BOIS DES FOSSÉS fallen too?
Has OWL'S NEST been sacked?
Has STILLPOND gone and now CHEVANNES?
Will SQUIRREL RUN be attacked?

Before MEOWN the wounded groan,
Beneath an angry sky;
Past YELLOW HOUSE and SHADOWBROOK,
The troops keep streaming by.

As BUENA VISTA rallies now,
At INVERGARRY'S side;
Hostile ranks assail their flanks,
Can PELLEPORT turn the tide?

Saved from loss is APPLECROSS,
STRAND MILLIS bars the way;
WINDMAR too now strives anew,
As PATTERNS joins the fray.

The arsenal at SQUARE HOUSE,
Explodes with fearful din;
Defenses fall at BELLEVUE HALL,
And DAUNEPORT burns within.

At GUYENCOURT, with each report,
All hopes of rescue fade;
As round on round, the skies resound,
In crashing cannonade.

At last the allies stand as one,
Their cannon in support;
A noble force of men and horse,
Now! on to GUYENCOURT!

A hail of shells the siege dispels,
As heroes spurn defeat;
Now ends the fray. We win the day!
The foe's in full retreat.

A mighty shout sweeps each redoubt,
And castle banners wave;
As maidens' cheers replace their tears,
For GUYENCOURT is saved!

The heavens clear, the stars appear,
As strife to order yields;
And battle's roar is heard no more,
Across the tented fields.

Our tale is clouded in the past,
And though the elders try;
It now befalls that none recalls,
Just who fought whom, or why.

Yet still today, when storms display,
Their terrifying show;
A fearful sight to rend the night,
'Tis good the children know:

That thunder, lightning fill the sky,
To herald, fort to fort;
A day again of gallant men,
"The Siege of Guyencourt."

> *Gordon Rust*[3]
> *January 1, 1973*

Notes

[1] Though Guyencourt is the subject of the poem, there is no evidence that there was a house by that name. It is a residential area north of Wilmington and shares the same zip code as Greenville. Population 2300.

[2] The house owned by Samuel and Victorine Homsey was named Tulip Hollow. It appears that Rust used poetic license in calling it Tulip Hill in order for it to rhyme with the second line of the verse.

[3] Gordon Rust was married to Francis du Pont Morgan Rust and they lived at Fair Hill in Pennsylvania, (mentioned in the poem), just over the Delaware border. As the DuPont business prospered and the family grew, their houses became larger as well, most of them referred to by name rather than street address. Within a twelve mile area, from the Brandywine River and Rising Sun Lane, extending north along Kennett Pike to Centreville and west to Red Clay Creek, were some ninety du Pont houses, fifty-four of which are mentioned by Rust in *The Siege of Guyencourt.* Copies of the poem were distributed at the 1973 New Year's Day Calling. (see Glossary)

Appendix 2

GLOSSARY

"Houses of the best taste are like clothes of the best tailors
—it takes their age to show how good they are."
— Henry James

Alicia. The name of Alfred I. duPont's first yacht. Purchased in 1910, it had been launched in 1902 as Coranto. DuPont renamed it *Alicia*, after his second wife. When it was sold, he sent the crystal and china back to Tiffany & Co. to have the name *Alicia* removed and replaced with the name of his new yacht, Nenemoosha.

American Country House (Place) Era. Late 1800s to mid-1940s, a time when the U.S. economy was enjoying a great growth spurt resulting in huge profits for those in top management giving them the opportunity to build expansive (and expensive) country estates and second homes.

American Eagle. The barely seaworthy schooner that brought Pierre Samuel du Pont and 12 family members to America. It left Rochelle, France, October 1, 1799, and arrived in Newport, RI, January 1, 1800, after a 91-day voyage (Christopher Columbus made it in 70 days). The ship was built in 1795 in Haverhill, Massachusetts. In 1964, Pierre S. du Pont III used the name for his 64-foot racing schooner entry in the America's Cup races. The eagle also has patriotic connections and is popular as a symbolic motif in many du Pont houses in forms including door knockers, sculpture, overdoor carvings, and even the hitching post at *Eleutherian Mills*.

barley mill. The barley mill, for which Barley Mill Road is named, was built in 1826-1827 by Samuel Kirk (Kirk Road) with financial help from E.I. du Pont. The miller's house was built at the rear of the mill and is still existent. The mill burned in 1897 and was not rebuilt.

Belted Galloway. A breed of hornless Scottish cattle distinguished by a broad stripe encircling their mid-sections. A herd of them grazes contentedly on Center Meeting Road across from the former Meown estate, built by Rodney Sharp for his wife Isabella (Bella).

Bidermann Golf Club. Located on Adams Dam Road between Routes 92 and 52. Originally the private golf course of Henry Francis du Pont; designed by Devereux Emmet. Named the Winterthur Golf Club, it opened in June 1929 with Henry as its sole member. In 1963, the Winterthur course was incorporated into a 40-acre tract of land donated by cousin, Emily, an avid golfer. It then became an 18-hole course designed by golf course architect Dick Wilson, later modified by George Fazio. The combined course was opened for play July 4, 1965. Another cousin, Bayard Sharp, gave Bidermann an additional 10 acres in the 1990s. The *Winterthur* estate leased 141 acres to the club for 50 years in 1963. The lease has now been extended until 2050. At Henry du Pont's suggestion the course was named for James Antoine Bidermann who built and named *Winterthur*. Membership is capped at 240 members.

Black Gates Road. A street beginning at the banks of the Brandywine Creek and the Iron Bridge and extending up the hill through the Black Gates at Rockland Road and on to Mt. Lebanon Road. It is a private road from the gatehouses to the Iron Bridge. The street name comes from black gates that at one time were in place between columns at Black Gates and Rockland Roads.

black powder. Black powder is the product on which E.I. du Pont based his business. It is a mixture of three components: potassium nitrate (75 parts), sulphur (10 parts) and charcoal (15 parts). In the 1800s it became standardized as 15/2/3. DuPont was the largest manufacturer in the world. Its Eagle brand of black powder was the premier brand.

Blue Ball Barn. Built by Alfred I duPont in 1914 as a dairy barn, it was a working part of the *Nemours* estate. Situated on the southwest corner of Rockland Road and Concord Pike, it was named for the Blue Ball Tavern that formerly occupied the site on the turnpike and was identified by a white post with a blue ball mounted on top. It is an element of the Nemours Historic District.

blue rock/Brandywine blue bock. According to Winterthur Museum, blue rock should be called Brandywine blue gneiss. When first quarried it is bright blue to blue-gray in color, which led 19th century stonecutters to call it Brandywine blue granite or blue rock. Gneiss is a metamorphic rock with a banded composition; granite is unstratified igneous rock. The rock was used extensively by the du Ponts in both construction of houses and in building the walls seen throughout the Brandywine Valley. It appeared 55 to 1.6 million years ago when the new Appalachian Mountains were formed

Bois des Fossés. Name of home of Pierre Samuel du Pont de Nemours, near the village of Chevannes, about 60 miles from Paris. Translated as "wood of the trenches," a reference to 2,000-year-old Roman trenches still visible on the property. Pierre S. du Pont III adopted it as the name for his Rockland Road estate.

Brandywine blue rock *(see blue rock)*

Brandywine Creek (River). A confluence of two streams, east and west, that come together in southeastern Pennsylvania forming a river 60 miles long that flows into the Christina River with a fall of about one thousand feet from stream to tidewater. In a space of 25 miles it falls farther than Niagara Falls' great drop. At the Delaware line it encounters ridges of hard granite and at Brandywine Gorge a series of rapids for four miles resulting in a superabundance of water power vital to operating 18th and 19th century mills. At one time there were said to be over 100 mills operating on the Brandywine, the majority of which were flour, textile and paper mills and, with the arrival of the du Ponts, powder mills.

Brandywine Creek State Park. At the intersection of Routes 100 and 92, the main entrances are on Adams Dam Road and Thompson Bridge Road. The section west of the Brandywine River was at one time part of the *Winterthur* estate farms. The stone walls within the park were built by DuPont workers who regularly worked at the powder mills and during down times were assigned to other projects.

Brandywine Hundred/Christiana Hundred. Established 1682. According to the Delaware Genealogical Society, "a hundred" is an old Saxon division of land originally comprised of the land holdings of 100 families. In Delaware "hundreds" once served as judicial districts, though they are now used primarily as the basis for tax assessment and their names still appear on all real estate transactions. Delaware is the only state that currently uses this division. There are 33 hundreds today. Brandywine Hundred is the portion of New Castle County that lies north of the Christina River and east of the Brandywine Creek. Christiana Hundred runs from the Pennsylvania border to the suburbs of Wilmington and from the Brandywine River to Red Clay Creek. Du Pont houses are located in both Brandywine Hundred and Christiana Hundred.

Brandywine Powder Mills Historic District. From the late 18th century through 1921 the mills were in continuous production of black powder, which was used from the War of 1812 through World War I as well as in major building projects such as the Erie Canal. The DuPont Company evolved into the largest supplier of black powder in North America and contributed significantly to the industrial and technological history of Delaware and the nation. Listed as a National Historic Landmark and on the National Register of Historic Places.

Brandywine River boats. During the 1880s the trip by railroad from Wilmington to Philadelphia was hot and uncomfortable. In 1885, the Wilson Line inaugurated a river trip as an alternate means of transportation between the two cities. Though it took longer, it was cleaner, quieter and cheaper. The one-way fare was 15 cents, round trip was 25 cents. In a few years its popularity increased and a second riverboat was put into service, the *City of Chester*.

Brandywine Valley. The Brandywine Valley extends from south of Wilmington (New Castle County) north to Pennsylvania. The Valley then follows the Brandywine River north to Chadds Ford (Delaware County), and west to Kennett Square (Chester Country). It is noted for its magnificent scenery—rolling hills, glorious gardens, and open tracts of land, as well as its superb estates, many of them owned by members of the du Pont family—all of which combined have earned it the name, "Chateau Country." *See* Chateau Country.

Breck's Mill. A brick and limestone building situated on the west bank of the Brandywine River between Rising Sun Bridge and the entrance to Hagley Museum. Built in 1813, it was originally a cotton-spinning mill. In 1832 Breck's Mill was sold to Charles I. du Pont who converted it to the manufacture of woolen goods. It now houses art and sculpture galleries, as well as the Montchanin post office (19807) and was added to the National Register of Historic Places November 5, 1971.

Carrere and Hastings. Architectural firm employed by Alfred I. duPont to design his 47,000 square-foot, 102-room mansion, *Nemours*. The firm is perhaps best-known for having designed the New York Public Library on Fifth Avenue. It also designed Whitehall, the Henry M. Flagler mansion in Palm Beach.

Centreville (Centerville). The Village of Centreville was founded in 1750 and is located north of Wilmington on Kennett Pike. In the 1920s, 48 per cent of the frontage on Kennett Pike was owned by du Pont family members. Many original houses are still standing, but have been converted into specialty shops. Buckley's Tavern, a popular Centreville restaurant, was founded in 1951 by William W. "Chick" Laird, Jr., a member of the du Pont family, and operated by Dennis Buckley. The restaurant is housed in a former house built in 1817. In the 1930s it was an ice cream store and tap room.

Chateau Country. The residential area of the Brandywine Valley surrounding *Eleutherian Mills*, and extending north along Kennett Pike to Centreville and the Pennsylvania border. It has long been nicknamed Chateau Country, a reference to the large du Pont estates, most of which were built between 1900 and 1950, and the family's connections to France's Loire Valley. Ferdinand Lundberg writes in *America's 60 Families* (Vanguard Press, 1937), "Owing to the many elaborate du Pont estates, Delaware and the immediately contiguous territory might aptly be termed the American "Chateau Country." In her book, *Wilmington: A Pictorial History (1982)*, Carol Hoffecker wrote: "Most members of the du Pont family resided on or near the original mill property, in time making much of the farm country along the Kennett Pike an expanded du Pont enclave, since dubbed 'chateau country'." Hoffecker further describes it as "sparsely populated, rolling country inhabited by many members of the du Pont family, high executives in the chemical industry, and other persons of wealth."

Chevannes. Village in Nemours District of France near location of *Bois des Fossés*, home of Pierre du Pont de Nemours, about 60 miles from Paris. The name was also used by Bessie du Pont for her estate south of Winterthur, built for her by Pierre S. du Pont following her divorce from Alfred I. du Pont as a thank you for writing an 11-volume history of the company, *Life of Eleuthere Irénée du Pont from Contemporary Correspondence.*

Chicken Alley. Chicken Alley, Duck Street, and Bedbug Row were row housing projects built by DuPont Powder Co. (c. 1812) for its workers on land purchased from Pierre Bauduy in 1802. It was not uncommon at the time for companies to build employee housing in industrial villages and company towns. Duck Street and Chicken Alley were located up the hill from the Louviers textile mill and across from and to the left of *Lower Louviers* with Bedbug Row (Bride's Row) at a right angle. The original Chicken Alley houses are now gone and the Duck Street houses are referred to as Chicken Alley. They have been combined into two, one-and-a-half story stuccoed houses. At one time there were six separate units of two rooms each. Many families kept chickens and it is possible that the lane between Duck Street and Chicken Alley could have been referred to as an alley.

The houses designated as Chicken Alley were placed on the National Register of Historic Places February 1, 1972. Workers used the Iron Bridge to cross back and forth from the east to the west bank. Charles' Banks row housing was on the east side of the river to the south of the Iron Bridge. Free Park (Flea Park) was between Christ Church and the Manufacturers' Sunday School. Three additional rows across the creek, Long Row, Diamond Row and Widow's Asylum, originally housed workers at the Rokeby Cotton Mill, but by the 1840s most of the tenants were powder mill employees.

Many DuPont employees were Irish and Italian. E.I. du Pont provided them with rent-free housing, medical care and education for their children as well as offering them loans to bring other family members and friends from Europe to Delaware to work at the mill.

Christ Church Christiana Hundred. Christ Church, as it is locally known, is an outgrowth of the Brandywine Manufacturers' Sunday School that began in 1815 in a building belonging to the DuPont Powder MIlls. Two years later a permanent Sunday School building was erected and instruction in several faiths offered. In 1848, a cornerstone was laid and Christ Church formally organized. The present church was constructed in 1856 and the first service held May 4 of that year. In the beginning worshipers were primarily members of the du Pont family, workers at the mill, and friends, giving rise to its reference as the "du Pont Church." Through the years it has been substantially enlarged and its congregation diversified.

During its construction in 1856 stone masons from the mill were assigned to work on the church during slow times and Alexis du Pont, a partner in the company and grandson of the founder, oversaw the building progress from time to time. On one of his visits he saw a bottle of whiskey passed among the men. When one of the masons noticed that they were being observed he hid the bottle in the wall they were building. Without saying a word Alexis stayed until that section of the wall was completed and sealed with mortar.

Christiana Hundred. *See* Brandywine Hundred.

Coffin, Marian. One of the country's first female landscape architects who was made a fellow of the ASLA in 1918. She met Henry Francis du Pont during their student years at Harvard and MIT respectively. In 1926, du Pont contacted her regarding landscaping at his home, *Winterthur,* and she worked with him from the 1930s until 1957. Her work there led to additional du Pont commissions; other clients included the Fricks, Huttons, Morgans, and Vanderbilts. Coffin was known for complete landscape design in her work including driving paths, walkways, woodlands, formal gardens, and the internal and external views from houses.

Colonial Revival. A style of architecture in great favor in the United States between 1876 and the 1950s that draws upon elements of Georgian architecture. Some of its distinguishing features include a rectangular design of two to three stories, brick or wood siding or a combination, gable roof, columns and pillars, multi-pane, double-hung windows, paneled doors with sidelights, fireplaces, and a center-hall floor plan. Notable examples among du Pont houses are *Bois des Fossés* and *Mt. Cuba*.

Consomme Bellevue. "It wouldn't be a New Year without Consomme Bellevue to usher it in," a family member told us. Following is the recipe for the traditional soup as served by Greenville Country Club at the New Year's Calling.

Ingredients:
4 lbs. soft shell clams
3 celery stalks
1 1/2 qts. chicken stock (not canned)
1/2 tsp. salt
1/4 tsp. white pepper
1/2 cup saffron whipped cream

Method: Wash the soft shell clams thoroughly in cold water. In a soup pot, combine clams, celery, chicken stock, salt and pepper. Bring to a boil and simmer for five minutes. Remove from fire. Let stand for 10 minutes. Strain the broth through a fine china cap strainer or cheese cloth. Clarify stock as you would consomme. Top each serving with whipped cream.

Saffron whipped cream: Bloom saffron threads in a small saucepan. Add heavy whipping cream and remove from stove. Let cool on kitchen worktable. Strain thread and refrigerate. Whip cream as usual with a pinch of salt and white pepper.

Crossing the Creek (Going across the river). DuPont Company powder houses situated along the Brandywine Creek were built of stone with a weak fourth wall designed to give way in case of an explosion. Employees outside the building would be afforded some protection while machinery and inside workers could be blasted across the river. Those who died in this manner were said to have "crossed the creek" (crick).

Dallin Aerial Survey Company. J. Victor Dallin, a former member of the Royal Air Force during World War I, formed his company in 1924 and operated it out of the Philadelphia Airport until 1941. His company took some 13,000 photographs in the mid-Atlantic region, though he concentrated on the Philadelphia area, including most of the du Pont houses in and around Wilmington. Photographs were taken at an altitude of between 400 and 1500 feet at an angle of about 45 degrees with a camera mounted on the side of the fuselage. Dallin controlled the shutter speed from the cockpit. Approximately 6000 images are included in the Hagley Library collection.

Duck Street. *See* Chicken Alley

DuPont Airfield. The DuPont Airfield was located at the intersection of Lancaster Pike (DE Rt. 48) and Centre Road (De Rt. 141) and was bounded by the old Reading Railroad and the Mt. Olive and Mt. Zion Cemeteries. The airfield had a single 1800-foot-long landing strip, a single-plane hangar and a workshop. An historic marker erected by Delaware Public Archives in 2003 reads in part:

> SITE OF DuPONT AIRFIELD. In 1924, a private airfield was established here by Henry B. du Pont. Charles Lindbergh landed here in 1927. With Richard du Pont's purchase of controlling interest in All-American Aviation and Henry du Pont's establishment of Atlantic Aviation in 1938, the airfield was expanded, becoming one of the most modern privately owned public-use facilities in the country. It was an important site for development and testing of military experimental projects. The final flight from DuPont Airfield was in 1958. The site was used by the DuPont Company for construction of the Barley Mill research and development center."

The hangars, control tower and other buildings were demolished and new buildings constructed. In 1952 All-American Aviation became known as Allegheny Airlines and successively as US Air (1979) and US Airways (1996). The DuPont Company recently sold the Barley Mill complex and is consolidating its operation at Chestnut Run. It is scheduled for mixed-use redevelopment by the new owner.

du Pont, Eleuthere Irénée. Founder of E.I. du Pont de Nemours and Company (DuPont). The name Eleuthere, often used by subsequent generations, translates as "the peaceful friend of liberty."

du Pont Family Reunion. The 150th Anniversary of the du Ponts arriving in America on January 1, 1800, was celebrated during the weekend of December 31, 1949 - January 2, 1950. Six hundred-thirty-two family members gathered from France, England, Italy, Switzerland and the United States.

Dinners were held at family members homes preceding a New Year's Eve dance held at Granogue, 9:00 PM to 2:00 AM. Meyer Davis and his orchestra provided the music. On January 1, New Year's Day, a sesquicentennial breakfast was held at Longwood. Placecards indicated where each guest was to be seated in the Sunken Garden of the Conservatory. The menu included johnnycake, terrapin stew, filet mignon and game pie. Claret and champagne were served. The charge, paid for by Delaware descendants as hosts, was fifty cents per year of the age of the person attending. Pierre du Pont paid forty dollars as he celebrated his 80th birthday on January 15.

du Pont Geneaology Committee. A registry for all du Pont family members with records maintained by two paid staff. Each member is assigned a coded number indicating his or her line of descent or ancestry. In the year 2000 there were some 3500 persons registered worldwide.

du Pont de Nemours Cemetery. *See* Sand Hole Woods

du Pont de Nemours, Pierre Samuel. Patriarch of the du Pont family in the United States. Father of Eleuthere Irénée (1772-1834), founder of the DuPont Company, and Victor Marie du Pont (1767-1827). Born in Paris in 1739 (d. 1817) the son of Samuel Dupont, a watchmaker, and Anne de Montchanin Dupont, daughter of an impoverished noble family in Burgundy. Beginning in 1763, he began signing himself Du Pont and later added de Nemours to prevent confusion with two other persons of the same name serving in the Chamber of Deputies.

duPont Motor Car. The first model of the duPont automobile was built in 1919 and was shown at the International Automobile Salon at the Commodore Hotel in New York. It was designed and spearheaded by E. Paul du Pont. In the years of production, 1919-1931, just 547 duPont cars were built. Mary Pickford purchased one for her husband, Douglas Fairbanks, Jr. Gloria Swanson, Will Rogers, Jack Dempsey and Fanny Brice were other owners. As the country sank into depression the luxury car market evaporated and duPont Motor Cars went out of business in 1932 along with a number of other manufacturers catering to up-market clientele. The 1931 Dual Cowl Phaeton Model H had a wheelbase of 146 inches and a Lalique hood ornament. Just three Model H duPonts were built.

Paul du Pont was also interested in motorcycles, designing and assembling one in a small room off of the living room in his house at 204 Buck Road. In 1928 he bought the Indian Motorcycle Manufacturing Co. that was once the world's largest manufacturer of motorcycles.

Dupont Song. As a community project during the 1920s, Pierre du Pont focused his attention on black education in Delaware. To this end he had 92 schools built or rebuilt in the state at a personal cost of some 2.5 million dollars. In appreciation for his philanthropy, in 1924 music teacher J. Matthew Coulbourne wrote the words and music to a composition he entitled "Dupont Song." It was included in a CD, *Music From the Banks of the Delaware*, recorded at the Amy E. du Pont Music Bldg., at the University of Delaware, January 17, 1993 by The New Tankopanicum Orchestra.

Eleutherian Mills. When Eleuthere Irénée du Pont first moved to the Brandywine Valley, he and his family occupied a small house already standing on the property he purchased from Jacob Broom. Soon after, plans were drawn for a new house, *Eleutherian Mills*, which was occupied in 1803. The two-story and attic dwelling had a center hall and was two rooms deep; it was built of grey stone, later stuccoed. E.I. and his family lived there until his death in 1834.

In the 1890 mill explosion, 30 tons of powder ignited, destroying 50 houses and killing 13 people. *Eleutherian Mills* sustained considerable damage and remained vacant until 1892. After repairs were made, it became a club house for DuPont workers until 1910. Because of disuse, the building was abandoned and remained empty until the first World War when it became a guard barracks. Later it became a farm manager's house. In 1921, the powder yards were closed and in 1922 the house was purchased by Henry A. du Pont for his daughter, Mrs. F.B. Crowninshield (Louise Evelina du Pont), who reconstructed it and created an elaborate Italianate garden on the site of the saltpeter refinery that had been destroyed in the 1890 explosion. She and her husband lived at *Eleutherian Mills* in the spring and fall months. At her death in 1958, ownership passed to the Eleutherian Mills-Hagley Foundation.

Eleutherian Mills, together with *Louviers*, the house E.I. had built for his brother, Victor, were the first of the du Pont houses that gradually evolved into the mansions lining Kennett Pike and the surrounding countryside. *See* Chateau Country.

Epping Forest. The name of the 58-acre riverfront Alfred I. du Pont winter estate in Jacksonville, Florida. Designed in Spanish-Mediterranean style, it was named after an ancestral house in the family of Jesse Ball, third wife of Alfred I. du Pont. Added to the National Register of Historic Places in 1973, it is now the home of the Epping Forest Yacht Club.

Essone. Town in France where Eleuthere Irénée du Pont learned his trade as a maker of black powder, the basis of the du Pont family fortune.

First Office. Business affairs of the DuPont Company were originally conducted from *Eleutherian Mills*. After the death of E.I. du Pont in 1834, his eldest son, Alfred Victor, built a separate office in 1837. An addition was made in 1849 and this became the office of his younger brother, Henry, who succeeded him in running the company. In 1891 the Second Office was built at 204 Buck Road. *See* Second Office.

game pie. Served each year at New Year's Day Calling (see below). In preparation for their original crossing from La Rochelle, France on the *American Eagle* (October 1, 1799), several very large pies (up to 35 pounds each) were provisioned. The voyage, expected to take approximately one month, actually took 91 days and the pies were of paramount importance to the group's survival. When the pies had all been eaten, the group was forced to exist on rat soup prepared by Pierre Samuel du Pont. His son, Victor, was later quoted as saying "the rats made excellent eating." Ingredients for game pie include wild turkey, duck, pheasant, partridge, quail, goose, etc. A recipe for its preparation is included in *The Hagley Cookbook*.

gneiss. A medium to coarse grained, high grade metamorphic rock with distinct banding that differs in color and composition, typically light and dark silicates. Because of its load-bearing capacity, hardness and resistance to weather, it is popular for construction of buildings and monuments.

Guyencourt. A residential area north of Wilmington bounded by Montchanin Road on the west and Thompson Bridge Road on the east. The Guyencourt (Center) railroad station on the Wilmington and Northern Railroad has been converted to a private dwelling. Anne Alexandrine de Montchanin, wife of Pierre Samuel, was descended from Jean-Baptiste, Seigneur of Guyencourt. Guyencourt is located in the north of France, 76 miles from Paris.

Hagley. To expand his property E. I. du Pont, founder of E.I. du Pont de Nemours & Co., purchased the Hagley property in 1813 from Rumford Dawes, a Philadelphia merchant. The name Hagley was probably given to the property by Dawes, who operated three mills on this site. It seems likely that the name came from an English estate in the West Midlands, well-known in the 18th century for its English style of landscape architecture created by Capability Brown, William Kent and Humphry Repton.

Hagley House. Built in 1814 for the first manager of the Hagley Powder Yard, Charles Dalmas. Members of the du Pont family occupied it until it was razed in 1950.

Hagley House (Jacob Broom House). Built c. 1794 for Jacob Broom, a signer of the Declaration of Independence. Purchased by Eleuthere I. du Pont and occupied by his daughter, Eleuthera and her husband, Thomas Mackie Smith, and by several succeeding du Pont families. It is still existent.

Henry Clay Village. A village downstream from the powder yards with approximately 80 buildings. Owned by the DuPont Company, it provided housing for mill workers and included stores, a dance hall, a Roman Catholic Church, and two saloons, the Blazing Rag on Rising Sun Lane and the William Penn on Creek Road The du Ponts chose the name out of admiration for the Kentucky senator and secretary of state ("that good Whig") who supported high tariffs on imported goods to stimulate the manufacture of American products and who was a visitor to *Eleutherian Mills* in 1833. It was not planned as a company town and, initially, most of the residents were textile workers, but later the black powder mills employed most of the workers. Roughly bounded by Breck's Lane, Kennett Pike, Rising Sun Lane and the Brandywine River. *See* Rising Sun Bridge.

Hotel du Pont. Constructed in conjunction with the proposed third section of the DuPont building at 11th and Market Streets in downtown Wilmington. The 150-room hotel opened January 15, 1913, the birthday of Pierre S. du Pont who, then a bachelor, built a suite for his own use on the executive floor and maintained it until his death in 1954. The exterior of the building is white stone and is an adaption of Italian Renaissance in design.

A 1919 addition added 115 more rooms and a large ballroom. A roster of famous guests who have stayed there reads like a Who's Who of politics, industry and show business and includes eight U.S. presidents, Amelia Earhart, Charles Lindbergh, Tommy and Jimmy Dorsey, Oscar Hammerstein, George M. Cohan, Bob Hope, Gregory Peck, Rex Harrison, Lena Horne, Elizabeth Taylor, Tallulah Bankhead, Bette Davis, Eleanor Roosevelt, Jacqueline Kennedy, and hundreds of other well-known celebrities.

Iron Bridge. A private bridge across the Brandywine River connecting the east and west banks between the Hagley Museum and privately owned estates. Initially the two points were connected by a ferry with a pulley system. It was called the "Rhine" ferry because of its resemblance to Rhine ferries in use at the time that moved with the flow of current. Legend has it that Pierre Samuel du Pont (1739-1817) fell into the Brandywine from this ferry and as a result contracted pneumonia that caused his death.

The first bridge, made of wood, was built in two stages. Stone piers were built in 1863 and the Pratt-type iron truss was completed in 1870. In 1874, the present wrought iron bridge was built by Wilmington shipbuilder Pusey & Jones. It was in daily use by mill workers living in the Louviers area (Duck Street, Chicken Alley, Charles Banks, Bedbug Row). Since 1935 it has been maintained by the du Pont family and is used exclusively by Black Gates Road residents. It is considered an element of the Eleutherian Mills National Historic Landmark and the Brandywine Powder Mills National Historic Landmark Register Districts. The bridge has an elevation of 115 feet, is 39.7 feet wide and 75.5 feet long.

Ives, Albert Ely. Wilmington architect who designed Chevannes, Bessie G. du Pont's Wilmington house, *Meown* (Mrs. H. Rodney Sharp), and his own house on Snuff Mill Road, later called Calmar (now Serendip). He moved to Hawaii in 1935 where he continued practicing his profession, designing Barbara Hutton's house in Cuernavaca, Mexico, and Samuel F.B. Morse's Pebble Beach, California house.

Kennett Pike. Route 52, designated as a Scenic Byway by the U.S. Dept. of Transportation's Federal Highway Administration. Kennett Pike was at one time a toll road. After paying the toll the keeper would turn the gate or pike to allow passage. Tolls were based on the width of carriages, number of wagon wheels, passengers, and horses passing through the gate. The toll and pike are gone, but the name remains. It became a public road in 1920-1921.

Louviers. The name of two du Pont estates. *Upper Louviers* was originally a small farmhouse bought by Peter Baduy in 1802 and later purchased by E. I. du Pont. During the 19th century it was the home of Admr. Samuel F. du Pont. It was razed in 1978 to provide additional acreage for the Louviers Course of DuPont Country Club.

Lower Louviers was built in 1811 for Victor Marie du Pont by his older brother, E.I. It was named either after a town between Rouen and Paris that was a center of wool manufacturing or for an islet across the road from Pierre du Pont's print shop. In 1921, Mary du Pont Laird purchased the house for her son, William Winder, Jr., then age 11. *Louviers* stood vacant for 14 years until major renovations to the house took place in 1935, the year William (Chick) married Winifred Moreton (Winnie) and it was their home for many years. It is still owned by a member of du Pont family. *Louviers* was added to the National Register of Historic Places in 1972.

Montchanin. A station on the Wilmington and Northern Railroad. Named by Col. Henry du Pont in honor of Pierre du Pont de Nemours' mother. The station remains in place, now adapted as an office building, and is the name of an inn nearby. The area was designated as the Montchanin Historic District June 9, 1978. A plaque erected on the site reads:

VILLAGE OF MONTCHANIN

Settled at the triangular intersection of three roads in the early 19th century by workers from the nearby DuPont Black Powder Mills, this village consisted initially of only 2.4 acres. The Wilmington and Northern Railroad established tracks through the vicinity in 1869, leading to a period of sustained growth in population and area. The village, known as DuPont Station, became a major shipping point for the mills and warehouse and rail sidings were built nearby to facilitate transport of the powder. In 1889, a new railroad station was constructed and a post office was established to serve the surrounding countryside. These signs of enduring settlement were commemorated with a new name for the village. Montchanin was chosen to honor Anne Alexandrine de Montchanin, who was the mother of Pierre Samuel duPont de Nemours, the founder of the American du Pont dynasty. The range of architectural styles and the history of the hamlet were recognized when the Montchanin Historic District was added to the National Register of Historic Places in 1978. Delaware Public Archives - 2008. NC-185

Montchanin Village, The Inn at. A 28-room luxury country inn consisting of 11 buildings dating from 1799 to 1910. Montchanin Village, across from the former Wilmington and Northern Railroad station, was basically a community occupied by workers at the DuPont Powder Mills. Because of its proximity to the powder mills it was called DuPont Station. The Inn is listed on the National Register of Historic Places.

Mrs. Pierre S. du Pont. A patron hybrid tea rose, *Rosa Mrs. Pierre S. du Pont,* bred in France and introduced in 1929. Bears medium yellow blossoms. It grows into a sturdy, upright plant and is well suited to cutting. Writing in *House Beautiful* magazine (June 1932), the author says it "bids fair to become the best yellow garden Rose."

Neighborhood, The. A nucleus of seven du Pont houses built within an area bounded by Kennett Pike (Route 52), Rising Sun Lane, and A.I du Pont Middle School (est. 1893). The seven houses were *Saint Amour, Elton, Spanish House, Copeland House, Square House, Still Pond,* and *Windmar.* Only *Windmar* remains.

Nemours (Old). The first *Nemours,* or *Old Nemours,* was built in 1824 by Eleuthere I. du Pont for his eldest son, Alfred Victor du Pont (1798 - 1856). The Federal style home was built by the same group that built E.I.'s 1802 *Eleutherian Mills* house.

Nenemoosha. The 97-foot yacht commissioned by Alred I. duPont following his marriage to Jessie Ball. Built by American Car & Foundry Co., it was launched in 1922 at a cost of $75,000. The name *Nenemoosha* is translated as sweetheart in the Iroquois language and might have been inspired by Henry Wadsworth Longfellow's poem, "Hiawatha" who "Called her sweetheart, Nenemoosha." Dissatisfied with the vessel, he replaced it with a second *Nenemoosha,* 130 feet in length, launched in 1925 and built by Newport News Shipbuilding. In 1934 the du Ponts purchased a 107-foot houseboat, *Gadfly,* berthed in Jacksonville, nearby their Florida residence, *Epping Forest.*

New Year's Day Calling and Receiving (usually referred to as New Year's Calling). The tradition of gentlemen calling on their female friends to renew or perpetuate friendship on New Year's Day, described by Rev. Issac Fidler in his pamphlet, *Observations in the United States and Canada, 1833.*

On this day in Wilmington, it has been the custom of du Pont men to call on ladies of the family in their respective homes, though today that has changed somewhat with groups of six or more women greeting callers in eight to 12 of the larger houses. *Granogue* is always a favorite among these. The custom now extends to the Greenville Country Club (formerly *Owl's Nest*, home of Eugene du Pont, Jr.), Vicmead Hunt Club, and sometimes the Inn at Montchanin, with these properties substituting for houses.

During the day some 250 du Ponts from the distaff side of the family, from Wilmington and elsewhere, greet about an equal number of du Pont men who come bearing small gifts for each lady. Typically these might include chocolates, boxes of tea, coffee mugs decorated with a logo of early du Pont Powder Mill advertising, notepads, or plastic glasses with the du Pont coat of arms. Baseball hats and mouse pads are recent, and very popular, additions to the list of gifts. Pierre S. du Pont III, when he was alive, brought Edam cheese to each lady and his son, Pierre IV, brought crackers as an accompaniment. At least two men creatively and thoughtfully provide bags imprinted with the family crest as gifts to help the women take home their bounty.

Game pie is a traditional dish served at two of the houses and Consomme Bellevue is served at Greenville Country Club. The Open House lasts from nine in the morning until two o'clock in the afternoon. One of the participants in the relays comments, "With about a dozen houses to visit and 300 cousins to shake hands with or kiss in a five-hour time span, it's a fast track." *See Consomme Bellevue.*

1921 Distribution, The. After World War I the DuPont Company stopped production of explosives at its Wilmington plant. The decision was made to sell off most of its land holdings and many company-owned houses and buildings to du Pont family members and DuPont executives in what became known as "The 1921 Distribution."

Okie, R. Brognard. Richardson Brognard Okie (1875-1945) was a Philadelphia and Main Line architect who specialized in houses based on Pennsylvania farmhouse traditions incorporating Colonial Revival style. His designs were identified by different roof lines, undressed fieldstone, and prominent chimneys. In Wilmington he designed houses for S. Hallock du Pont (*Squirrel Run*), H.B. du Pont, Jr. (*Ashland Red Clay Creek*), and Nicholas du Pont (Ridgely) as well as additions for several others.

PADLE-A-MIOW. An anagram made up of the names of du Pont cousins who produced a series of 21 homemade movies 1927-1931. Working from original scripts, e.g. Veni Vidi Vindbag (I Came I Saw I Gossiped) or satirizing events of the day, e.g. The Honey-Teeney Prize Fight (Gene Tunney vs. Tom Heeney) they created highly amusing and innovative productions ranging in length from three to 70 minutes.

People's Railway. Name given to one of the interconnecting trolley systems serving Wilmington. Established in 1901 with the initial terminus being Rockford Park. Extended in 1906 to Henry Clay Village across Barley Mill Road, uphill through Squirrel Run Village and terminating at Buck and Montchanin Roads at Hunter's Corner (Wagoners Row). Service was discontinued in 1928, six years after the DuPont powder mills were closed down. The car barn and repair shop were located at Delaware Avenue and DuPont Street, now known as Trolley Square.

Pontiana. The name chosen by Pierre Samuel du Pont for the land development company and "rural society" he hoped to establish in the new world, at first in northern Virginia, later in Kentucky near the Ohio River.

Rising Sun Bridge. The original Rising Sun Bridge was built of timber in 1833 and was covered. Signs over the entrances read "Walk Your Horses Over This Bridge." Its abutments were made of the same Brandywine granite as that used in constructing the nearby DuPont powder mills whose workers lived in the surrounding hamlets of Rising Sun (Henry Clay Village), Rokeby, Breck's Lane, Walker's Bank, Squirrel Run Village, and Louviers. Over 1,000 workers lived within sound of the powder mills. The bridge was used primarily by them and served as a community gathering place. It was replaced by a truss bridge in 1928.

According to Charles A. Silliman in his book, *The Story of Christ Church Christiana Hundred and its People*, "In the locality of Rising Sun there were several taverns including Thomas Toy's and Jeff Blakeley's. ... They were lighted by coal oil lamps ... and the whiskey was kept in barrels behind the bar. A good shot cost ten cents, and if you wanted to take a bottle with you, the bartender would fill it from one of the barrels. ... Everyone knew one another, and having a drink at one of the many taverns was one of the few forms of entertainment available to a man in those days. ... There were never any women around taverns in those days."

Rockland. The manor of Rockland was a tract of land given by William Penn to his daughter Letitia, who sold pieces of it to settlers. It was styled the Manor of Rockland and Strand Millis. The Rockland Historic District was one of the earliest and longest functioning mill sites on the Brandywine River with gristmills established by John Gregg and Adam Kirk on the west bank as early as 1724. The village was originally called Kirk's Ford. A fulling (scouring and milling) mill was built by Jonathan Strange in 1733. The river was dammed in 1794 and a paper mill was built on the east bank by William Young, who built workers' housing and a church and changed the village name to Youngstown. The mansion he built for himself at 507 Black Gates Road is still standing. Following Young's death in 1829, the land and mills were sold to Augustus Jessup and Henry du Pont and the name changed back to Rockland.

Rockland Historic District was added to the National Historic Register February 1, 1972. It includes the Town of Rockland and its environs along Rockland Road and the Brandywine River and includes the 18th century Rock Spring house at the corner of Rockland and Adams Dam Roads.

Sand Hole Woods. Early on a sand and gravel pit in the woods east of the Hagley Yards became the burying ground for members of the du Pont family. Sand from this location was used in mixing mortar for the stones used in building company mills. The first grave was that of Pierre Samuel du Pont de Nemours, patriarch of the family who died at *Eleutherian Mills* on August 17, 1817. As time went by it became a formally laid out cemetery and was landscaped by Marian Coffin in 1915. Most of the headstones are made of plain marble. A broken Greek column marks the grave of Lammot du Pont who was killed in an explosion in Gibbstown, New Jersey in 1884. The first wife of Alfred I. du Pont, Bessie Gardner, is buried here, but her former husband is not. He is interred in the Carillon Tower at *Nemours*. There is an open-air chapel of Gothic design; the cornerstone was laid in 2005. The cemetery is now called the du Pont de Nemours Cemetery. There are on average five interments annually.

Second Office (New Office). Having outgrown its first 1837 office, the company built 204 Buck Road in 1890-91 to be the corporate office building or, the Second Office. Eventually this also became too small and, in 1902, an office building in downtown Wilmington was constructed. Later, the Buck Road property was converted to a private residence, first for William K. du Pont, and, after extensive alterations, in 1911 became the home of E. Paul du Pont, his wife, Jean, and their children. A motor cycle enthusiast, he acquired the Indian Motorcycle Company and is said to have designed and built a motorcycle in a small room off the living room. In 1992, the house was offered for sale at the price of $988,000 and was advertised as having 10 bedrooms, five-and-a-half bathrooms, and eight fireplaces. In 2010 it was again offered for sale, this time at an asking price of $3,890,000. Extensive renovations have brought the total number of rooms to 26.

Shipman, Ellen Biddle. Noted landscape architect who designed the gardens at *Owl's Nest*. In her 32-year career she planned over 650 gardens throughout the United States for families that included the Astors, Fords, and Dukes, in addition to the du Ponts.

Squirrel Run. A stream that flows into the Brandywine at a point just above Old Barley Mill Road and below Christ Church. At one time it provided the power for a mill on the Brandywine, probably a cotton or wool factory. A village, inhabited primarily by Italian and Irish workers, grew up along the stream and was designated on early maps as Sqerrel Run. Most residents worked at cotton or woolen mills, a keg factory, or for DuPont. It was acquired in the 1920s by Samuel Hallock du Pont.

Tankopanicum Musical Club. Group organized by Alfred I. du Pont and generally considered to be the forerunner of the Delaware Symphony Orchestra. DuPont took the name Tankopanicum from the Native American name for the Brandywine River, more specifically, "rushing waters." The group originally was composed of friends and mill workers and included cousin Pierre who played the piano, though not very well according to Alfred who played the violin. It played for dances at Breck's Mill and at *Eleutherian Mills* after it had been converted into the Brandywine Club for millworkers. It was also known as the Tankopanicum Orchestra and the Tankopanicum Musical Society and is thought to have been the same group that called itself the Eleutherian Cornet Band.

Tower Hill School. Tower Hill was founded by brothers Irénée and Lammot du Pont, joined by cousins, A. Felix du Pont and Eugene E. du Pont, brothers-in-law William Winder Laird, Hugh Rodney Sharp, and R.R.M. Carpenter, Carpenter's brother, Walter S. Carpenter, Jr., and three colleagues, Charles M. Barton, Albert Robin, and Josiah Marvel. The school was legally incorporated February 27, 1919, with the named men comprising the Board of Trustees. In March of that year construction began and the school opened in September 1920; however, costs estimated at $300,000, exceeded twice that amount.

Lammot du Pont lived across the street from the school on Rising Sun Lane at *St. Amour,* the estate built by his mother. At his death the house became the property of Tower Hill. It was razed in 1972 to make room for athletic fields, though the *St. Amour* garden, designed by Marian Coffin and built in 1918, was restored in 2004 and is a popular venue for teas, parties and wedding receptions.

Valley Garden Park. Hundred-acre garden, approximately one-quarter mile long and several hundred yards wide, created in natural style on an abandoned farm off Campbell Road. Many of the plants were salvaged from the site of Hoopes Reservoir before it was flooded in 1930. Given to the public by Ellen du Pont Wheelwright. The park was designed by her husband, landscape architect Robert Wheelwright.

Vicmead Hunt Club. Private hunt club organized in 1920 by four du Pont women—Mrs. A Felix du Pont, Sr., Mrs. H. Rodney Sharp, Mrs. Victor du Pont, and Mrs. Hollyday Meeds, the latter two whose names were contracted to form the club name. Mrs. Meeds had been Ellen Coleman du Pont and after her divorce from Hollyday Meeds she married Robert Wheelwright. Merged with Bidermann Golf Course in 1977. At each club a Colonial farmhouse serves as the clubhouse.

Wagoners Row. A group of row houses located at the corner of Montchanin Road and Buck's Road originally built to house DuPont Powder Mills wagon drivers. Two of the houses are still existing. While waiting for their house (Wagoner's Row) to be built in 1938, one was occupied by Mr. & Mrs. R.R.M. Carpenter, Jr., A trolley line was built in 1906 to connect Wagoner's Row to the Rockford Park line. From downtown it ran parallel with the Brandywine River through Rising Sun Village and Squirrel Run and across fields to the Montchanin and Buck Roads intersection. Fare was five cents. Service was discontinued October 8, 1928, for lack of ridership and a bus route substituted.

Walker's Bank, across from the mill, dating to 1813, is a connected row of stone dwellings that housed mill workers. Both the mill and the bank are part of the Eleutherian Mills National Historic Landmark District, It is recorded in the Historic American Bldgs. survery, Site DE-65 and DE-67.

The name "bank" used in Walker's Bank, Charles' Bank (at Louviers) and Upper Banks (at Upper Yard of DuPont) was adopted because employee row houses were sometimes built facing the river with the back of the house against a bank or slope of a hill. These were often built in units of four houses with a concrete slab porch across the front. A typical floor plan would have two rooms on the first floor, one room on the second and two rooms on the third floor, plus a garret.

Walker's Mill. Located across the Brandywine River from Breck's Mill in Henry Clay Village. When advertised for sale in 1825, it was described as "of stone, built in 1814, being 65 feet front by 45 deep, four stories high, besides a basement story and two garret floors." It was originally used for manufacturing cotton goods and was known as Simsville Mill, named for owner Joseph B. Sims. On November 15, 1840, the mill was purchased by Alfred du Pont at a sheriff's sale. It was refitted with looms in 1848. It was given by DuPont to the Hagley Foundation in 1955. Walker's Mill was added to the National Register of Historic Places February 1,1972, and its measurements listed as 40 by 75 feet.

Wawaset Park Historic District. A residential area developed by the DuPont Company on 50.48 acres formerly occupied by Schuetzen Park, a fairground, and racetrack, initially for horses, later for auto racing and the former site of Delaware State Fair. There are some 200 houses bounded approximately by Greenhill, Woodlawn, and Pennsylvania Avenues and West 6th and 7th Streets. The area was designed by Edward L. Palmer in the tradition of Frederick Law Olmsted and was marketed as "a suburb within a city." DuPont chose Palmer based on his work in the development of Roland Park in Baltimore.

Most of the houses were built in the 1920s, though construction of the first house was in 1918. Many of the houses were designed by Wilmington architect Leon Wilde Crawford, for whom Crawford Circle in Wawaset Park is named. Preference was given to DuPont employees. Houses are mostly designed in what would be called "period" architecture in Georgian, Dutch Colonial, or Tudor style. It was listed on the National Register of Historic Places in 1986.

Westover Hills. Wealthy residential neighborhood in Wilmington developed by William duPont, Sr., through the Delaware Land Development Co. in which he held controlling interest, and to which he transferred 600 acres. After the crash of 1929, when some homeowners were having difficulty

with finances, it was jokingly referred to as "Leftover Bills." Among its millionaire residents was Pierre S. du Pont III, who lived at 1102 Hopeton Road from 1933-1935 while his Rockland Road house, *Bois des Fossés,* was under construction.

Wilmington and Reading (Northern) Rallroad. The Wilmington and Reading Railroad was organized in 1864 for operation from Wilmington to Coatesville. Service began in 1869 and was extended to Birdsboro in 1870 and Reading in 1874. The DuPont Company and du Pont family members were major investors and it was reorganized by Lammot du Pont and the name changed to Wilmington and Northern. Service resumed in 1877 and Col. Henry A. du Pont became president in 1878. It was nicknamed the "Weak and Nervous."

Under the colonel's presidency stations were renamed drawing upon the family's French connections. DuPont Station became Montchanin, Adams was changed to Winterthur, Smith's Bridge to Granogue, Center to Guyencourt and Pyles to Cossart. The principal purpose of the railroad was to carry freight; however, there was a brief period when passenger service was offered with a few coaches outfitted with wicker seats. Passenger service was discontinued about 1928.

Winterthur. In 1837, Jacques Antoine Bidermann and his wife, Evelina Gabrielle du Pont, purchased 450 acres from the estate of Evelina's father, Eleuthere I. du Pont. A three-story Greek Revival house was built in 1839 and named *Winterthur* after the Bidermann ancestral home in Switzerland. From the original 450 acres the estate grew to 2400 acres in 1927; it now has approximately 1000 acres. *Winterthur* houses one of the country's most important collections of American antiques. Developed by Henry (Harry) F. du Pont, it is displayed in 175 period settings. Most of the museum's rooms are open to the public. There are approximately 85,000 objects in the collection spanning the period from 1640 to 1860.

The estate has 60 acres of naturalistic gardens that began in 1912 with H.F. du Pont planting daffodils in the gardens. In the 1930s he began working with landscape architect Marian Coffin to create an overall plan for the grounds. In 1914 Harry took over management of the farms from his father and produced a prize-winning Holstein herd which at one time numbered 450 cows.

Xanadu. House on Cuba's Hicacos Peninsula built by Irénée du Pont, Sr. In 1927 du Pont purchased 180 hectares, including eight kilometers of virgin beach, and hired architects Covarrochas & Govantes to design the four-story house, situated on the San Bernardino Crags and protected by sea walls. It has three terraces and seven balconies. Marble from Cuba, Italy and Spain was used for floors and columns and exotic Cuban woods for paneling. In 1931 du Pont had an 18-hole golf course built (re-designed to nine following a 1933 hurricane) and in 1932 had an organ installed, reputed to be the most expensive one in Latin America. Du Pont's last visit was in 1957 and the property was confiscated by the Castro government in 1959. It is now a guest house open to the public.

Appendix 3
DIRECTORY OF DU PONT HOUSES

For as long as the du Ponts have lived in this country, records have been kept of the houses they lived in, the location of these houses and the years in which they were first occupied by family members. Wilmington, Delaware is where the DuPont Company started, and it is here that most of the family built their houses and chose to remain, though there are also houses close by in Maryland and Pennsylvania, as well as in other more distant locations. Houses are located in Delaware unless otherwise indicated

Name of House	Original du Pont Occupant	Location
Addlestone (2004)	Mr. & Mrs. Henry E.I. du Pont II	Greenville
Applecross (1807, 1929)	Mr. & Mrs. Donald Peabody Ross (Wilhelmina H. du Pont)	Montchanin Road
Ashland Red Clay Creek (1934)	Mr. & Mrs. Henry B. du Pont, Jr.	Red Clay Creek
Ball Farm (c.1802, 1921)	Mr. & Mrs. R.R.M. Carpenter III	Montchanin Road
Bellevue Hall (1855,1930s)	Mr. & Mrs. William duPont, Sr.	Carr Road
(formerly Woolsey Hall)		(Holly Oak)
Big Bend (1640, 1750, 1920s)	George A. Weymouth	Chadds Ford, Pennsylvania
Bohemia Manor (1920)	Mr. & Mrs. Thomas F. Bayard (Elizabeth Bradford du Pont)	Chesapeake City, Maryland
Bois des Fossés (1936)	Mr. & Mrs. Pierre S. du Pont III	Rockland Road
Boxwood (1928, 1994)	Mr. & Mrs. George P. Edmonds (Natalie W. du Pont)	Greenville
Brantwyn	DuPont Company (1990)	Rockland Road
(renamed, see Bois des Fossés)		
Brookdale Farm (c.1800)	T. Coleman du Pont	Greenville
Buck and Doe Run Farm (1919)	Lammot du Pont	Coatesville, Pennsylvania
Buck Hill Farm	Mr. & Mrs. Stephen du Pont	Greenville
Buena Vista (1846, 1914, 1924, 1930, 1937)	Gov. & Mrs. Clayton Douglass Buck (Alice Hounsfield du Pont)	New Castle
Calmar (1928)	Mr. & Mrs. Alfred V. du Pont	Snuff Mill Road
(renamed Serendip)	Lisa Dean MacGuigan Moseley	
Cherry Knoll (1919) (razed)	Mr. & Mrs. Willliam duPont, Jr.	Whitehorse Pike, Newtown Square, Pennsylvania
Chestertown House (1926)	Mr. & Mrs. Henry F. du Pont	Southampton, Long Island, New York
Chevannes (1928)	Bessie Gardner du Pont	Kennett Pike
Copeland House (1904) (razed)	Mr. & Mrs. Charles Copeland	Kennett Pike
Copeland House (1964)	Mr. & Mrs. Lammot du Pont Copeland, Jr.	
(2nd house on same foundation)		
Coverdale Farm (1927-1930)	Mr. & Mrs. Crawford Greenewalt (Margaretta du Pont)	Greenville
Crestlea	Eleuthera du Pont Bradford du Pont	Ardmore, Pennsylvania
Crooked Billet (1684)	Mr. & Mrs. James H. Tyler McConnell (Jean Ellen du Pont)	Kennett Pike
Dauneport (1932)	Amy Elizabeth du Pont	Old Kennett Pike
Dilwyne Farms (1922) (razed)	Mr. & Mrs. R.R.M. Carpenter, Sr. (Margaretta Lammot du Pont)	Buck Road
Doe Run (1934)	Sir John & Mrs. Esther du Pont Thouron	Unionville, Pennsylvania
Doe Run Inn (c. 1740, 1828,1968)	Mr. and Mrs. Richard I. G. Jones (Ann Lunger)	Doe Run, Pennsylvania
Doggone (1930)	Mr. & Mrs. George Tyler Weymouth (Dulcinea Ophelia Payne du Pont)	Kennett Pike
(renamed Twin Lakes)		
Dogwood (1917) (razed)	Mr. & Mrs. Eugene Eleuthere du Pont	Kennett Pike
Eleutherian Mills (1802)	Mr. & Mrs. E. I. du Pont	Hagley
Elton (1902) (razed)	Mr. A. Felix & Mrs. Mary du Pont	Kennett Pike

Name of House	Original du Pont Occupant	Location
Elton (1970)	Mr. & Mrs. A. Felix du Pont, Jr.	
(new house with same name)		
Fair Hill (1929-1930)	Mr. & Mrs. Gordon A. Rust (Frances du Pont Morgan Rust)	Fair Hill, Pennsylvania
Fair Hill (1926)	William duPont, Jr.	Fair Hill, Maryland
Fairthorne	Mr. & Mrs. Harry Clark Boden IV (Marguerite du Pont Ortiz)	Newark
Farfields	Mrs. Victor du Pont (Josephine Anderson)	Rising Sun Lane
Fiskekill (1934-35)	Mr. & Mrs. Richard E. Riegel (Edith "Skippy" du Pont Riegel)	Guyencourt
(renamed, see Staglyn)		
Foxcatcher Farm (1925)	Mr. & Mrs. William duPont, Jr. (Jean Liseter Austin)	Newtown Square, Pennsylvania
Foxwood	Mr. & Mrs. Wm. Glasgow Reynolds (Nancy Bradford du Pont)	Greenville
Gibraltar (c. 1844, 1909)	Mr. & Mrs. Hugh Rodney Sharp (Isabella du Pont)	Pennsylvania Avenue
Goodstay (1740, 1868)	Margaretta E. L. du Pont	Pennsylvania Avenue
Granogue (1921-1923)	Mr. & Mrs. Irénée du Pont, Sr.	Wilmington
Great House Farm (1680)	Mr. & Mrs. Richard "Kip" C. du Pont, Jr.	Chesapeake City
Greenville House (1934-1935)	Mr. & Mrs. Francis Victor du Pont (Octavia du Pont)	New London Road
Hagley (1794, 1823)	Mr. & Mrs. Thomas Mackie Smith (Eleuthera du Pont)	Greenville
(Jacob Broom House)		
Hagley House (c. 1814) (razed)	Mr. & Mrs. Charles Dalmas (Evelina du Pont)	Greenville
Happenstance Farm (1737, 1952, 1956)	Alice du Pont Buck	Greenville
Harry's Gate (c. 1780, 1920s)	H. R. Sharp, Jr. (Ada B. Ward du Pont)	Centreville
Hayloft, The (c. 1900)	Mr. & Mrs. Francis George du Pont (Beatrice Churchman)	Fairfield, Connnecticut
Hexton Hall (1936)	Mr. & Mrs. Samuel F. DuPont	Georgetown, Maryland
Hod House (1931)	Mr. & Mrs. Crawford H. Greenewalt (Margaretta du Pont)	Greenville
Invergarry (1960-1961)	Mr. & Mrs. Ellice MacDonald, Jr. (Rosa Laird Hayward)	Montchanin
Iris Brook (1902) (razed)	Mr. & Mrs. Lammot du Pont	Kennett Pike
Letdown (1935)	Mr. & Mrs. Robert Norton Downs III (Alletta "Letty" d'Andelot Laird)	Centre Road
L'Hermitage (c. 1930)	Mr. & Mrs. Elbert Dent (Victorine duPont)	Wilmington
Limerick (1815,1934,1936)	Mr. & Mrs. Ellason Downs III (Mary "Molly" Belin Laird)	Lancaster Pike
Limestone Farm (c. 1920)	A. Felix du Pont	Limestone Road
Liseter Hall (1922)	Mr. & Mrs. William du Pont, Jr. (Jean Liseter Austin)	Newtown Square, Pennsylvania
Longwood (1730, 1764, 1824, 1914)	Mr. & Mrs. Pierre S. du Pont	Kennett Square, Pennsylvania
(renamed Peirce-du Pont House)		
Louviers (1810-1811)	Mr. & Mrs. Victor M. du Pont	Wilmington
Lyndham (1901)	Evelina du Pont	Kennett Pike
Meadow Wood (1936-1937)	Marion du Pont Somerville Scott	Carr Road
Meown (1930)	Isabella du Pont Sharp	Centreville Road
Montmorency (1937)	Mr. & Mrs. Henry E.I. du Pont (Martha "Muffin" Verge)	Walnut Green Road
(formerly Stockton)		
Mount Cuba (1936-1937)	Mr.& Mrs. Lammot du Pont Copeland	Barley Mill Road
Mount Harmon (c.1651, 1937)	Mr. & Mrs. Henry C. Boden IV (Marguerite du Pont de Villiers-Ortiz)	Cecil County, Maryland
Nemours (1909-1910)	Mr. & Mrs. Alfred I. duPont	Rockland Road
Nemours House (1824)	Mr. & Mrs. Alfred V. P. du Pont	Greenville
New Poems (1980)	Jane du Pont Lunger	Centreville
Oberod (1935-1937)	Mr. & Mrs. Harry W. Lunger (Mary Jane du Pont)	Burnt Mill Road
Old Mill, The (1909-1910) (razed)	Thomas Coleman du Pont	Greenville
Owl's Nest (1915-1920)	Mr. & Mrs. Eugene du Pont, Jr.	Owl's Nest Road
Patterns (1966-1967)	Gov. & Mrs. Pierre S. du Pont IV	Rockland Road
Pelleport (1881) (razed)	Mr. & Mrs. William du Pont	Kennett Pike
Peirce-du Pont House – see Longwood		
Point Lookout Farm (1902)	Francis G. du Pont	New Castle
Randalea (c. 1940)	Mr. & Mrs. Reynolds du Pont	Hillside Road
Renaud (c. 1880)	Mr. & Mrs. Victor du Pont, Jr.	Kennett Pike
Rencourt (c. 1890) (razed)	Mr. & Mrs. Alexis Irénée du Pont	Rising Sun Lane
Ridgely (1940)	Mr. & Mrs. Nicholas R. du Pont	Snuff Mill Road
Rock Manor (1913)	Alfred I. duPont	Wilmington
(Rock Farms)		

Name of House	Original du Pont Occupant	Location
Rock Spring (1930-1931)	Mr. & Mrs. J. Avery Draper (Irene "Renee" Carpenter)	Rockland Road
Rocky Hill	William K. du Pont	Newark
Rokeby (1836)	Mr. & Mrs. William Breck (Gabrielle Josephine du Pont)	Breck's Mill Lane
Rounds, The (c. 1800s)	A. Felix du Pont II	Cecil County, Maryland
Saint Amour (1891-1892) (razed)	Margaretta du Pont (Mrs. Lammot du Pont)	Kennett Pike
St. Giles (1900, 1923) (razed)	Mr. & Mrs. Walter S. Carpenter	Rising Sun Lane
(formerly Square House)		
Second Office (c.1891)	DuPont Company	Buck Road
(renamed Squirrel Run Hill) Mr. & Mrs. E. Paul du Pont		
Serendip – see Calmar		
Shadowbrook (1939	Mr. Gerret & Mrs. Ann Copeland	Snuff Mill Road & Old Kennett Pike
Spanish House (1910) (razed)	Mr. & Mrs. Ernest du Pont	Kennett Pike
Square House (1900)	Mr. & Mrs. Irénée du Pont, Sr.	Rising Sun Lane
(renamed St. Giles) (razed)		
Squirrel Run (1926-1927)	Mr. & Mrs. Samuel Hallock du Pont	Old Barley Mill Road
Squirrel Run Hill – see Second Office		
Staglyn (1934-1935, 2005)	Mr. & Mrs. Brock Vinton	Guyencourt
(renamed, see Fiskekill)		
Still Pond (1899) (razed)	Mr. & Mrs. William K. du Pont	Kennett Pike
Stone's Throw (1650, 1820, 1935, 2010)	Mr. & Mrs. Peter Hayward	Centre Road
Strand Millis (1694)	Henry F. du Pont	Rockland Road
Swamp Hall (c.1800, 1864) (razed)	E. I. du Pont II	Breck's Mill Lane
Sycamore Lodge (c.1800)	DuPont Company	Breck's Mill Lane
(renamed Swamp Hall)	Eleuthere I. du Pont II	
Tulip Hollow (1939-1940)	Mr. & Mrs. Samuel Homsey (Victorine du Pont)	Lancaster Pike
Upper Louviers (c. 1802) (razed)	Gabrielle du Pont	Blackgates Road
Up-the-Hill	Mr. & Mrs. Richard "Kip" C. du Pont , Jr.	Greenville
Valley Garden Park (1930)	Mr. & Mrs. T. Coleman du Pont	Campbell Road
Valmy (c. 1906) (razed)	Mr. & Mrs. Julien de Villiers Ortiz (Alice Eugenie du Pont)	Greenville
Vireaux (1877) (razed)	Mr. & Mrs. Antoine Lentilhon Foster (Victorine du Pont)	Greenville
(Winterthur estate)		
Wagoners Row (c. 1890)	Mr. & Mrs. R.R.M. Carpenter, Jr.	Montchanin Road
Walnut Hall (1927)	William duPont, Jr.	Boyce, Virginia
White Eagle (1916-1917)	Mr. Alfred I. & Mrs. Alicia duPont	Wheatley Hills, Long Island, New York
Windmar (1906-1907)	Mr. & Mrs. W.W. Laird, Sr. (Mary Alletta Belin du Pont)	Kennett Pike
Winterthur (1839)	Mr. & Mrs. James A. Bidermann (Evelina "Lena" du Pont)	Kennett Pike
Winterthur Cottage (1951)	Mr. & Mrs. H.F. du Pont	Kennett Pike
Woodstock Farm (c. 1794)	Helena Allaire du Pont (Mrs. Richard C.)	Chesapeake City, Maryland
Xanadu (1928-1930)	Irénée du Pont, Sr.	Republic of Cuba
Yellow House (1967)	Mr. & Mrs. Daniel C. Lickle (Nancy "Missy" Kitchell)	Rockland Road

Houses without names:

Thomas Francis Bayard house (1908)	Sen. & Mrs. Thomas F. Bayard (Elizabeth Bradford du Pont)	Rockford Park
Archibald du Pont house (1913)	Mr. & Mrs. Archibald M. du Pont	Montchanin
E. I. du Pont III house (c. 1930)	Mr. & Mrs. E. I. du Pont III	Westover Hills
Richard S. du Pont farm (1900)	Richard S. du Pont	Newark
Victor du Pont house (c.1910)	Mr. & Mrs. Victor du Pont, Jr.	Centreville
Crawford Greenewalt house (1939)[1]	Mr. & Mrs. Crawford H. Greenewalt (Margaretta Lammot du Pont)	Old Kennett Pike
Ernest May house (1933)[1]	Mr. & Mrs. Ernest N. May (Irene Sophie du Pont)	Smith Ridge Road
808 Broom St. (1890, 1906)	Mr. & Mrs. T. Coleman du Pont	Wilmington

[1] Sisters Margaretta Greenewalt and Sophie May did not follow the trend of naming their houses, but within the family jokingly referred to their respective houses as *Dripping Spigots* and *Belly Acres*. Nancy Greenewalt Frederick, Margaretta's daughter, relates a story about delivery of the Mays' new station wagon by a proud salesman. Incredulous when he heard the house name, he had taken it upon himself to interpret the spelling. Across the side of the new "woodie" was emblazoned *Bellee Acres*, causing much hilarity among family members.

ACKNOWLEDGMENTS

Three years ago, when I considered writing *Chateau Country*, I learned that more than fifty books have been written about the du Pont family or have major sections devoted to it. I was further concerned that the title I long had in mind might not apply to all of the houses to be included. As it happened, the insight and interest of my editor, Nancy Schiffer, and the wisdom of the patriarch of the du Pont family, Irénée du Pont, Jr., came to my rescue. *Chateau Country* is written from a different point of view than other books and covers different material, it was pointed out. As for the title, *Chateau Country*, Mr. du Pont commented, "Well, that's what it is and that's what people call it. I think it's fine."

Greatly relieved and newly energized, I proceeded, in concert with the help and encouragement of many du Pont family members and support from numerous persons who have been associated with the du Ponts directly and indirectly. To all of them, and especially the owners and residents of the houses, past and present, who have warmly welcomed me into their homes, I owe an enormous debt of gratitude and I thank them. It is often said, but nonetheless true, without their help and interest this book could not have been written.

Chateau Country could also not have been written without the help and interest of my wife, Anne, who was always ready to offer suggestions, read the manuscript, and bring extra cups of tea.
—D.D.M.

In particular I would like to extend a special thank you to:

Nancy Schiffer
Irénée du Pont, Jr.
David Laird Craven
Marion and Kai Lassen
Missy and Dan Lickle
Charles F. du Pont
Ruly Carpenter
Keith Carpenter
Phoebe Craven
Henry B. du Pont IV
Mary Laird Silvia
Jon Williams
Chris Patterson
Geoff Halfpenny
Ronald Finch
Crystal Jester
Don Homsey
Debra A. Adelman
Grace Gary
Francesca Bonny
Lisa and David Frankel
Linda and Steve Boyden
Tatiana and Gerret Copeland
Brock and Yvonne Vinton
Kent and Betty Riegel
Calhoun W. Wick
Jeff Groff
Lou Ann Carter
Patty McCoy
Andrew W. Edmonds, Sr.
Andrew W. Edmonds, Jr.
Annie L. Jones
Katharine Gahagan

Beatrice C. du Pont
Nancy G. Frederick
Caroline duP. Prickett
Beatrice "Beasie" du Pont
Rosie McFadden
Larry C. Hampton
Pierre D. Hayward
Nathan Hayward III
Jeannette McGlothlin
Maggie Littleton
Meg Marcozzi
James R. Davis
Deborah Hughes
Adam Albright
Carolyn F. Grubb
Joanna L. Arat
Heather A. Clewell
Sean Bavol-Montgomery
Todd Bavol-Montgomery
Jason Hummel
Janet Huntsberger
Pierre S. du Pont IV
Renee O'Donnell
Lynn Williams
Geoffrey Gamble
Colvin L. Randall
Carol and Chris Jording
LeDee Wakefield
Bobbie Harvey
Ken Geist
Vera C. Palmatary
Joan Hughes
Justin M. Carisio

Francine Solomon
Anna Helgeson
Andrew Huber
Robert Conte III
John Schoonover
Catherine Wheeler Bowen
Brett Jones
Rachael DiEleuterio
Vicki Vinton King
William D. Owens
David Thompson

and especially to:
Hagley Library and Archives
Wilmington Library Reference Desk
Winterthur Archives
Longwood Gardens, Inc.
Delaware Historical Society Research
Delaware History Museum
Delaware Art Museum Library
Cruising Club of America
The Museum of America and the Seas
Christie's Auction House New York
Freeman's Auctioneers Philadelphia
The Ninth Street Bookshop

Finally I thank Terence Roberts, whose photography shows the houses as beautifully in print as they are in actuality and Joe Melloy, whose line drawings illustrate perfectly that each house is as individual as its owners.

RESOURCES

A Genius for Space
    Robin Karson
    University of Massachusetts Press, 2007
A Man And His Garden
    George F. Thompson, Sr.
    Longwood Gardens, Inc., 1976
Alfred I. du Pont — The Family Rebel
    Marquis James
    Bobbs-Merrill Company, 1942
Alfred I. Du Pont - The Man & His Family
    Joseph Frazier Wall
    Oxford University Press, 1990
America's 60 Families
    Ferdinand Lundberg
    Vanguard Press, 1937
American Country House, The
    Clive Aslet
    Yale University Press, 1990
American Country House in the Brandywine Valley (Thesis), The
    Karen Marshall
    Heritage Preservation Coordinator
    Chester County Dept. of Parks & Recreation
American Eden
    Wade Graham
    Harper Collins, 2011
American Elegance
    Cheryl Gibbs and Lucinda Costin
    Abbeville Press, Inc., 1988
American Estates and Gardens
    Barr Ferree
    Munn & Co., 1906
Architect & the American Country House, The
    Mark Alan Hewitt
    Yale University Press, 1990
Autobiography of Du Pont de Nemours, The
    Translated by Elizabeth Fox-Genovese
    Scholarly Resources, 1984
Black Powder, White Lace
    Margaret M. Mulrooney
    University of New Hampshire, 2002
Blood Relations —The Rise and Fall of the du Ponts of Delaware
    Leonard Mosley
    Bobbs-Merrill Company, Inc., 1941
Brandywine, The
    Henry Seidel Canby
    Schiffer Publishing Ltd., 1975
Brandywine Valley Scenic River and Highway Study
    New Castle County Department of Planning, 1987
Bridges
    Marjorie G. McNinch
    Cedar Tree Press, 1995
Buildings of Delaware
    W. Barksdale Maynard
    University of Virginia Press, 2008
Centreville: The History of a Delaware Village:1680-2000
    Centreville Civic Association, 2001
Colorful Du Pont Company, The
    P.J. Wingate
    Serendipity Press, 1982
Country Houses Along the Brandywine: The Du Pont Legacy
    Maureen Quimby
    Thesis, May 1988

Delaware — A Guide to the First State
    American Guide Series
    Federal Writers' Project
    Works Progress Administration
    First published June 1938
Delaware Aviation History
    George J. Frebert
    Dover Litho Printing Co., 1998
Discover the Winterthur Estate
    Pauline K. Eversmann with Kathryn H. Head
    Winterthur Museum, 1998
Discover the Winterthur Garden
    Denise Magnani
    Winterthur Museum, 1998
Du Pont — Behind the Nylon Curtain
    Gerald Colby Zilg
    Prentice-Hall, 1974
Du Ponts, The: Houses and Gardens in the Brandywine
    Maggie Lidz
    Acanthus Press, 2009
Du Pont De Nemours: Apostle of Liberty and the Promised Land
    Pierre Jolly
    The Brandywine Publishing Company, 1956
    Translated from the French by Elise Du Pont Elrick
du Pont Domain, The
    E.Paul du Pont
    F.Wm. F. Fell Co., Philadelphia, 1945
Dupont Dynasty, The
    John K. Winkler
    Reynal & Hutchcock, New York, 1935
Du Pont Dynasty, The
    Gerald Colby (Zilg)
    Lyle Stuart, 1984 *(Re-release)*
Du Pont Family, The
    John Gates
    Doubleday & Company, 1979
Du Pont Family Legacy of Horticulture in the Brandywine Valley
    Eliabeth Varley
    Thesis, 1995
Du Pont Family, The: Two Hundred Years of Portraits
    Brandywine River Museum
    An Exhibition June 10 Through September 4, 2000
DuPont: From the Banks of the Brandywine to Miracles of Science
    Adrian Kinnane
    E.I. du Pont de Nemours and Company, 2002
DuPont Highway, The
    William Francis and Michael C. Hahn
    Arcadia Publishing, 2009
Du Pont — The Autobiography of an American Enterprise
    E.I. Du Pont de Nemours & Company
    Charles Scribner's Sons, New York, 1952
Du Pont — 200 Years of an American Family
    Michelle Ferrari
    Winton du Pont, 2001
du Ponts — From Gunpowder to Nylon, The
    Max Dorian
    Little, Brown Co., Boston, 1961
Du Ponts of Delaware, The
    William A. Carr
    Dodd Mead, 1964
Du Pont — One Hundred and Forty Years
    William S. Dutton
    Chas. Scribner's Sons, 1942

Du Ponts — Portrait of a Dynasty, The
    Marc Duke
    Saturday Review Press
    E.P. Dutton & Co., 1976
Educating today ... preserving for tomorrow: A 40-Year History of the Delaware Nature Society
    Joan W. Priest
    Delaware Nature Society, 2005
E.I. du Pont, Botaniste: The Beginning of a Tradition
    Norman B. Wilkinson
    The University of Virginia Press, 1972
Eleutherian Mills
    Maureen O'Brien Quimby
    rev. Debra Hughes and Carol Hagglund
    Hagley Museum and Library, 1999
Explosions at the Du Pont Powder Mills
    William Hulbert du Pont
    Privately printed
First State, First Lady's Recipe Book, The
    Francis O. Allmond
    Charles Printing Company, Inc., 1975
Forever Green: A Commemorative History of Tower Hill School
    Tower Hills School Association, 1994
Genealogy of the du Pont Family 1739 - 1949
    Pierre S. du Pont
    Hambleton Printing & Publishing
    Wilmington, DE
Golden Age of American Gardens, The
    Mac Griswold and Eleanor Weller
    Harry N. Abrams, Inc., 1991
Great Estates: The Lifestyles and Homes of American Magnates
    William G. Scheller
    Universe, 2009
Guide to Winterthur Museun & Country Estate
    Pauline K. Eversnann
    University Press of New England, 2005
Hagley Cookbook, The: Recipes With A Brandywine Tradition
    Hagley Volunteers Cookbook Committee
    Charles Printing Co., Wilmington, DE
Hagley Museum; A Story of Early Industry On the Brandywine
    Eleutherian Mills Hagley Foundatiion, 1957
Henry Francis du Pont
    John A.H. Sweeney
    Henry Francis du Pont Museum, The 1980
Henry Francis Du Pont Winterthur Museum, The
    Joseph Downs and Alice Winchester
    Antiques Magazine, 1951
Henry F. Du Pont and Winterthur
    Ruth Lord
    Yale University Press, 1999
Heritage of Longwood Gardens, The
    Pierre S. du Pont & His Legacy
    Longwood Gardens, 1998
Historic Houses and Buildings of Delaware
    Harold Donaldson and Cortlandt Hubbard
    Public Archives Commission, Dover, DE, 1962
History of Delaware
    J. Thomas Scharf
    K.L.J. Richards & Co., 1888
History of the State of Delaware
    Henry C. Conrad
    1908
Horse On Rodney Square, The
    Lee Reese
    The News-Journal Company, 1977
Hotel du Pont Story
    Harry V. Ayres
    Serendipity Press, 1981

Jessie Ball Du Pont Papers
    Department of Special Collections and Archives
    James G. Leyburn Library
    Washington and Lee University
    Lexington, Virginia
Lammot Du Pont and the American Explosives Industry: 1850-1884
    Norman B. Wilkinson
    University Press of Virginia, 1984
Life At Winterthur: A Family Album
    Maggie Lidz
    Winterthur Museum, 2001
Life of Alexis Irénée du Pont, The: Volumes I and II
    Edited and compiled by Allan J. Henry
    William F. Fell Co., Philadelphia, 1945
Longwood Gardens: 100 Years of Garden Splendor
    Colvin Randall
    ,Longwood Garfdens, 2005
Millionaires, Mansions, and Motor Yachts
    Ross MacTaggart
    W.W. Norton & Company, 2004
Money, Manure & Maintenance: Ingredients for Successful Gardens of Marian Coffin
    Nancy Fleming
    Country Place Books, 1995
Montpelier and the Madisons
    Matthew G. Hyland
    History Press, 2007
Nemours: A Portrait of Alfred I. duPont's House
    Dwight Young and Grace Gary
    Rizzoli, 2011
100 Most Beautiful Rooms in America
    Helen Comstock
    Bonanza Books, 1958
Stone Houses: Traditional Houses of Pennsylvania's Bucks County and Brandywine Valley
    Geoffrey Gross, John Milner, Margaret Richie, Gregory Huber
    Rizzoli, 2005
Story of Christ Church Christiana Hundred and its People, The
    Charles A. Silliman
    Humbleton, 1960
Treasure House of Early American Rooms, The
    John H. Sweeney
    Introduction by Henry F. du Pont
    Bonanza Books, 1978
Two Hundred in Two Thousand: A Du Pont Family Reunion
    Robert Rebensky
    The Du Pont De Nemours Cemetery Company, 2000
Vanished Estates of the du Pont Family
    Barbara E. Benson
    The Hunt, June-July 2000
Within the Reach of All
    Susan M. Chase
    Friends of Wilmington Park, 2005
Winterthur's Culinary Collection
    Anne Beckley Coleman
    Henry Francis du Pont Winterthur Museum, 1983
Winterthur Illustrated
    John A.H. Sweeney
    Chanticleer Press, 1963
Winterthur In Bloom
    Harold Bruce
    Chanticleer Press, 1968
Women's History: A Guide to Sources at Hagley Museum and Library
    Lynn Ann Catanese
    Greenwood Press, 1957

INDEX

A

Addlestone, 260
Aeolian organ, 94, 96, 170, 245
Alapocas, 6
Alfred I. duPont Institute, 144
American Car & Foundry Co., 94, 133, 257
American Eagle, 5, 40, 41, 53, 75, 101, 144, 165, 192, 254, 256
American Youth, 18
Amy E. du Pont Music Building, 55, 256
Anderson, William, 89
A Piece of Cake, 134
Appalachian Piedmont Region, 134
Applecross, 9-17, 253, 260
Architectural Record, The, 142
Arthur Bernardson & Associates, 33
Artilleryman, The, 18, 19
Ashland Red Clay Creek, 17-23, 132, 181, 257, 260
Austin, Jean Liseter, 25, 47, 48, 261

B

Bach, Oscar, 54, 161, 163
Ball Farm, 9, 59, 64, 65, 260
Ball, Jessie B., 143, 257
Baltimore & Ohio Railroad, 21
Barbaro, 26
Barber J., 117
Barlovento, 40
Barlovento II, 40
Bauduy, Peter, 5
Bayard, Thomas Francis, house, 262
Bear Lodge, 182, 188
Beaver Dam Marble Co., 82
Beitel, Jeffrey, 10, 11
Bellevue Hall, 6, 24-29, 48, 205, 253, 260
Bellevue State Park, 25, 27
Belly Acres, 262
Bernardon & Associates, 122
Bethlehem Steel Co., 154
Bidermann Golf Club, 238, 254
Bidermann, Jacques Antoine, 259, 229
Big Bend, 260
Binfield Park, Bracknell, 25, 51
Blackgates Road, 39, 125, 217, 218, 224, 262
Blue Bottle Inn, 47
Boca Grande, FL, 74, 82, 239
Bohemia Manor, 252, 260
Bois des Fossés, 38-45, 73, 205, 252, 254, 259-260
Bon Sejour, 73, 87, 88
Boone & Crockett Club, 60

Boudin, Stephane, 238
Bowman-Biltmore Hotels Corp., 117
Boyden, Steve & Linda, 3, 196-203, 232
Boxwood, 30-37
Bradford, Eleuthera du Pont, 17, 126, 260
Brandywine blue rock, 16, 65, 81, 254
Brandywine Club, 74, 258
Brandywine Creek State Park, 229, 238, 254
Brandywine River, 5, 6, 26, 73-74, 78, 130, 182, 197, 211, 217-218, 253-255, 257-258, 263
Brandywine River Museum, 40
Brandywine School of Art, 245
Brandywine Valley, 5, 6, 40, 73, 81, 87, 93, 141, 146, 153, 181, 197, 211, 254-256, 263-264
Brantwyn, 39-45, 260
Breck, William, 180-183, 217, 262,
Breck's Lane, 257-258, 262
Breck's Mill, 181. 183, 255, 258, 262
Bredin, Bruce & Octavia (Tibi), 102, 238
Bredin, Octavia M. (Tibi), 102
Breese, Vinton, 60
Brinckle, John Rodney, 81-83
Brinckle, Samuel C., Rev., 81
Brindley, James, 47-48
Brookdale Farm, 260
Broom, Jacob, 5. 73, 256
Brown & Whiteside, 59, 65, 169
Buck, Alice du Pont Wilson, 182
Buck, Clayton D., Sr., 181, 260
Buck and Doe Run Farm, 260
Buck, Dorcas Van Dyke, 126-127, 182
Buck Hill Farm, 260
Buckley's Tavern, 108, 125
Buena Vista, 181, 252, 260
Bushnell, Robert, 134

C

Calmar, 252, 257, 260, 262
Campbell, John, 191
Carpenter, Irene (Renee), 59-60, 122
Carpenter, Keith, 58, 61-63, 65
Carpenter, Louisa d'Andelot (Jenney), 212
Carpenter, Margaretta Lammot du Pont, 59, 123, 191, 260
Carpenter, Nancy, 59
Carpenter, R. R. M., Jr., 59, 61
Carpenter, Robert Ruliph Morgan Sr., 59-61,122
Carpenter, R. R. M. III, 63, 65, 260
Carpenter, Ruly and Stephanie, 65
Carpenter, William, 59

Carillon, The (Nemours), 205, 258

Carrere & Hastings, 141-145, 255

Carter, Jimmy, Pres., 134

Casa del Sueno, 54

Center Meeting Road, 6, 254

Centreville, 6, 82, 107-109, 155, 163, 253, 255, 261-263

Chamberlin, Noel, 10, 11

Chandler, Theophilus P., Jr., 53, 229

Charles & Co., 142

Charleston, SC, 125, 143, 218

Chateau Country, 153, 156, 191, 255, 256

Cheval de frise, 142

Cherry Knoll, 260

Chestertown House, 233-234, 260

Chevannes, 6, 39, 94, 252, 254, 255, 257, 260

Chicken Alley, 127-129, 224, 255, 277

Christ Church, 11, 81, 162-163, 198, 255, 258, 264

Christiana Securities, 197

Christiana Stables, 154

Christina River, 19, 116, 254

Christie's Auction House, 102, 239

Ciarrocchi, Charles J. Jr. and Diane, 32-33, 35

Clark, Katherine, 101

Clayton Hotel, 115

Clenny Run, 229, 234, 237-238, 242

Clenny, William, 229

Coffin, Marian Cruger, 10, 82, 85, 134, 162-163

Consomme Bellevue, 255, 257

Copeland, Charles, 40, 76, 260

Copeland, Gerret and Tatiana, 181-182, 184, 187-188

Copeland House, 182, 184, 223, 257, 260

Copeland, Lammot du Pont, 19, 82, 101, 133, 182, 261

Copeland, Lammot du Pont, Jr., 260

Copeland, Pamela C., 19, 82, 101, 133, 182, 26

Corbit-Sharp House, 82

Covarrocas and Giovantes, 245, 247

Coverdale Farm, 260

Craig, James Osborne, 53

Craig, Mary, 53, 55

Craven, David S., 223-225

Craven, Rosa Laird, 223, 225, 260

Craven, Wilhelmina Wemyss Laird, 223, 225

Crawford, Leon Wilde, 223, 259

Crestlea, 260

Crooked Billet, 46-51, 252, 260

Crowninshield, Frank, 74-75

Crowninshield, Louise, 74-76

Cyane, 18

D

Dalmas, Charles, 74, 256, 261

Dauneport, 52-57, 260

Davis, Jr., F.B., 31, 33

Davis, Jean Ellen, 47

Davis, Meyer, 40, 163, 256

Davis, Zack, 61

Dean, Paulina du Pont, 10

DeArmond, Ashmead & Bickley, 81, 83, 153, 155

Delaware Land Development Company, 31, 47

Delaware Park Racetrack, 9

Delaware River, 26, 116

de Montchanin, Anne Alexandrine, 18, 121, 256-257

de Pusy, Bureaux, 5, 6, 88

Dilks, Albert W., 191, 193-194, 224

Dilwyne Badminton Club, 60

Dilwyne Farms, 9, 58-63, 65, 122, 260

Dilwyne Kennels, 60

Distribution, The 1921, 59, 76, 224, 257

Dixon, Jeremiah, 198

Dixon, Joseph, 181, 183

Doe Run, 260

Doe Run Inn, 260

Doggone, 252, 260

Dogwood, 163, 252, 260

Domville, Paul, 206-207

Donaghcumper House, 102

Dripping Spigots, 108, 262

Duenling, Louisa, 134

du Pont, Ada B. Ward, 261

du Pont, Adelaide Camile Denise, 144

du Pont, Aimee, 162

DuPont Airfield, 18, 256

du Pont, Alice Elsie, 181

du Pont, Alice Houndsfield, 181, 260

du Pont, Alicia Bradford, 141, 143-144, 218, 254, 262

duPont, Alfred I., 79, 141-144, 218-219, 255-259, 261-262

du Pont, Alfred Victor Philadelphe, 191, 192, 219, 229, 257, 260

du Pont, Alice Belin, 82

du Pont, Amelia Elizabeth, 53

du Pont, Amy E., 52, 256, 260

du Pont, Archibald, 262

du Pont, Beatrice C. 261

du Pont, Bessie Gardner, 255, 257, 260

duPont, "Boss" Henry, 25, 47

du Pont, Charles I., 181, 182, 219, 255

du Pont, Charles Jr., 181, 183

DuPont Company, 5, 134

DuPont Country Club, 29-41, 217-219, 257

du Pont de Nemours Cemetery, 10, 256, 258

Du Pont de Nemours Pere, Fils et Cie, 5

du Pont de Nemours, Pierre S., 6, 39, 88, 121, 125, 191-192, 254-258

du Pont de Nemours, Samuel, 18

du Pont, Dulcinea Ophelia Payne, 260

du Pont, E. Paul, 181, 218, 256, 258, 262

du pont, Edith "Skippy," 204, 261

du Pont, Edward, 18

du Pont, Eleuthere Irénée, 19, 72, 79, 133, 169, 205, 218, 219, 254-257, 259-260, 262

du Pont, Sr., Eleuthere Irénée, 229

du Pont, Jr., Eleuthere Irénée, 262

du Pont, Eleuthere I. III, house, 262

du Pont, Elizabeth Bradford, 260, 262

du Pont, Elise, 219, 220

du Pont, Ellen C., 88-89, 259

du Pont, Eleuthera, 261

du Pont, Emma Paulina, 88-89

du Pont, Emily du Pont Tybout, 18

du Pont Ernest, 262

du Pont, Esther, 260

du Pont, Ethel Fleet Hallock, 224

du Pont, Ethel Pyle, 161

du Pont, Eugene E., 163

du Pont, Eugene H., 33, 141

du Pont, Eugene H., Jr., 53-54, 122, 161-163, 258, 260

du Pont, Eugene III, 55, 56

du Pont, Evelina (Lena) Gabrielle, 229, 259, 261, 262

du Pont, Francis G., 253, 261

du Pont, Francis I. and Marianna Rhett, 218

du Pont, Francis Victor, 261

du Pont, Gabrielle Josephine de la Fite de Pelleport, 180-181, 217, 219, 262

du Pont Gold Cup, 54

duPont, Helena, 262

du Pont, Henry Algernon, 141, 192, 205, 211-212, 229, 233, 234, 235, 256-257, 259

du Pony, Henry Belin, 163, 199, 229, 234, 256, 258, 260

du Pont, Henry Belin IV, 18

du Pont, Henry Belin, Jr., 17, 19, 22, 23, 182

du Pont, Henry E.I. II, 260

du Pont, Henry Francis, 134, 162, 234, 237-239, 254-255, 259-260, 262

du Pont, Hubert, 218

du Pont, Irene, 95, 262

du Pont, Irénée, Jr., 93-95, 108, 261

du Pont, Irénée, Sr., 95, 105-107, 244-247, 250-251, 259, 261-262

du Pont, Isabella Mathieu, 81, 261

du Pont, Janet G., 101

du Pont, Jean Kane Foulke, 181

du Pont, Jean Ellen, 260

duPont, Jessie Ball, 143-144, 257

Du Pont, Julia Sophia Angelique, 40

du Pont, Lammot, 153, 191, 193, 205, 229, 258-262

du Pont, Lammot, Jr., 260

du Pont, Louisa G., 74

du Pont, Louisa d'Andelot, 59, 79, 191, 199, 211, 212

du Pont, Evelina, 256

du Pont, Margaret Flett, 192

du Pont, Margaretta E., 212, 261

du Pont, Margaretta Lammot, 87, 260-262

du Pont, Marion, 25, 48, 108, 261

du Pont, Mary Alletta Belin, 191-193, 223-224, 262

du Pont, Mary Jane, 153, 261

du Pont, Mary Sophie, 181

du Pont, Mary Van Dyke, 181, 260

duPont Motor Car, 181, 256

du Pont, Nancy Bradford, 261

du Pont, Natalie, 205, 260

du Pont, Nicholas, 199, 258, 261

du Pont, Octavia Mary (Tibi), 239, 260

du Pont, Pauline L., 233

du Pont, Pierre S., 59, 81, 108, 168-171, 255, 257, 261

du Pont, Pierre S. III, 27, 38-41, 76, 205, 254, 258, 260

du Pont, Pierre "Pete" S. IV, 40-41, 261

Du Pont Powder Mills, 5, 6, 9, 74, 121-122, 126, 142, 183, 217-218, 254-255, 257-259

du Pont, Reynolds, 261

du Pont, Richard "Kip" C. Jr., 261, 262

du Pont, Richard S., 199, 256, 262

du Pont, Ruth Ellen, 234

du Pont, Ruth Wales, 237

Du Pont, Samuel Francis, Admr., 218-219, 230, 257

du Pont, Samuel Hallock, 197, 199, 258, 262

du Pont, Sophie Madeleine, 78, 247

DuPont Station, 121-122, 257, 259

du Pont, T. Coleman, 141, 181-182, 260-262

du Pont, Victor Jr., 181, 261, 262

du Pont, Victor Marie, 181, 219, 256, 257, 261

Du Pont, Victorine, 262

du Pont, Wilhelmina Haedrick, 260

du Pont, William H., 74

du Pont, William, Jr., 24, 262

du Pont, William, Sr., 261

duPont, William III, 27

du Pont, William Kemble, 197, 224, 258, 262

E

Edison, Thomas, 27, 141, 199

Edison, William, 27

Edmonds, Sr., Andrew, 32, 263

Edmonds. Jr., Andrew, 32, 263

Edmonds, George P., 31, 33, 260

Edmonds, Natalie Wilson, 31-32

E.I. du Pont de Nemours & Co., 5, 73, 229, 257

Eleutherian Mills, 5, 6, 72-76, 79, 125, 219, 229-230, 252, 254-259

Elrick, Elise du Pont, 218-220, 264
Elton, 252, 257, 260-261
Emmet, Devereaux, 234, 254
Episcopal Diocese, 154, 155
Essonne, France, 256
Exhibition of the Industry of All Nations, 218

F

Fairfield Farms Horse Show, 54
Fair Hill (MD), 26, 252, 261
Fair Hilll (PA), 253, 261
Fairthorne, 252, 261
Farfields, 261
Farquhar, Donald K., 182
Ferrier, Gabriel, 142
Finch, Ronald, Dr., 211-212
Fiskekill, 205-207, 252, 261-262
Fouilhoux, J A, 117
Fountain Plaza, 18
Foxcatcher Farms, 25
Foxwood, 252, 261
Frankel, Steven and Lisa, 107-110, 263

G

Garden Club of America, 10, 31, 76, 88
Gate houses, Blackgates Road, 218-220
Gibraltar, 10-11, 80-85, 224, 261
Gilchrist, Edmond, 88-89
Gilliand, Maurice, 239
Godley, F., 117
Go For Wand, 154
Goodstay, 5-6, 73, 87-90, 191, 252, 261
Gram, Janet, 101
Granogue, 2, 92-98, 205, 245-246, 252, 256, 258-259, 261
Green Hill, 87
Greenville, 6, 9-11, 26, 48, 61, 65, 101-102, 135, 161-163, 182, 199, 205, 225, 253, 255, 258, 260-262
Greenville Country Club, 162-163
Greenville House, 100-103
Greenewalt, Crawford Hallock, 107-109, 260-262
Gregg, John, 212, 258
Gregg, William, 11, 211-212
Griggs, Clark Robinson, 25, 27
Guernsey cattle, 25, 171, 230
Guyencourt, 205, 207, 252-253, 257, 259, 261-262
Guyencourt, The Siege of, 252-253

H

Hacienda, The, 82
Hagley, 18, 56, 75-76, 79, 95, 126, 128,152, 193-194, 211, 216, 220, 224, 229, 234, 244, 248-252, 255-261

Hagley House, 126, 229, 257, 261
Happenstance Farm, 261
Hart, Mrs. Walter T. (Doris), 27, 75
Harry's Gate, 155, 261
Harvey, André, 10, 15, 93, 182
Hayloft, The, 261
H.B. du Pont Park, 18
Henry Clay Village Historic District, 181-182, 257-259
Herter, Adele, 54
Hexton Hall, 252, 261
Hicacos Peninsula, 244-245, 259
Hilgartner Marble Co., 54
Hirons, John, 87, 89
Hod House, 107-112
Hodgson Houses, 107-108
Holcomb, Frederick W., 39-41, 44
Holden, McLaughlin & Associates, 9
Hollahan, Cornelius, 133
Homsey, Samuel and Victorine, 101-102, 126-127, 132-133, 135, 154, 253, 262
Hoopes (Edgar) Reservoir, 101-103, 259
Hotel du Pont, 114-119
House Beautiful, 54, 257
Howard, Robert A., 17-18
Hurd, Henriette Wyeth, 108
Hurd, Peter, 108

I

Ile Louviers, 217
Indian Motorcycle Co., 102, 181, 256, 258
Inn at Montchanin Village, The, 121-123, 258
Invergarry, 252, 261
Iron Bridge, 125, 127, 217-218, 254-255, 257
Iris Brook, 192, 261
Italian Ruin Garden, 75
Ives, Albert Ely, 31, 80-81, 85, 233, 257
Ives, Burl, 54, 212

J

Jardin des Plantes, 73
Jefferson, Thomas, Pres., 73, 125, 130
Jekyll, Gertrude, 234
Jenney, John King, 212
Johnson, Reginald, 54
Jones, Annie Lunger, 154, 260, 263
Jumbles, 79

K

Kelsey, Seth, 134-135
Kemble, William, 9, 191
Kennedy, Jacqueline, 40, 75, 238, 257

Kennett Pike, 6, 9, 4653, 55, 74, 88, 93, 108, 153, 155, 161-163, 190-193, 234, 239, 253, 255-257, 260-261

Kershner, Vance V., 155

King Baudouin I (Belgium), 134

King Ranch, 261

Kintzing, Peter, 142

Kleberg, Robert J., Jr., 26

Krazy Kat's, 120, 122

L

Laird, Bissell and Meeds, 223

Laird, Mary A.B. du Pont, 183, 126-127, 183, 223-255, 257

Laird, William Winder, 183, 223-225, 258, 262

Laird, William "Chick", W., Jr., 108, 126-127, 129, 142, 144, 181, 183, 197, 224, 255

Laird, Winnifred "Winnie", Moreton, 126-127, 129

Lassen, Kai, 48

Lassen, Marion du Pont, 48

Latrobe, Benjamin, 125, 130

Lee, Maurice du Pont, 192

Lenape Indians, 141, 169, 212

Letdown, 252, 261

L'Hermitage, 261

Lickle, Nancy (Missy) and Dan, 60, 131-122, 262

Life Magazine, 40, 108, 163

Limerick, 252, 261

Limestone Farm, 261

Lina, Andrew, 87, 89

Lindeberg, Harrie T., 160-161, 163

Lindbergh, Charles, 18, 117, 256-257

Liseter Hall, 25-26, 48, 261

Longwood Farms, 169, 171

Longwood Gardens, 10, 40, 82, 117, 169, 170-172, 174, 176, 178, 198, 224, 229, 252, 256, 261

Lord & Burnham, 10, 88, 94, 107, 111, 206, 224

Loseley Park, Surrey Co., England, 25

Louviers, France, 217

Louviers gate houses, 218-220

Louviers, Lower, 124-130, 182, 186, 217-218, 229, 252, 255-261

Louviers, Upper, 126, 181-182, 186, 216-221, 224, 257, 262

Ludowicki Roof Tile Co., 206

Lunger, Harry W., Mary Jane, 153-155, 159, 261

Lyndham, 261

Lyons, Dr. & Mrs. Garrett B., Jr., 55

M

Madison, James Pres. & Dolley, 6, 24-26, 48, 108, 265

Maddux, Alicia Bradford and George, 141

Maillol, Aristede, 88

March Bank, 230, 234

Marie Antoinette, 142, 143, 170

Mason, Charles, 198

Massena and du Pont, 31, 39, 41, 144, 192, 205-207

May, Ernest, house, 262

McLane, George R., 87, 89

McConnell, Jean Ellen du Pont, 47-48, 260

McConnell, J.H. Tyler, 47-49, 260

McCoy, Ann Wyeth, 108

McDonald, Rosa Laird Hayward, 192

McHugh, Marie L., 55

Meadow Wood, 261

Meeds, Ellen C. du Pont, 88-89, 259

Meeds, Hollyday, 223, 259

Mellor, Meigs & Howe, 74

Meown, 6, 82, 252, 254, 257, 261

Mills of Liberty, The, 59, 61

Montchanin, 6, 9-10, 18, 65, 121-122, 205, 212, 255, 261-262

Montchanin Design Group, 10-11

Montchanin Railroad Station, 59, 162, 257, 259

Montchanin Road, 47, 59, 95, 121, 181, 257-260, 262

Montchanin Village, The Inn at, 120-123, 258, 262

Montmorency, 261

Montpelier, 6, 24-26, 48, 108, 265

Moreton, Winnifred, 126-127

Mount Cuba, 2, 133-139, 261

Mount Cuba Center, 133-135

Mount Harmon Farm, 261

Mount Vernon, 53

Murillo, Bartolome Esteban, 142

N

National Historic Trust, 47

National Trust for Historic Preservation, 75

Nemours, 5, 6, 217, 254, 261

Nemours Foundation, 141, 144

Nemours Gardens, 39, 144, 150-151

Nemours House, 10, 53, 74, 87, 138, 141-151, 205, 218, 224, 252, 254-255, 257-258, 261

New Castle Air Force Base, 18

New Castle County, 19, 26, 153-154, 205, 254-254, 264

New Poems, 154, 155, 261

Newtown Square, PA, 25, 47-48, 260-261

New Year's Calling, 32, 224, 227, 255, 257

New York Crystal Palace, 218

New Yorker, The, 60

New York Times, 60, 144, 181, 183, 239

1921 Distribution, The, 59, 62, 76, 126, 224, 258

Nor'easter, 18

North Bergen, NJ, 5, 73, 88

O

Oberod, 2, 153-156, 159, 252, 261

Off Soundings Club, 18
Ogle, Thomas, 47-48
Okie, Richardson Brognard, 17, 19-20, 31, 196-197, 199, 212, 258
Old Kennett Pike, 53, 55, 108, 162, 260, 262
Old Mill, The, 181, 183, 261
Old Nemours, 10, 53, 138, 224, 257
One Hundredth Anniversary Celebration, 192-193
Osborne, Margaret, 27
Owl's Nest, 53-54, 82, 94, 117, 160-163, 252, 258, 261

P

Parke Bernet, 142
Parks, Charles C., 10, 18
Parrish, Maxfield, 87, 94, 96, 245
Patterns, 40, 253, 261
Peacock Alley, 116
Peale, Rembrandt, 18, 23, 94
Peirce's Park, 40, 169, 171
Peirce, George, 169
Peirce, Joshua, Samuel, 168-169, 171
Peirce-du Pont House, 168-171, 261
Pelleport, 6, 53, 74, 126, 217, 252, 261
Penn, Letitia, 133
Penn, William, 11, 19, 46-47, 133, 153-154, 169, 197, 211, 257-258
Pennsbury Manor, 19, 197
Philadelphia Flower Show, 94
Philadelphia Phillies, 61
Physiocracy, 18-19
Pirates Picnic Ashore, (The Party Ashore), 246, 251
Point Lookout Farm, 261
Pontiana, 73, 258
Point-to-Point Steeplechase, 18, 207
Pratt, Richard, 75, 257
Preservation Delaware, 83
Prickett, William and Elizabeth, 108-109, 263
Pyle, Howard, 108, 114, 245
Pyle, William, 87, 89, 259

Q

Queen Theatre, 115

R

Radnor Hunt Club, 206
Randalea, 252, 261
Raskob, John J., 115-117
Reagan, Ronald, Pres., 134
Rectitudine Sto, 143, 161
Red Clay Creek, 16-20, 132-133, 154, 182, 253-254, 258, 260
Rehoboth Beach, DE, 82
Renaud, 261
Rencourt, 252, 261
Ridgely, 252, 258, 261
Riegel, Richard E. and Edith, 204-207, 261, 263
Rising Sun Lane, 91, 94-95, 190, 253, 257, 259, 261-262
Rising Sun Village, 259

Robinson, Hanson, 25, 27
Rock Manor (Rock Farms), 141, 144, 261
Rockland, DE, 41, 162, 205, 211-212, 217-219, 258
Rockland Road, 39-40, 59, 121-122, 124, 141, 144, 238, 254, 258-262
Rock Spring, 252, 258, 262
Rocky Hill, 262
Rodney, Caesar, 81, 115
Roentgen, David, 142
Rokeby, 180-189, 217, 252, 255, 258, 262
Rollins, John W., 55
Roosevelt, Franklin D., Pres., 122, 162-163, 257
Roosevelt, Franklin D., Jr., 117, 122, 162, 165
Roosevelt, Theodore, Pres., 60
Rosemont, 25, 31
Ross, Donald Peabody, 9-11, 26, 260
Rounds, The, 262
Route 52, 93, 257

S

Saint Amour, 6, 11, 190-195, 257, 262
St. Giles, 262
Samuel T. Freeman, 239
Santa Barbara, CA, 54, 55
Saridakis, Christopher and Penny, 9-11
Saunders, Rikki, 205
Savery & Cooke, 237
Scott, Marion du Pont S., 48, 108, 261
Schoonover, Frank, 87, 108, 117, 245-247, 251, inside cover
Sears, Thomas W., 134-135
Second Office, 9, 59, 74, 256, 258, 262
Siege of Guyencourt, The, 252-253
Serendip, 257, 260, 262
Sezincote House, 239
Shadowbrook, 252, 262
Sharp, Bayard, 9, 254
Sharp, Hugh Rodney, 11, 55, 81-83, 170, 254, 257-259, 261
Shields, Jean, 134
Shipman, Ellen Biddle, 161-163, 166-167, 258
Silvia, Mary Laird, 126-127, 224, 263
Sleeper, Henry Davis, 233
Smyth, James M., 141
Soda House, 59, 60, 63, 76
Sotheby's New York, 134
Southern California Tennis Assn., 27
Spahr, Albert H., 93, 95
Spanish House, 223, 257, 262
Spruance, William Corbit, 94
Square House, 81, 223, 253, 257, 262
Squirrel Run, 197-199, 202, 252, 258-259, 262
Squirrel Run Hill, 196, 262
Squirel Run Village, 197, 199

Staglyn, 205-207, 261-262
Stedham, Adam, 47-49
Still Pond, 9, 10, 223-225, 257, 262
Stone's Throw, 262
Strand Millis, 59, 211-214, 253, 258, 262
Street, Gerald, 246-247
Strong, Herbert, 246
Stuart, Gilbert, 142
Stuart, Captain Sidney, 218
Swamp Hall, 141, 262
Sweeney, Joseph, 238-239
Sycamore Lodge, 262

T

Tankopanicum Musical Club, 141, 144, 256, 258
Tsaraskoya Selo, 142
Thompson, George, 169, 171
Thompson, James, 9, 11
Thouron, Esther du Pont, 260
Thouron, Sir John, 260
Tiffany Studios, 142
Tower Hill School, 59, 192-193, 224, 258
Town & Country, 142, 144
Tulip Hollow, 253, 262

U

UNIDEL Foundation, 55
University of Delaware, 10, 55, 81-82, 87-87, 94, 197-198, 212, 256
Upper Louviers, 126, 181, 182, 186, 216-219, 257, 262
Up-the-Hill, 262
U.S. Rubber Co., 31
USS *Montauk,* 218

V

Valley Garden Park, 259, 262
Valmy, 252, 262
Van Dyke, Dorcas, 126, 182
Van Dyke, Mary, 181
Varadero Beach, Cuba, 245-247
Varadero Golf Club, 246
Vicmead Hunt Club, 18, 88, 258-259
Village of Montchanin (marker), 121
Vinton, Brock J. and Yvonne, 205-207, 262
Vinton, Vicki, 10, 65, 69, 206, 209
Vireaux, 262

W

Wagoners Row, 252, 258-259, 262
Waldorf-Astoria, 115, 117
Wallace & Warner, 31, 33

Washington, George, Pres., 53, 143
Waterman Thomas T., 237, 239
Webb, Electra Havemeyer, 230
Westover Hills, 9, 27, 31, 33, 47, 205, 259, 262
Wedding trees, 127
Weymouth, George A. (Frolic), 17, 206-207, 262
Wheatley Hills, 127
Wheelwright, Ellen Meeds, 88-89, 259
Wheelwright, Robert, 88-89, 259
White Clay Creek, 19, 154
White Eagle, 144, 262
Whitely Farm, 198-199
Wimbledon Manor House, 142
Wilmington Morning News, 115
Wilmington and Brandywine Railroad, 205
Wilmington and Northern Railroad, 60, 93, 121-122, 162, 205, 207, 224, 234, 257, 259
Wilmington and Reading Railroad, 259
Wilmington Blue Rocks, 61
Wilmington Country Club, 88, 229, 234, 238
Wilmington Garden Club, 94
Wilmington Trust Co., 31, 33, 59
Wilson, Alice, 181-182
Wilson, Paul, 181
Windmar, 223-225, 253, 257, 262
Winterthur, 2, 6, 10, 18, 74, 82, 94, 102-103, 117, 121-122, 133-134, 146, 162, 171, 192, 205-206, 224, 228-240, 252, 254-255, 259, 262
Winterthur Cottage, 237-239, 248
Winterthur Farms, 230, 234, 238
Woman's Home Companion, 87
Woodstock Farm, 262
Woolton Manor, 25-26
Wright, Frank Lloyd, 54-108
Wyeth, Andrew, 93, 108, 117, 238
Wyeth, Carolyn, 108, 117
Wyeth, Jamie, 117
Wyeth, N.C., 87, 108, 117

X

Xanadu, 108, 244-251, 259, 262

Y

Yellin, Samuel, 94, 224
Yellow House, 252, 262
Young's Pier, 54

Z

Zinn, Annie Rogers, 25

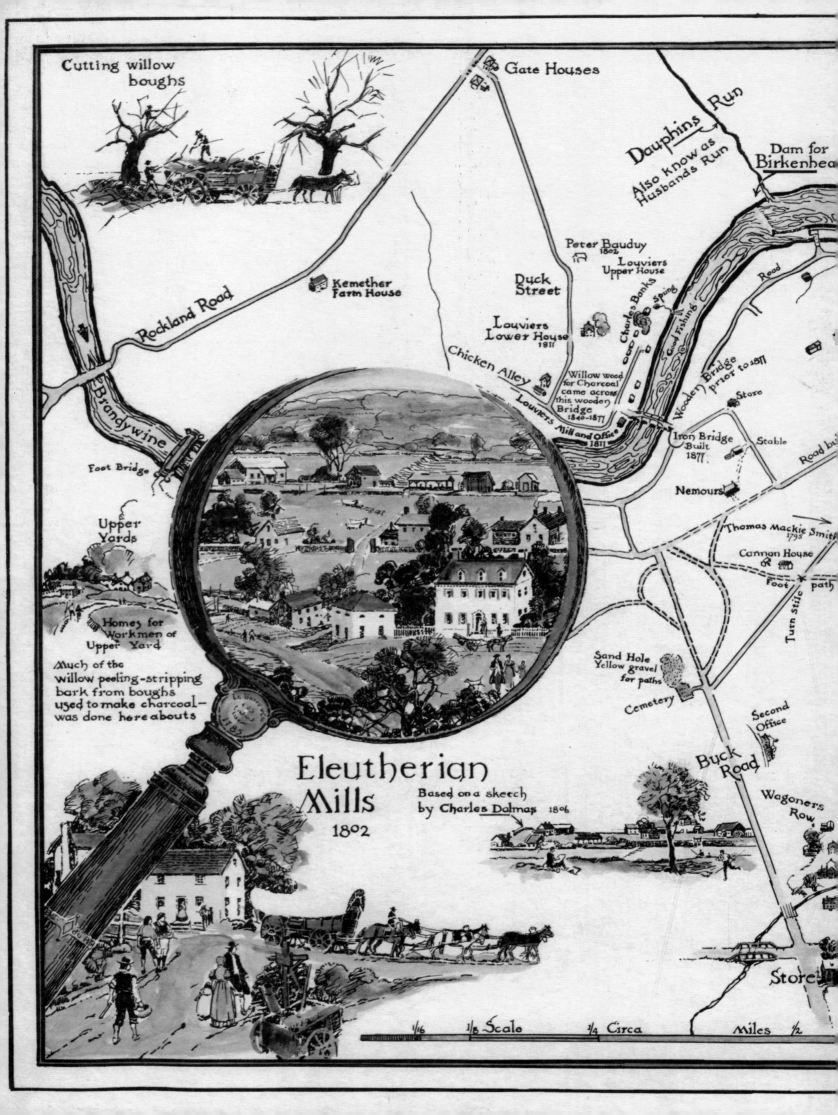

Cutting willow boughs

Gate Houses

Dauphins Run Also know as Husbands Run

Dam for Birkenhea[d]

Peter Bauduy 1802

Louviers Upper House

Rockland Road

Kemether Farm House

Duck Street

Charles Banks

Spring

Good Fishing

Road

Louviers Lower House 1811

Chicken Alley

Louviers Mill and Office 1811

Willow wood for Charcoal came across this wooden Bridge 1840-1877

Wooden Bridge prior to 1877

Store

Brandywine

Foot Bridge

Iron Bridge Built 1877

Stable

Road bu[ilt]

Upper Yards

Nemours

Thomas Mackie Smith 1795

Cannon House

Homes for Workmen of Upper Yard

Foot path

Turn stile

Much of the willow peeling-stripping bark from boughs used to make charcoal- was done here abouts

Sand Hole Yellow gravel for paths

Cemetery

Second Office

Buck Road

Eleutherian Mills 1802

Based on a sketch by Charles Dalmas 1806

Wagoners Row

Store

1/16   1/8 Scale   1/4 Circa   Miles 1/2